SPEAK HUMAN

Outmarket the Big Guys by Getting Personal

ERIC KARJALUOTO

smashLAB

For my lovely wife Amea, who pretends she's paying attention to all of this stuff—sometimes even convincingly.

Contents

Preface

A lot of companies are stuck. They find marketing bewildering and unpredictable and just don't know how to connect with customers. So they look to big companies and start imitating. Most times this goes over like a lead balloon. Fact is, the big guys have more firepower. Pretending you're one of them only makes you look like an also-ran. Worse yet, it forces you to give up a power those guys would kill for.

Being small makes you fast, agile, and responsive. Most importantly, it allows you to get personal with your customers in a way no multinational can match, using tools that have never existed before. As natural as it should be for you to take advantage of them, it's not easy to know how to start.

After a lifetime of ridiculous ads, phony marketing, and outrageous exaggerations, we need to step back and relearn how to communicate... in a way that actually works. This isn't a textbook with a complicated marketing plan. It isn't a marketing checklist either. It's a one-on-one conversation full of zigs and zags. In it, I share many stories that are practical and sometimes personal. I believe they'll help you find a way to take advantage of your small, smart, strategic advantage.

Ultimately, this book is about finding your own voice, articulating it clearly and using it to connect with your customers. My hope is that when you finish it, you'll find yourself excited by the astounding opportunities that have only now become available to you. Get ready to do something with them. All you have to do is Speak Human.

SPEAK HUMAN

PART ONE

SMALL IS BEAUTIFUL

Bigger is better—well, that used to be the case. The game is changing, with power shifting to small companies like yours. In this section, we'll reflect on how you can make these changes work for you and consider what can be learned from tiny startups: like the 10 year old sneaker shop that sold a billion dollars of product last year. Along the way, you'll learn how marketing is being shaken up, and why this makes advertising way less important. Let's begin with Starbucks: a big, famous company that's getting tripped up by its size.

CHAPTER 1

Big Isn't
the Only Option

EVERY COMPANY STARTS WITH A DREAM. Some of these dreams are about making a great product. Others signify liberation from an unfulfilling day job. And a few are solely about generating wealth. Whatever the dreams are, they tend to be infectious. I think we all admire entrepreneurs for breaking from the status quo and embarking on a riskier path… just because they believe in something.

The dream goes awry

Espresso is a treat I've grown to love. That and scotch bookend many of my days, and I could likely fill a chapter detailing my likes, dislikes, and general preferences when it comes to these two distinct liquids.

I don't know many espresso drinkers—most seem to prefer brewed coffee, or one of those froofy coffee and milk concoctions that have hazelnut or cinnamon added. I think they're missing out. I'm of the opinion that espresso is the essence of coffee. It's strong, condensed, and rich. It's the coffee and nothing else. Something about that really appeals to me.

I thank Starbucks for opening me up to the pleasure of espresso. Without them, I doubt that our general knowledge and standards regarding coffee would be where they are. Sadly Starbucks' success has compromised its core product, and there's little they can do to combat this.

"Expresso"

Howard Schultz was the Director of Marketing at Starbucks when he traveled to Italy and fell in love with espresso. At the time, Starbucks didn't sell any coffee beverages on site and Schultz became committed to bringing the espresso experience to America. Despite positive early indicators, the owners were unwilling to grow and take on the debt associated with such an addition. This led Schultz to forge out on his own and start a shop called Il Giornale. (In time, Schultz acquired Starbucks, and his startup became the precursor to the Starbucks shops that are now seemingly everywhere.)

A visit to Il Giornale in April of 1986 would have likely been a little messy. Howard and his staff were just getting started with their new shop and had lots to work out. What's particularly notable is the purist sensibility found amongst them. Schultz says, "We didn't want to do anything to dilute the integrity of the espresso and the Italian coffee bar experience in Seattle. For music, we played only Italian opera. The baristas wore white shirts and bow ties. All service was stand up, with no seating. We hung national and international newspapers on rods on the wall. The menu was covered with Italian words. Even the decor was Italian."[1]

Later he notes the troublesome logistics found in doing some of this; what's interesting is how committed he was to preserving an experience he held dear. I never sampled an espresso at Il Giornale but I feel pretty safe in presuming that they served up a rather good cup. With only one shop, the founder present, and a deep desire to create the most authentic espresso possible, it must have been impressive.

Given a problem, they could fix it and adapt their methods on the fly. All of the "knobs" were in their hands, ready to be tweaked at a moment's notice. Clearly they were on to something, as they subsequently experienced enormous success. Love them or hate them, you have to admire how Starbucks has redefined a category and scaled to meet the demands. That said, with growth comes dilution. As each new store opened, piece of equipment added, and employee hired, the distance from Howard to those knobs lengthened. It shows. Today's Starbucks runs efficiently, but the love of craft doesn't appear to be what it once was.

Not long ago I went to a Starbucks and ordered a double espresso in a ceramic cup. I do this from an environmental standpoint, and I also prefer this to a paper cup. When the order was up, the barista called out my "expresso," presenting me a cold, oversized mug with a dribble of espresso at its bottom. This seemed like a pale shadow of the promise I had learned to associate with Starbucks.

This may sound like a lot of fuss around something rather unimportant, and that's not entirely inaccurate. It is also a symptom of greater challenges. First of all, you have to understand that espresso comes in small quantities, and it cools off very quickly. In all probability, the barista had little sense of any of this. My guess is that he was a university student who needed a part-time job, but had little personal interest in coffee. This is all understandable enough: why would he care about coffee as much as the founder of the company?

My thought is that at Il Giornale, this wouldn't have happened, though. My cup would have been heated and sized correctly to maintain the integrity of the espresso. The barista would have known the characteristics of the drink and perhaps even had experience in roasting coffee beans. At very least, he would have known how to pronounce the name of the drink upon which the franchise was founded.

What happened

Starbucks announced a massive closure of 600 stores in July 2008.[2] The following year, they closed another 300 locations noting that they had all been underperforming.[3] A slow economy could certainly be what forced the closures at Starbucks. One could ask if there might be another consideration: could Starbucks' growth and streamlining have resulted in their stores feeling a little less special and personal to their customers?

In early 2007, Howard Schultz released a now infamous memo titled: "The Commoditization of the Starbucks Experience."[4] He discussed the challenges the organization faced as it raced to meet demand. He also made special note of how the more tactile and sensory experiences had been compromised in their shops. Streamlining operations had changed the retailer, and it showed. This thought led to him addressing how some had referenced the stores as "sterile" and "cookie cutter"—personally admitting that there was little evidence to visitors that they even roasted their own coffee.

So the brand's crop was thinned, and a set of measures were put in place to get back to basics. They worked to reinstate simple gestures like "grinding and brewing fresh batches of coffee more frequently throughout the day." Perhaps more telling is Starbucks' recent experimenting with new "stealth" shops.[5] The 15th Avenue Coffee & Tea and the Roy Street Coffee & Tea in Seattle subtly note that they are "Inspired by Starbucks" but other than that appear to be deliberately divorced from the mother ship. While many license big names to help sell their products, Starbucks seems to perceive some value in breaking away from the behemoth.

The issue of dilution

Although some of the comments I make regarding espresso may seem like small details, they quintessentially change the experience for the espresso drinker. Then, of course, Starbucks isn't really in the espresso business any longer; they're in the growth business. In order to do this well, they just have to forego some troublesome details. Every barista can't be a coffee aficionado when you have more than 175,000 employees,[6] over 15,000 locations, and annual revenues approaching $10 billion.[7]

Starbucks' growth has been the stuff of legend, and something that most all of us can admire in one way or another. They've created a business success that few of us will ever achieve. They also seem to understand the inherent challenges that their growth presents. Howard Schultz himself has noted, "The battle within the company is making sure growth doesn't dilute our culture."

A comment like this seems almost counterintuitive, doesn't it? Here's a famous brand that seems to have the Midas touch. Most of us would reason that such a position would be absolutely dreamy. What do these guys really have to worry about? Well, it turns out that too much of anything can prove a problem.

As companies grow, their promise is diluted, and it's very difficult—perhaps impossible—to counteract this. If your company fares well, this is a problem you too may have to face. Growth always comes with some form of compromise and for most people, this is an acceptable trade off. Starbucks offers consistency so we frequent them as we would any other large, convenience based, fast food provider. My point is that scaling as they did comes with a price. To some, this isn't a concern. For the small provider, a window of opportunity is opened.

You used to have to be big

Some of us look at this scenario and find ourselves asking why so many are so obsessed with size. For a long time growth seemed like one of the few business rules universally agreed upon. In part, the thinking behind this can be defended as simple pragmatism. As industrialization took hold, vast fortunes were amassed by those who applied principles of centralized manufacturing to their businesses. The efficiency and economies of scale made growth a sensible choice.

Such processes afforded greater quality control, as is evidenced in Ford's Rouge Factory. In it, Ford brought together every aspect of manufacturing that it could, in order to control the process and maintain quality. Journalist Charles C. Mann explains, "Initially, the complex was Ford's attempt to solve a manufacturing problem; in the days before networked communication, coordinating precisely with small suppliers was impossible, which meant that he couldn't ensure that all parts for his cars would be ready at the right time and in the proper condition. Ford's answer: total control. By trusting as little as possible to outside entities, he was able to guarantee that his factories got what they needed when they needed it." Ford went as far as purchasing an Amazonian rubber plantation, in an attempt to make their own tires.[8]

In the past, size was a prerequisite for operating at a certain level. More people creating products, faster (and sometimes better) than an individual could, became the predominant model. We therefore saw this take hold almost everywhere as assembly lines became a standard of efficiency even applied to the preparation of food products. There were few operations that didn't have something to gain by being bigger than the other guys.

This carries through to advertising as well. Reaching customers was a big company's game until very recently. Running ads in major media came with very high associated costs, making it the domain of only those with substantial resources. So without size you probably didn't have ample funds; and without funds, your message was likely left unheard.

We love a challenge

I ask if the desire to be big isn't fueled by pragmatism alone; moreover, I posit that it is deep rooted in the human condition. Why do people climb Everest, race performance cars, or play video games? We want to challenge ourselves and see how we rank amongst those around us. Such competitions allow us to measure where we fit, and provide an opportunity to potentially feel good about ourselves.

Tell me that this isn't the case for many of us who run businesses. Who wants to say that they're a partner in a company of three people? Alternately, I'll bet you'd feel pretty proud to say that you've built a company of 500.

A few of us—who are also rather competitive—have started to ask whether we are playing the right game. If that business owner runs a company of 500, but operates consistently in the red, should we really champion his success? Some of us think the answer may be found by measuring this differently. In considering it, perhaps a lower head count in favor of a bigger pay day would be more admirable. I'm getting ahead of myself. *Forgive me—I do that sort of thing.*

Growing pains

If you've started your own company, the first memories are likely ones held dear. The liberation and excitement felt in taking direct control of your fate is hard to match. Yet while many of us are thrilled by starting new ventures, new companies have their share of rough edges. They can't handle too many customers and often fumble because they don't quite have things figured out. Most times we forgive this, knowing that it comes with the territory, but the patience of most customers is finite.

Those companies who survive tend to get pretty smart about how they operate, and in doing so find ways to be as consistent as possible. By establishing systems and processes, they're better able to run efficiently and offer service that their customers can depend on. Such steps are essential for any company to take, but can easily go too far. Many of us have experienced the challenges associated with getting even the simplest things done when a company becomes overly bureaucratic in nature. Those same systems that began with the hope of streamlining can at times start to feel like an anchor.

This becomes particularly evident in marketing. A small company with clear purpose can implement a plan rather quickly. Sure, these plans might suffer from a lack of exhaustive strategy or limited resources; nevertheless, implementing a plan and gauging success can be both rapid and direct. As companies become larger, such efforts become more cumbersome as the pool of stakeholders grows and get harder to manage. So we find multiple department managers who seem more intent on battling for space on the company's home page than conveying a singular message, even though doing so might best suit the whole organization's needs.

Youth and bravery

Just out of college, the world seemed a little like a playground. Most of us didn't have many responsibilities, so we didn't think there was much to lose. This made it the perfect time to go exploring and see what we might find. Some of us saw wildly exciting things, and a few of us had some scares. For the most part we went a little outside of our comfort zone because the risk/reward ratio seemed worthwhile.

Most of us returned, happy to sleep in our own beds again, wondering what our next adventure might be. It's so much fun to meet different people and see new places; why wouldn't you do so all the time? Upon returning, some find that fate has other plans. One might start to work in order to save money and pay down student loans. Perhaps the new job requires a car, resulting in monthly payments. Along the way, a relationship might evolve, necessitating the purchase of a home. With time, friendships form and life settles into a pattern. Who knows? Perhaps kids enter the picture as well.

All of these are fine things, and pattern is comforting. The one thing it does typically tend to limit is one's proclivity for risk. With a mortgage, car payment, work responsibilities, and a couple of toddlers running around the house, one rarely thinks, "Hmmm... I wonder if I should take a few months off to visit Borneo's Valley of the Headhunters and get an authentic tattoo?" Nope, as we become entrenched in these patterns, that risk/reward ratio starts to look quite different, and most of us seek out stability.

This shift isn't altogether that different for companies. Ones that previously embraced risk and disruptive thinking find that they can't quite do the same as they grow. There's now a responsibility to all of the people involved. Employees have families, mortgages, and bills; suppliers need to be paid consistently; and clients need to know that our companies are dependable and here to stay. As a result, growing organizations often find themselves in a straightjacket within which movement is slow, painful, and sometimes seemingly impossible.

So many voices

In no way do I mean to suggest that growing a company isn't without challenges and rewards. I'm just trying to illustrate that making changes becomes more difficult as a company gains mass, because of the increasing number of goals and needs to be considered. Surely this can be combated by having a crystal clear purpose, brand strategy, and marketing plan. These sorts of things do require discipline to stick with, though. As more voices clamor to be heard, the company's core messaging goals can become abandoned, replaced by erratic seeming gestures.

Almost everyone in a company believes that their message is the most important. To mitigate stress and try to keep everyone happy, we sometimes respond by just putting everything in the pot. This leaves us with a big pile of marketing soup: lots of messages get mixed together, limiting any of them from making a direct connection with the audience. With so many people wanting to say so many different things, the message gets lost. As that erodes, so does the organization's voice.

Most small companies have a voice that's largely an extension of the founder's personality. When I go down the street to The Revel Room—which has a rather wicked veggie burger—I get the real deal. The owner talks about what they're doing to build up the business and jokes about how I order the same thing almost every time. Yet when I call my bank, it's unlikely I'll speak with the same person twice. Although the operator today may be helpful, the next one might not be. In an effort to manage this, companies institute policies and procedures for dealing with customers. As laudable as these efforts may be, they tend to feel forced. As a result, niceties are thrown about with abandon, but most customers are left feeling as though they're being read a script.

Handcrafted versus mass-produced

In a world in which experiences are increasingly streamlined, processed and even virtual, we often find ourselves turned off by mechanical interactions. I'm of the mind that what we really crave are tactile, human, and personal touchpoints. These add color to our lives, particularly when details seem to be commonly glazed over in favor of operational efficiency.

Some of us are quite disinterested in a Kindle or digital reader, as we'd rather hold a real book. Most of us pay greater attention to a handcrafted card than some corny sentiment mass-produced by Hallmark. Likewise, some prefer the idiosyncrasies of the local sandwich shop owner over that of the pimply, bored teenager lumping mayonnaise on our Cold Cut Combo at Subway. While the logistical advantages for mass-production are clear, it can come at the cost of delighting customers

For most large companies, this is a manageable compromise. Given the choice of being more personal with customers or building a bigger company, the latter will almost always win out. But as Starbucks' recent closures evidence: getting too big can come with its own perils. This becomes a challenge for many growing operations: how do you maintain the personal connection with your customers when there are so many of them? How do you maintain the personal touch? How do you remind customers that there's a little soul in your company and that it's not just a machine?

Small is powerful

For all of the thrills that must come with growing a large business, I have to say that small ones are closest to my heart. Typically I find the people within them closer to the action, and that's almost always more fun than being around middle managers who seem more interested in office hockey pools. I like it when the dream is alive, and the people in the room are engrossed in the work at hand. That's where the magic is, and I feel like these are *my* people.

Small businesses in the United States alone "produce 13 times more patents per employee than large patenting firms" and "create more than half of nonfarm private gross domestic product."[9] They're a huge economic driver, and they add to the cultural fabric and diversity of our communities. But for some reason we tend to think they should all try to get bigger. Systemize, grow, franchise, retire, and get a boat somewhere; is this really all there is to business? Grow as fast as you can and push everything else in your life aside in order to be rich in retirement? I don't know, it all seems so… hopeless. Do we really benefit by sacrificing all the great things we have today just for financial wealth in our old age? Clearly, there's more to living a rich life than a large number attached to one's bank balance.

I'm of the mind that small businesses are actually much better equipped to excel than many of their larger counterparts. (I've likely made that pretty clear.) I'll come back to this several times, as I think it's something you need to ask. What's the perfect size for you? What do you want out of your company? Given any option, what would you prefer to actually do all day?

If you're in it for the rush of growing the biggest thing you can, great. I think you should do it, and I appreciate the rush you'll experience. On the other hand, if you want some balance, or simply enjoy the work and the people you get to do it with, size may not be the only thing to concern yourself with. More than that, there are advantages to being small; let me get to those.

The new deal

Thankfully, you're still small, and this leaves you with a huge advantage when it comes down to getting personal. Plus, in recent years, the tools have changed drastically. As a result, your size becomes a little like a superpower you didn't even know you had. (Personally, I would have asked for x-ray vision, but this ain't bad either.)

Every once in a while something changes and reorders the landscape completely. It wouldn't be an overstatement to say the advent of the internet is precisely one of those changes. What's curious about this development is how it has played out to date. While many thought the web would replace traditional shops, we've found that the opposite has happened. Instead of the predicted Borg-like assimilation of all products and services, we've witnessed the emergence of a new era. Today's web brings us an increasing number of unique offerings, cottage industries, and easier methods for everyone to promote and distribute their wares.

What they're doing

Rob Kalin, Chris Maguire, Haim Schoppik, and Jared Tarbell started the website Etsy in 2005, with a mission to "enable people to make a living making things, and to reconnect makers with buyers."[10] Or, said otherwise: four friends got together to make a web-based craft fair. In 2008, over $100 million of goods were sold through Etsy— not too bad, eh? Curiously, I've never even seen an advertisement for their company. Hmmm…

When I was a kid, getting in the newspaper or on TV was sort of a big deal. You know, you might even call a friend and congratulate her if you spotted her in a background shot on the nightly news. So the notion of making it in Hollywood always seemed to me like a fool's mission, but don't tell Mario Armando Lavandeira that. In 2004 he had been fired by Star Magazine, and was having "the worst year of *his* life."[11]

While visiting an internet cafe, he stumbled upon some personal blogs and decided that he too might have something to say. He created a site on Blogger (for free) and started to create an online persona. In time he became known as Perez Hilton. By 2008, his site was averaging 198 million page views a month and ads on his homepage were earning up to $54,000 a day. By October 2009, Quantcast ranked his site the 212TH most popular on the internet.[12] Star Magazine (his former employer) ranks #4,236.[13] To my knowledge, he has never employed an ad agency to help connect with customers or build his brand.

Perhaps you've heard of Zappos? They sell sneakers online—a business few would have bothered to start. Most would (wrongly) assume that such a market was too small, and that customers wouldn't actually want to buy shoes they hadn't tried on. In 2008, Zappos definitively proved any naysayers wrong. In less than ten years they became a company with annual revenues of $1 billion. In the summer of 2009 Amazon announced the acquisition of Zappos, in a deal valued at approximately $928 million.[14] Along the way, they have advertised a little, but not really that much. As CEO Tony Hsieh notes, "We actually take a lot of the money that we would have normally spent on paid advertising and put it back into customer experience."[15]

You can do it too

These examples are amongst the most remarkable in this new landscape. Nevertheless, there are countless other stories of companies who started small and used the new tools to gain success. As you may have noticed, I've harped on one other point I believe to be particularly important: they hardly used any traditional media to spread their messages. They've (rather quickly) created powerful brands, in ways that were almost unheard of ten years ago.

I don't suggest that everyone who starts a company using the web will fare as handsomely. In truth, I suspect that the ratio of companies that fail to those that succeed on the web likely isn't all that different than we'd see amongst less wired businesses. What I do feel is important to note, is just how different these sorts of enterprises are from the factory model that we used to think of as the only option. Each of these organizations started small and used digital methods to help amplify their voices and better connect with their respective audiences.

Twenty years ago, small companies had limited access to the tools employed by multinational brands. There were fewer advertising venues and the cost to access them was terribly prohibitive. Some advertising is still very expensive, but it's no longer the only way to spread one's message. The tools that have become available in recent years are as readily accessible to a small organization like yours as they are to any major corporation. Better yet, you might be able to use them far more effectively than your larger counterparts—*more on that later.*

We can get personal

In recent years, most of the discussion surrounding the web has concentrated on social media. If you're not familiar with this subject, it can be effectively encapsulated as, "media designed to be disseminated through social interaction, created using highly accessible and scalable publishing techniques."[16] The important part of that definition relates to the words "social interaction." With social media we find ourselves better able to communicate than we ever were with advertising, because two-way discussion is enabled.

For big companies, this might be seen as a drag. They're likely already burdened by an inordinate amount of incoming calls, email, and regular mail. As new methods of communication open up, the big guys find themselves with an even greater number of messages to contend with. Some of this can be worked around, but I bet some of the folks in these companies are rather wary of giving their customers even more ways to call in and complain.

For small operations like yours, this is—in a word—awesome. The battle for many small organizations is in building trust with customers in order to become a "known quantity." Few will buy from a stranger if they can instead work with someone they know on a first name basis. The reason some of us get so excited about social media is that it can help erase the lines between our companies and our customers. This allows them to get to know us and perhaps love what we do.

Are you playing the same game?

As you work your way through this book, you might wonder if my suggestions are conflicting. In one section I'll tell you to openly experiment and embrace change; in the next I'll caution that doing unnecessarily wild things is not the best course of action. There's little actual confusion here—just different sides of the same coin. My argument is that while many conventions exist for a reason, some are actually just bad habits. We need to carefully examine the things we do as well as the standards that we work with. In doing so we can best determine what should be maintained and what we'd be better off to rethink or perhaps abandon.

One thing that demands special attention is our dangerous fixation on what everyone else is doing. It's my firmly-held belief that by imitating how others market and do business, we miss out on opportunities. On countless occasions, I've met with great small companies who were so obsessed with being like someone else that they missed all of the possibilities right under their noses.

If you aren't a big company, don't act like one. You're probably better off to do the exact opposite of what they do. They're big, so they probably need to concentrate on being professional and (sorry) boring. This means they've left you with plenty of room to differentiate and connect more personally with clients—most likely at a significantly lower cost than they're able to achieve.

Plans

The means by which you'll connect with customers—more effectively than the big guys do—are well within your reach. Although sheer brawn was previously a determining factor in a company's marketing success, the new landscape seems to favor those who act more intelligently. Having access to new tools is just one part of the equation; you need to use them well in order to reap the rewards.

You'll need to craft a smart plan to outmarket the big guys. This means the alignment of your brand, the development of an appropriate voice, and a peripheral understanding of the new tools that are emerging. That's really what this book is about: helping you clarify what your company does and says, and focusing on appropriate methods for spreading that message.

CHAPTER 2

THANK GOODNESS YOU'RE SMALL

WHILE MANY BUSINESSES are madly chasing growth, I want to take a moment to convince you that the size you're at is quite possibly perfect. You have agility, speed, and a personal touch that large companies would kill for. Are you ready to sacrifice that just to say that your company has more people on the payroll?

Let me tell you about my mom

Believe it or not, cross-country skiing in North America (circa 1983) wasn't as big a deal as major league baseball. I know… I know… given how we're riveted by the sport today, it's hard to believe this, but I assure you it's true. My dad was one of those rare few who really liked skiing; he even raced competitively. At the time, spandex had just come to market, and a few one-piece suits (like those seen on speed skaters or in bobsledding events) had become available. These were lighter, breathable, and more flexible than other garments, helping skiers achieve a wider range of movement. As you can imagine, my dad wanted one of these.

For Christmas, my mom put one on order. It was shipped from Finland and one of very few you'd see at ski races. Given the hassle involved, my mom saw an opportunity and toyed with the idea of creating her own. I can't stress how much I respect the way she went about doing this. Today it would be much simpler. We have the internet, which can help us locate clients, suppliers, plans, and resources on legal matters, taxation, and business advice. In 1983 it was all quite different. My mom went down to Fabricland and bought a few bolts of fabric, and then had skiers like Dave Wood (now the head coach of the Canadian National Team) come over and help her figure out the sizing. She'd bribe skiers with homemade lasagna, and they'd be guinea pigs who'd help her test out her most recent iterations.

Mom had grown up with an interest in starting businesses; she was also handy at sewing. In addition to some night classes in accounting, this formed her business "toolkit" when she started Lumi. It wasn't exactly easy for her. I still remember how hard she had to work to get things off the ground. She put everything into that business and toiled into the wee hours many nights to fulfill orders.

She did quite well for herself. Over the years she adapted and grew, building systems to help manufacture more efficiently and better service clients. For a while she rode a small wave when spandex tights became a fashionable item for women; later, she worked directly with figure skating clubs whose members needed warm up suits. Mom and I have talked about business a lot, and I watched as she worked through many different struggles that first-time entrepreneurs face: hiring issues, workflow challenges, and clients who went into receivership and were unable to pay.

Lumi didn't have an IPO, nor is it a household name. For twenty years, though, it ran in the black, making a good product (I still see the odd person wearing one of her jackets from fifteen years ago). The revenues from that business in part allowed my parents to invest, send their kids to college, and even retire a little early. We all like to hear about the riches found in business, but unfortunately most companies fold within the first year. This leaves founders with either a nasty loan that takes years to pay off, or bad debt resulting in bankruptcy. We rarely talk about all of those little companies that pay their bills and generate reasonable returns, but they are a really big deal. (They're the ones that keep most of us employed.)

Aside: If you call smashLAB, my mom might pick up the phone. She's our bookkeeper now and lends a hand every here and there.

Temptations of success

I remember a drive to Edmonton when my mom had a meeting with a chain of sports retailers. She was so thrilled I thought she might pass out. The trip resulted in a substantial order, so there was some deal of excitement for her. Such instances weren't uncommon, and each time they resulted in discussion around how she could make the most of the opportunity. Our dinnertime conversations often revolved around the orders at hand and ever-looming delivery dates. Such demands brought on issues of hiring and the associated challenges given the seasonal nature of her business. I made all kinds of simplistic suggestions for how to address such issues. I now know first hand how challenging it is to balance staff and workflow.

With each of these opportunities came a real thrill and opportunity for advancement. I know the exhilaration of this rush and how it leads you to think about growth. "If I get three more orders like this, I can hire another person to do X, which will allow us to take on that many more orders…" and it goes on. It's awfully difficult to not get sucked up by the possibility of growth and the promise it may hold. The notion—not always accurate—that added staff will allow you to fill out certain roles and have individuals specialize on key tasks is incredibly seductive. Many of us start to grow our companies before we've determined whether that's what we actually want.

For the many reasons there are to grow, I argue that there are just as many to stay small. Increased size means added bureaucracy, management, office politics, and training—not to mention the need for additional equipment, space, health plans, phone lines, insurance packages, and so on. From the outside, running a business may seem like a license to print money. On the inside it often feels quite the opposite. Some may think I'm being whiny about this, but I have to say that after costs are paid out, many find that there's little left over.

When you're small…

With all of the attention the Googles, Nikes, and Cokes get in the press, we often think the only measure of an operation relates to its size. This is changing and I think that we in part have technology to thank, in conjunction with the buzz we see around startup culture.

Consider the venture capitalist Paul Graham. He's one of the key people in Y Combinator: a venture firm that funds early stage startups. Although their investments typically amount to less than $20,000 of actual funding, participants find benefit in having access to the team's connections and collective expertise. In the past such a sum might have seemed offensive but this is no longer the case. As a result of the low barrier to entry for today's startups, many eagerly apply to the Y Combinator program. Paul espouses starting companies from the standpoint of "smaller, cheaper, faster."[17]

As a small company, you can turn on a dime. That's a good thing as it allows you to correct course easily while larger companies are still trying to get their bearings. Let's say you have a little software company that competes with one of Microsoft's products. Along comes a new innovation that you choose to implement in your application. All you have to do is get down to work. Sure, Microsoft has nearly 90,000 people to do the same, but do you think it's really that easy?[18] How many meetings, proposals, surveys, and assessments need to happen before a single line of code is written? It's like arranging a get-together: a dinner for two is easy, a gathering of 12 friends is no big deal, but planning a wedding for 100? That's a kind of torture.

Another great thing about small companies is that they can be highly focused. This doesn't mean that all are, but for the most part, they should be. Without all those hundreds or thousands of staff members to keep paid, you don't need quite as much cash coming in. See where I'm going with this? Lower operating costs mean that you also don't need as many customers. This allows you to concentrate on just a few great customers in a more lucrative market. While a large department store might need to service many different customers with varied needs, your small company might be able to make a single product the core of its business.

For example: hats. I'm bald you see, so covering my noggin has become a bit of a thing for me. Instead of going to a massive department store for this sort of purchase, wouldn't it be nicer to find a little shop where hats are all they sell? These people know the product better, have the nicest hats before they're available in the chain stores, and tend to have a greater selection.

Minimum wage passion

Small companies are often fueled by passion. To best contextualize this, I think we have to begin by looking at what most companies have instead. While she was in high school, my wife Amea worked in a location of the Canadian Tire franchise. If you're not Canadian, you'd likely be led astray by the name. It's a cross between a car parts shop and hardware store, which also sells yard items, camping gear, household essentials, insurance, and pretty much anything else you can think of. The thing is, that's a lot of stuff to know about, and Canadian Tire tends to mostly hire students who don't know that much about any of these products. Amea sometimes recounts how angry customers were with her for not being able to help them better. Believe me, I understand their complaints. Service at Canadian Tire makes me want to scream, too.

But is this realistic? She was a teenager making minimum wage who had received hardly any training. There's typically little passion in big companies because the people there aren't invested in the product. You, with your small company—did you start it just to make money? Maybe, but most don't. It seems to me that those who go into business for themselves do so in an area they love. This shows, and customers enjoy buying from people who are excited and knowledgeable about what they do. Teaching passion to a staff of thousands isn't easy though. In a way it's like trying to force love en masse. Most times it's there or it's not—case closed.

Although I don't intend to touch upon every advantage a small company has, I do think it's important to hit a few of the high points. The one that I haven't addressed yet relates to the sub-title of this book and it's my favorite: being personal. When you're singing to an audience of thirty, you can hang out with everyone and grab a beer once the show's wrapped up. What about The Beatles? How personal could they get with their fans? Right—not very. Everyone was crazy about those guys, so it didn't matter too much. How about General Electric? Do you think they can get personal with their customers? I don't think so either, and unlike the Beatles, I'm less excited to invest much of my own enthusiasm in GE.

Getting personal is something that some big companies try to do through their ads, marketing, staff training programs, and so on. It's not that they shouldn't try, but sometimes it's like teaching a humpback whale how to do the tango.

Make it an unfair fight

My dad and I were in the car the other day, talking about small shops. He noted his belief that for most of these companies, the possibility of success is negligible given the prevalence of large box stores and mega malls. We continued to discuss this on the drive to my parents home and even had a little debate about it. I disagreed with him, and it became a pretty good discussion.

In my mind, the only thing that kills a small shop is when it tries to be something it's not. If you're not stronger, you have to be smarter. Head-to-head, Walmart will crush you. Let's pretend that you sell books. If your strategy is to undercut Walmart on the price of best sellers, you are on a suicide run. First of all, they have more fire power than the rest of us. They can buy their inventory for less than anyone else because of their purchasing power, and they have no problem with loss leaders (something sold at a loss to get you into the store and presumably buy more stuff).

Most of us see the inherent problem here. To fight a bigger enemy with limitless resources on equal ground is like courting a certain death. No one ever said that business against the big guys would be a fair fight. Perhaps we need to turn this into a street fight that's less about following rules, and more about who walks away at the end.

My friend Jim owns a book store, and it's a great one. It's eclectic, personal, and very much the polar opposite of a Walmart, or a big bookseller. The shelving is bric-a-brac in nature, there are no uniforms, and there's isn't a corporate identity system to speak of, although it certainly has a strong brand presence.

You'd go to Books & Co. (Jim's store) on a Friday night and grab a coffee and shortbread cookie at the adjoining cafe. Then you'd settle in for an evening of local musicians playing folk music while sharing stories and enjoying a couple of laughs. Or you'd be one of the parents who brings their kids in on the weekend for story time, allowing you to grab a bowl of soup, magazine, and maybe even chat with a friend. You might talk with one of the staff members who'd suggest a good book to bring home for your mom.

I met Jim when I was working as a painter. I asked him if I could use some of his space for an exhibit of my artwork. I noted that I could bring in paperwork, a portfolio, and contracts if he wished. Really, I was willing to do whatever I needed to gain access to that space. Jim just paused for a moment and said, "OK."

I was surprised by how casual he was about it. I offered to come back with the papers I had promised. He explained that it was entirely unnecessary and noted again that the space was mine for the exhibit.

Compare this to Walmart. Would they be able to put on these fun community nights? I suppose, but I can't imagine anyone going. Are you interested in a night of folk music at a box store? I didn't think so. Could they offer suggestions on other books? I doubt it. My guess is that most of the people working there don't care about books that much. Would they know their customers by name? Maybe, but the number of customers would certainly make doing so more difficult. Might they special order that book you were looking for but couldn't find anywhere? Um...

I could go on, but I don't think I have to. In this fight of Walmart vs. Books & Co., the only clear advantage Walmart has is price. For some people this is enough, but the rest of us want more than to just save a few dollars on a purchase.

I've come to feel like Jim's brand is directly related to the community. I could easily buy my books online, but I instead pay more to get them from Jim. It's not that I have to, and I'm not trying to be nice. It's that Jim supported me, and I know how important his store is. It makes the community better, and I also believe that my purchases help support something that I believe in. (Really, I'd feel like an ass to buy a book anywhere else.)

No more pointing fingers

When you get bruised in business, it's easy to point the finger and blame the big guy. This often feels comforting and there's very little possibility of an actual altercation ensuing. We can all blame a big company for being "stupid" as they're (at least in an abstract sense) so far from us. You'll often hear small retailers singing the blues about how a big box ruined their business. Don't get me wrong, I've been there, and it sucks, but if you weren't ready for a bit of a fight, you were never cut out for business in the first place.

Keep in mind, big companies are so far from their customers that you have countless opportunities to get in there and fight for the business. Maybe you take your loyal customers out for lunch to thank them for working with you. Or, how about this? You could just make a vastly superior product. (Those big boxes often offer a low price, but at the cost of other nice things like personal service and lasting quality.)

In Seattle a few weeks ago, my wife, sons, and I walked by a little ice cream shop. It was hard to identify from outside, but it was memorable for the amazing vanilla scent that wafted through the air and the massive line up of people waiting to step inside. I pass by a Dairy Queen twice daily and have never seen a line up like that outside its doors. We were in a rush and were unable to wait. (It was a pretty long line up, after all.) Still, I'll hazard a guess that their ice cream was available in fewer flavors than at an ice cream franchise, and that they didn't have any kind of movie tie-in promos. They might not even have had seats or napkins with their logo on them. Really, I don't know and I don't care. All that sticks in my mind was a warm afternoon and a lovely fragrance that passed through the air. The next time we're in Seattle, I'll find that place.

You can complain perpetually about the hardship in your life, or you can do something remarkable.

Something interesting

I was just out of town for a speaking engagement. These trips aren't particularly fun. I often find myself at odds with just finding a reliable Wi-Fi connection and a healthy meal. Although business travel comes with the promise of a getaway, it has very little in common with a holiday. Additionally, I perpetually find myself with the dubious task of finding gifts I can return home with for my wife and kids.

On this particular occasion I forged out bravely, in search of a local shop containing something unique to bring home. I finally came across a large collection of stores; unfortunately, it turned out they were all part of a large outdoor shopping mall. I'm not a fan of malls. Being a thousand miles from home, I figured there had to be something of interest there, but the mall directory proved me wrong. Bed Bath & Beyond, The GAP, Victoria's Secret: every name on that list was familiar, in fact omnipresent. I sulked, feeling somewhat beleaguered, asking myself if this same list might be in every city around the world. I had to wonder if I'd find some variation of it in Dubai, Helsinki, or Madrid. Maybe not—I've never been to Dubai or Madrid, but I wouldn't be surprised. I have yet to travel to a city these brands haven't penetrated.

All I wanted was to find something just a little unique from the place I was visiting. Sadly, these big brands seem to have wiped out such a possibility. As a result, I temporarily gave up and instead made my way to a nice little Mexican restaurant. As I worked through my second glass of wine, I found myself asking why it had come to this, and what it all might mean.

The loss of local color

This is the power these brands have. They are everywhere, and we know precisely what to expect when we see their names. In many respects I admire them—the clarity in their messaging and their reach. No matter how boring the Banana Republic may be, I still spend at their shops and I know that I'll generally find something suitable there.

You should likely stop me here, because I feel a rant coming on. My parents are from Finland, and we've traveled back on a number of occasions. The first time I was in second grade, and after that we returned every few years. By the time I was sixteen, something there had changed. My Dad and I were out for a run, when we came upon a gas station. I can't remember which multinational brand it was, but it hardly matters. At that moment Finland felt a little less "Finland" to me. I think this gas station marked a personal tipping point at which I realized just how much this country was changing. The brands here were looking increasingly American, and that seemed sad.

Odd as it may sound, I want Finnish gas stations in Finland. I don't want a Starbucks in the Forbidden City (others felt similarly, which seemingly influenced its closure in 2007).[19] I dread the notion of boring, homogenized Budweiser being equated as the "king of beers." Be that as it may, the convenience and awareness of big brands allow them to effectively clearcut local cultures. Soon (if not already) we'll all know, have, and buy exactly the same things. A rational counterpoint to my argument might be that this hardly matters as shops are just one part of what one finds in a particular region. I'd argue that it's like a virus that spreads easily. You'll hear more about American entertainment in Finland than that crafted by locals; similarly, Canadian films are routinely sorted into the "Foreign" category, even in Canadian movie rental shops. (This isn't a good thing.)

My fear is that we in ways court a rather gray and bland future by supporting the big brands. Many bring convenience, but at the cost of variety, color, and delight. The travesty is that the convenience and consistency of these major brands has in many respects superseded the possibility of something interesting and compelling.

The power of a community

Arguably, the most interesting street in Vancouver is Commercial Drive. Our little city has some hippy roots, and they're most visible in this area. Calling it "The Drive" (as locals often do) is perhaps a better moniker for it, as the term "commercial" isn't particularly accurate. In actuality, it's a rather messy collection of shops that has captured the interest of residents by being the "anti-mall." Dining there ranges from the Honduran place that will only accept cash payment, to the Italian cafe famous for its great coffee and tacky decor. *(Interesting note: I met my wife Amea at this cafe and later proposed to her in the same spot.)*

"The Drive" is a funny place—some might consider it the polar opposite of the air conditioned suburban shopping mall. Curiously, it has gotten so successful that some franchises have become attracted to it. In recent years a Starbucks and Tim Hortons (a popular Canadian coffee/donut shop) have opened on the Drive. Shops like these could threaten the nature of the community, but I doubt they'll ever open there en masse, given how cynical many are of their presence. The fact is, those who choose to live around Commercial Drive enjoy Little Nest. It's noisy and chaotic, and you can let your kids play while you have a delicious breakfast. Similarly, they love the energy found at the street parades, and the wildly creative costumes that are to be seen there at Halloween. There are countless vivid, real, human experiences to be found on The Drive, because it hasn't been sanitized, regulated, and contained in a perfectly sealed box with ample parking.

There's a lesson in this: individually, we can strike up a fight against those brands we've come to see as soulless, anonymous machines that do little for the communities within which we live. That being said, individual efforts often remain disconnected, making it harder to win. This makes the links we have with our neighbors even more important, as they can serve to propel our efforts much further and faster than we could otherwise.

Such movements probably won't be the result of municipal revitalization plans, nor do they need to be limited to a physical community. Whether it's those shops on The Drive, Seattle grunge in the early '90s, or technology in Silicon Valley—organically formed collectives can move mountains. Look to your neighbors; what are the common threads that can lead you to join forces?

What if my organization isn't small?

Then you have your work cut out for you. For all the perks and resources available in large companies, these can prove hard positions for marketers. First of all, many find themselves mired in stifling bureaucracy that severely limits their ability to make bold moves. What's worse is the difficulty such groups have in rewriting perceptions about their organizations.

While we all strive to be known for something, doing so comes at a cost. Once an idea about a company is cast, it's very difficult to change. I can't overstate the challenge that marketers in this spot face. I think the Korean car company Hyundai serves as a good example of this. You may very well think that Hyundais are great—I can only speak for myself here. When I hear the name Hyundai, the image that comes to mind is of a rickety old tin can that an acquaintance of mine once drove. It was poorly styled, perpetually in need of repair, and seemed to be comprised more of rust than metal. Sure, this was a "beater" and therefore not a fair example, but their struggles with quality have tainted the way some think of them.

Fast-forward fifteen or twenty years, and we find that Hyundai has addressed many of these quality issues. They established new quality control measures, reportedly investing "$6.5 billion to improve quality"[20]; they even started to warranty their cars for 10 years or 100,000 miles. As a result, in J.D. Power and Associates' 2009 Initial Quality Study, Hyundai placed fourth in overall quality, only bested by Lexus, Porsche, and Cadillac.[21] Meanwhile, the Genesis, their first luxury offering, "was voted car of the year by a panel of journalists at the Detroit Auto Show."[22]

Still, I can't shake that notion that Hyundai is a "cheap" brand. This is clearly an inaccurate belief, and it's not as though they aren't going to lengths to change it. In addition to their quality improvements and positive reviews, they market aggressively, even buying expensive ad spots during the Super Bowl. Clearly, they're doing things right. Between 1998 and 2006 their unit sales increased by 400 percent[23] and they've stated their goal to be one of the world's top five automakers by 2011.

I think they will do it. Similarly, I think that in time they'll be free of the negative associations related to their poor quality, now many years in the past. Few of us remember when the name Toyota wasn't synonymous with dependability, but such a time did certainly exist. Negative brand associations can be rewired when the process is steered nimbly. Doing so just isn't easy or cheap. Hyundai may come out of this on top; nevertheless, don't you think it would have been easier if the same fleet of vehicles were to appear on the market under a wholly new and untarnished brand?

CHAPTER 3

Startup Thinking

I'D LIKE TO LOOK MORE CLOSELY at just how small you can go. I think the most interesting example of this is found in startups. While many companies are small as a result of circumstance, startups are a little different. They are abundant in the tech space, as it's so easy to start one on a shoestring budget with just a couple of founders and some sweat equity. These operations tend to run extremely lean in order to extend runway (the amount of time you have before your cash runs out). Many founders even abstain from basic comforts like independent living, proper nutrition, and family life just to make it work.

The potential benefit of all this sacrifice comes to a lucky few who experience meteoric success in their operations—sometimes to the extent of becoming internationally recognized brands within just a few short years. Startups are risky and are often headed by those just out of college. With little to lose, these people make perfect candidates for dropping out of the mainstream for a while and making a big bet. For the sake of this book, we'll look at how these groups approach their operations with the notion that we might find something to borrow and apply to our own companies.

Looking for role models

When we start our companies we often lack role models; unfortunately, we often pick the wrong ones. I can't speak for you, but I readily admit that this was one of the greatest mistakes we made in starting our company. As two guys in their early twenties with little business experience, we became fixated with looking *like* a business. (We should have just concentrated on running a good business.)

In spite of limited funds, we still tried to buy a phone system, conference table, set of desks (for our seemingly inevitable expansion), enterprise-level software, suits, presentation folders, and all the rest. To this day, I still wish that we had taken my dad's advice on the topic more to heart. He suggested that we concentrate on our service and clients, and not worry about other stuff until it became absolutely necessary to do so.

It's not like we didn't put adequate—or exemplary—effort into doing good work. For the first five or six years we rarely clocked less than 80 hours a week. And it's not as though our interests in "looking like a company" were intended as a substitute to doing a good job. It's just that when we looked at every company we admired, all of them seemed to "look" like big companies.

The simple fact is, we mimic the behavior of those who have achieved a position we too would like to reach. The challenge with this is that we confuse the affectations with the cause. Although a wealthy person might have a Bentley, it's unlikely the car made them rich. Similarly, a big company may have really nice offices, but it's a mistake to think they are successful because of those offices.

My one caveat

You might think I'm asking you to ignore how your company is perceived. Allow me to stress that this is the furthest thing from the truth. For small companies these concerns are often more vital than they are for their larger counterparts. Committing to a purchase from a large company is generally more reassuring for buyers than taking a chance on a lesser-known option. As a small business owner, it's your job to ensure that your offering is seen as different and in some way markedly better than those of your more established competitors.

My suggestion is twofold: first, you have to act smarter than the big guys in order to get the most bang for your buck. Second, trying to look like a big company when yours is small will only result in you looking foolish. (Imagine: a gangly adolescent in a pinstriped double-breasted suit.) Most small companies just don't tailor their messages and marketing to fit their "body styles." Is there anything more ridiculous seeming than meeting someone from a three-person company who introduces himself as the CEO?

Sure—for the buyer, there's a sense of security to be had by working with a company that has a large number of employees. Still, I say it's wiser to openly state who you are than later be found out an imposter. There's nothing embarrassing about being small, and there's certainly no need to hide this fact. Instead, embrace it, use it as a strength, and look *fabulous* in it. If you're a three-person company you can likely offer more personalized service and access to higher levels of expertise than a company of 500 can. Being small isn't a bad thing by any means; that said, it also can't serve as an excuse for offering a product that isn't better than that of the dominant players in your market.

The purest form of business

As businesses get larger, it's easier to hide bad people in them. This is because there are so many things going on, alongside numerous coworkers who can shield one's dismal performance. Toss in some memos, meetings, office politics, and it gets harder to determine whether a staff member is kicking ass or just great at kissing it. In a company of one, there's little room for any of this. When you're that tiny, you have little choice but to be exemplary.

Most startups have limited time before their money runs out. I don't know why—perhaps I'm a compulsive gambler at heart, but there's something about this notion that excites the bejesus out of me. Without funding or a wealthy family, this means you just have to do it. Sink or swim. Hunt or starve. Succeed or get a job.

Anyone's singing voice can sound great once ample processing and effects are applied in the studio. Put that same person in front of twenty listeners with nothing but a crummy microphone, and see what happens. Startups are like this: business unplugged. This makes them wildly exciting, and often terrifying, but the notion of anything else seems a little lame after you've felt it for yourself. Every move matters and the only person handling the controls is you.

Kodak didn't think like a startup

When I grew up, the name Kodak was synonymous with photography. Their bright red wordmark surrounded by a warm yellow backdrop is etched in my mind, and I don't think it will ever be shaken. Sadly for Kodak, the same can't be said for the company.

Kodak fell into the same trap that many other successful companies have. They had dominated photography, and dabbled in other areas as well. They concentrated largely on film, and until the late 1990s this worked well. As a 2005 *BusinessWeek* article notes, "...Kodak was in denial. The company had supposedly been on a decade-long journey to digital technology, yet very little had actually been done. The pressure to rethink the business didn't seem that great."[24]

Being an amateur photographer at the time, I found it difficult to imagine the quality of digital photography ever matching that of film. I doubt that any of us could have predicted the speed with which this actually did occur. Digital cameras initially seemed like a novelty, hardly worth forsaking a time-tested standard for. At the time, I reasoned that if it took 17 years for us to get from DOS to Windows 95, we could expect it to take equally long to move from these low-quality photos to ones that matched a professional-grade camera. At the time I'd go to photo shoots with our shiny new digital camera and people would gather around me exhibiting an almost childlike fascination. Within three years no one would have even batted an eyelash around that same device.

My guess—entirely unquantified, but probably right—is the people at Kodak *did* anticipate the imminent succession of digital over film. They just didn't think the change would come barreling at them so fast. Kodak was hit by a surprise left hook before the fight even started.

I say the bigger problem for Kodak was their size. They had built a juggernaut that *was* film. They conceivably had complex systems, refined processes, and massive infrastructure. Changing that wasn't going to be cheap or easy. Few there were initially ready to accept the kind of change at hand, and this left them slow to adapt. By the time they did, they learned that their new direction simply wasn't profitable enough. At around the same time, film sales dropped off faster than anticipated. To adapt again would force a massive rethinking of their business model.

They've since done bold and ambitious things, but with seemingly little success. By early 2009, the company's stocks had lost 76 percent over the prior 12 months. They planned to cut another 14 to 18 percent of their staff, after already having reduced their workforce by 50 percent two years earlier.[25]

Big companies do well with certainty. In the face of change, all of those systems, people, and infrastructure can get in the way. If you think about it, Kodak should have been years ahead on this one. They had the money, knowledge, and reach to lead the pack when it came to imaging. To their detriment, they lost sight of what they really offered (imaging) and got stuck in a soon to be antiquated technology. The problem is that technologies change. Kodak thought it was a *film* company and was unable to transition quickly enough—that will probably kill it.

Startups are easier to turn

There are plenty of failed startups out there, and I'm certainly not proposing that they are inherently better or run by smarter people than large companies. In my mind, people are overwhelmingly people: some good, others bad—some successful and others less so. It's awfully challenging to put forth a single hard-and-fast rule for why some companies are successful while others fight to stay alive.

A certain number of things happen in companies that seem like laws of nature. The law that most relates to you, as a small company is that gravity exists in business. We like to fantasize about large organizations not having any problems, but that's simply not the case. I suggest that gravity in business means that problems scale with the organization. In time, the weight of an organization becomes a burden. The crushing gravity felt by Kodak was one that most startup founders could hardly fathom.

Startups don't typically suffer from baggage, bureaucracy, or legacy. On the other hand, they are hampered by a lack of consistency and process that might be assuaged by more experienced managers. In my mind, this is an acceptable trade off. Startups often make clumsy mistakes, but because they're such "light" organizations, they are an awful lot easier to correct. They can move at lightning speed and quickly outrun bigger, more slovenly-natured titans of industry.

A startup might not have been as stuck in a "film" mentality as Kodak was. This is in part because a startup wouldn't have spent more than a century building a hundred-ton machine and legacy. By only being in business for months (or perhaps a few years), a startup could easily cut bait and change direction when the writing was on the wall.

Small means fast

Small companies don't have to contend with "turning the Titanic" at critical, game-changing moments. This leaves them more agile when the unforeseen occurs. Even on a more day-to-day basis, though, small operations maintain certain advantages.

Management is Hell. Sure, it's often necessary, but it's filled with waste. Let's imagine the process involved in getting an ad campaign to press for a well-established brand. How about... I don't know... a video rental shop like Blockbuster? Let's pretend that they devised a partner program with Domino's Pizza.

This is a completely hypothetical situation, but let's run with it anyway. Suppose that a couple of young managers at their respective head offices came up with an idea to have your videos and pizza delivered by one driver, by making a single phone call. (Actually, this isn't a bad idea. I'd use a service like this; wouldn't you?) This is the kind of thing that would likely take an awfully long time to work out from a logistical perspective, so let's skip past that and look solely at the associated marketing.

Each company's marketing people would likely get together with their agencies and start to talk about strategy, creative, and all of that other good stuff. A batch of agency folks would put some deal of effort into forming a strategy, some smart ideas, and perhaps even examples of implementation. The companies' marketing teams might then bring all of this back to their execs and internally debate the approach. Afterwards it goes back and forth from agency to client until everyone's OK with the campaign. From there it will likely to go to legal departments, focus groups, production houses, media buyers, medium-specific teams (digital, broadcast, print, direct mail).

After likely months of exchanges between an ever-expanding number of parties, the campaign is launched. Millions are spent, and no one even knows if it's a success for many months to come. It's all terribly slow, cumbersome, and unforgiving. Just imagine the brouhaha that arises if the thing doesn't work, or if someone's made a mistake.

Small companies often complain that they don't have the budgets to advertise like the big guys, but they really shouldn't. A startup might also be frustrated by this exercise, but probably wouldn't be quite as paralyzed. Startups know they're up against the odds, so they *change the rules*. Let's pretend that these two organizations are instead a local pizza shop and a video store (they don't have to be startups to think like startups). They have the same idea, and have also worked out the operational logistics.

In a situation like this, there would be no ad agency, legal department, sound editors, media buying department, or any of that stuff. They'd be left with a very clear challenge: implementing a great idea that no one knows about. Given their limited funds and resources, they'd simply have to think their way around the problem. Perhaps they'd hire a few impersonators of film stars to walk around a local park, giving out free slices, and coupons offering discounts. If they did it well (and it was a slow news day), they might even get some interest from the local press and some free publicity. Maybe they'd call up some existing customers, tell them about the service, and arrange a free first order. They might even create an online contest, in which people could win pizza and movies for joining a Facebook group.

Clearly, I'm glazing over some big points here. (For example, the fact that some don't even rent DVDs from bricks and mortar shops any longer.) While I generalize liberally, I hope that my point still comes across. You might not have the resources of a large company, but you also aren't burdened so much by size. With a little ingenuity and elbow grease, you can get your message out an awful lot faster.

Adapt

If these little guys found their efforts weren't working out, you know what they'd do? They'd change course, and instead of taking months to do so, they could alter their approach in days—or even hours. "Hey, no one's joining our Facebook page. Want to try a small ad in tomorrow's paper to direct people to it?" Without an executive team watching your every move, you can really change the speed with which you react. But of course marketing is only a small part of any company. Startups benefit from being agile in all ways.

One thing that drives me crazy about helping people with their marketing is that they put so much stock in it. While bad marketing can certainly damage a good company, great marketing can't save a bad one. Blame is easy to place in a large company—sometimes I think it's like a game of "hot potato." (e.g., "It doesn't matter how much I screw up as long as I'm not the one who gets shit for it at the end of the day.")

The owner of a startup isn't interested in who gets the blame; her single concern in such situations is how to adapt. If the product isn't getting interest, she has to find out what's wrong with their marketing and adapt. If people know about the offer but aren't buying, she has to look critically and adapt. If they buy, but don't do so again, she has to ask why and adapt. Like a traveller landing on an alien planet with few familiar reference points, the founder of a startup has to test, learn, and adapt until it works.

I don't know your company. What I do know is that a lot of companies try to hide mediocre (and sometimes bad) products and services behind glossy and misleading marketing. Doing this when you're up against the big guys is suicide. Startup thinking forces you to look past excuses and find the true problems with your business; it then asks you to sacrifice what isn't working.

Why are you telling me this? I already know what small is about!

We had been in business for seven years before we really started to think in startup terms. For almost all of that time, we used larger companies as the benchmark for what we should aspire to, and mimic. We tried desperately to do so as we believed they had found some kind of answer. My guess is that you probably do the same. You check larger competitors' websites, examine their methods, and secretly wish you could do it as well as they do.

Startups are the mavericks of business. They tend to behave quite differently than other small companies. Talk to someone in a startup—particularly at a hard time—and you tend to find a few common things: most startup founders are a little nervous and not terribly sure of how they'll achieve their dreams. They also tend to be quick to act and adapt, and are burning with excitement and urgency.

CHAPTER 4

Marketing is a Big Load of Bologna

WE'VE ESTABLISHED THAT BIG COMPANIES have some huge challenges to deal with. If you're anything like me, you probably see opportunity in this. If they're slow and hard to move, there must be room for little guys like us, right? I'm with you—really, I am. Actually, from the articles I've read and conversations I've taken part in lately, I get the feeling that many are onboard with this notion.

"Everybody's talking at me. I don't hear a word they're saying."

Those words, from Harry Nilsson's recording of the song *Everybody's Talkin'*, float about in my mind when I think about most marketing.[26] I'm just trying to do my work, walk down the street, or eat my dinner. But, it feels almost impossible to do so, as so many want to say something pointed in my direction. Most of them aren't actually talking to me, nor are they in any way interested in me—even if they might pretend to be. They just want me to do something for them: buy their stuff, vote for them, watch their movie... you get the picture.

This is made worse yet for me personally, because I'm a marketer too. I like to think I'm on the less irritating end of the spectrum, but the fact is, I have to spread the word about smashLAB and the projects we work on. I wish I didn't have to, and I appreciate that most of our work comes from referral. But little of it happens without some marketing at one point or another. We all need to make a little money, and in order to do so, we have to tell people about what we do.

Some feel weird, bad, or even embarrassed about having to get the word out, but that doesn't make it any less necessary. The funny part is there really isn't anything inherently problematic with this. It's just that so many of us have chosen to utilize crummy methods. Some lie, others don't shut up, and most just scramble about, trying to make things like newsletters do all of the work for them.

New! Improved! Ultra grease fighting formula! (Lies)

In your gut you know that most marketing is a load of crap. It's vague, inhuman, and backed by nonsense that seems designed to bamboozle. It is about exaggerating wildly and telling lies. Take a walk through any shopping mall and look at the messages found in promotional materials. The first thing you'll notice is that they're founded on hyperbole.

Sure, I understand that Nike sells more Air Jordans by advertising them with that epic icon of Jordan in flight than they would by just calling them "good shoes." Truth be told, most of us don't mind a little exaggeration as it really isn't such a terrible thing. We all like to embellish at one time or another: "It was so funny I peed my pants!", or "I'm so hungry I could eat a cow!", or "Totally… he's so stupid he put a peep hole in a glass door." We try to make our stories colorful, and marketers do the same.

Playful exaggeration can be fun, and sometimes even sparks our imaginations. The problem with this comes with how easily it goes too far. When this happens, we find ourselves surrounded by messages that aim to outdo the rest with increasingly questionable claims. Although I may believe that Cheerios are reasonably healthy, I sincerely doubt that eating them will reduce my cholesterol by 4–6 percent. (The FDA seems to feel similarly. They recently "scolded" the company for making such claims.)[27]

I know what you're thinking: If even the people who make Cheerios perhaps aren't telling the entire truth, maybe all marketing messages are suspect! Am I to believe my underwear won't result in women clamoring just to get near me? Could it be that the contractor who's renovating my house isn't actually the best in the business? Worse yet, those emails I get offering to add seven inches to the length of my penis—are even those questionable? Damn! I wish I could get that check back!

The old model is inherently flawed

Just for fun, take a moment to google some ads created in the fifties, sixties, or seventies. This time is fawningly referred to as "The Golden Age of Advertising," and the ads from it offer amazing examples of collective delusion. Ad agencies concocted fantasies with hardly any connection to reality and established whole new standards for deceit.

I'd like to share with you the ad that was my introduction to the cruel world of advertising. Like many of the kids of my generation, I loved comic books and I had a collection of them that I adored. One of the staples of comics at that time were the ads for x-ray goggles, Hypno-Coins, and of course... Sea Monkeys. I was too young to be particularly critical of advertising; nevertheless, I did think these ads were a little questionable. Curiosity got the better of me, though, so I pulled together a few dollars and ordered my very own Sea Monkeys.

I eagerly awaited their arrival and imagined the things we might do together. I pondered their size and demeanor, while wondering if they would share the same diversity in gender and age as illustrated in the ad. I was particularly excited to gather my family around our new bowl of Sea Monkeys, to join in the excitement and revelry of observing our new waterborne friends. They'd swim, dance, toss balls, and perhaps even take a break on occasion and simply lounge about, making idle Sea Monkey chitchat.

Finally the day came and the package arrived. I followed the marked instructions diligently and waited for my new friends to "hatch." From that day forth I would race home from school, anticipating the fun I had been promised by the fine people who advertised in the comic books I held so dear. That day never came.

After a few days (I can't remember exactly how long) I did see some miniscule flecks of dust floating about the bowl, but they never amounted to much. No dancing, no games, no interspecies shindigs. I soon lost all interest in my bowl of murky water. It turns out that brine shrimp aren't nearly as exciting as one might be led to believe.

This story, or some variation of it, is a good example of how many of us were introduced to advertising. As a result of this, a strange reciprocal arrangement was formed. We became cynical of advertising, seeing it as little more than fanciful exaggeration; meanwhile, advertisers learned that for no clear reason we'd endure even the most ridiculous lies. With time, these ads lost some of their power. The frequency, funds, and exaggeration they now demand in order to make an impact results in the medium becoming largely unworkable for any party without vast resources.

Turn up the volume!

Lying like this has become an addiction of sorts for many marketers, and it seems that one fix only leads to a bigger one. Worse yet, it becomes a kind of perpetual one-upmanship in an effort to stem the diminishing returns. A lie may be heard once but will probably be ignored upon being repeated. We all know what to do when no one can hear you, though... you SPEAK LOUDER!

So instead of a few people standing around talking about what they do, we're left with a whole room full of folks trying to outyell one another. The lies also follow suit, become increasingly obscene. Once down this road, it seems no one can speak human at all any longer. New fantasies are barfed out in rapid succession and hardly a sentence is uttered without a healthy scoop of superlatives and flowery adjectives.

Perceptive marketers even work to dip into the psyche in an effort to uncover people's greater problems; they then pretend to have the answer to said problems. They tell us how we can be better people: more complete, more content, perhaps even the best versions of ourselves. Sadly, there are very few products that truly solve any of the deeper challenges we face.

Ultimately, it's the business version of *The Little Boy Who Cried Wolf*. As an increasing number of unrealistic promises are made and broken, we turn off and believe very little that's said. Even worse, we become suspect of true messages just because we're so strongly predisposed to thinking everything must be a lie.

Blah, blah, blah, blah-ba-dee-blah, blah, blah!

When everyone's talking and no one's listening, we're not left with communication; we're left with noise. Before you do any marketing, I want you to consider how little *signal* you find amidst this *static*. Did you watch television this morning? Were there any ads that made you buy something or even take some kind of action? If not, can you at least remember one of those ads? I can't hear your response, but my suspicion is that you're quietly thinking, "no." I admit I'm picking on advertising here, but I certainly don't think this mess is limited to ads.

I find almost the exact same thing in resumes from job applicants. Every once in a while we need to hire someone at smashLAB. At these times, we receive hundreds of resumes from candidates who go on at length about how they'll be a greater employee than we can possibly imagine. Their enthusiasm is seemingly difficult to contain. Yet if you ask me to recommend a designer or developer at this moment, I'd be hard pressed to think of even one.

Why? Is it that they are all hacks? Hardly—many of our applicants seem amply qualified. Is it that they weren't polite? No—almost all of these letters were pleasant and positive. Is it that I'm just a big jerk? That might be it, but I'd like to think the problem can once again be tracked back to noise levels. It's really hard for me to differentiate between most applicants, as they tend to exaggerate in exactly the same way. Here I have a few hundred resumes, all largely identical, each trying to outplay the next one. How am I to tell the difference?

The question then might be: what would I need to see, in order to break through the noise? Some have thought about just that, and they've effectively "turned up the volume." One sent us a package containing an umbrella, another formatted their resume to like a newspaper, and one even packaged up a small bottle of alcohol. The strangest berated us for being, "so fucking predictable I could puke" in an effort to stand out. (By the way, that last approach didn't work out particularly well.) The question still stands, though: how do you get past all of the noise, given that every resume claims its owner is better than the next one in the stack?

Showing and telling

I studied under a sometimes curmudgeonly painting instructor during my time at the Emily Carr Institute (now University). Bob was a little older than his fellow faculty members and often seemed out of his element, given the direction art was headed. While others worked on a more conceptual level, Bob was primarily concerned with forming an emotional connection through his paintings. At the time this resonated with me.

There were aspects of Bob's instruction that didn't jibe with me, but one lesson that I've held on to—and will continue to—relates to Bob's perception of the difference between showing and telling. I'd often tell him that a painting I had made was supposed to be fun; he'd counter that it just didn't work. I'd get very frustrated by this, but he continued to remind me that just saying something "was" didn't make it so. Bob's contention was that the most powerful art didn't need an artist's statement to accompany it, as it would make you feel a certain way, free of any verbal crutches.

As we explore this notion of showing versus telling, we see that it applies almost everywhere. It's easy to say you have a great band, but it means more if you play songs that are as great as those written by the Rolling Stones. Telling people you have a great sense of humor isn't a big deal, but making them laugh is. Likewise, telling us your company has great service means nothing, because everyone says that. Those who *show* us remarkable service are much more rare.

Prove it!

Let's address the quandary posed earlier: how might a job applicant break through the noise? To which I'd suggest that one might concentrate on establishing *proof*. Claiming to be a talented, hard working, and insightful candidate isn't any more challenging than saying you've climbed Everest. On the other hand, exhibiting a snapshot from the peak changes everything.

You might respond that this is harder for candidates to do, as they are only being differentiated by a resume. If we work strictly with the traditional application process, you'd be right. I ask whether we should play by such rules. Personally, I'd look at what it would take to get past all the noise and into a space of one's own. Here the message might actually be heard, and proof could be presented.

One might do this a number of different ways. Perhaps they'd seek out a person who could vouch for them, and ask if they might make contact on their behalf. A qualified and respected individual or shared connection can often elevate one beyond the noise and lend validity to their claims. For newcomers, it might not be so easy to call on such a connection; they might have to do something less traditional.

Perhaps they'd start by investing some time in the prospective employer's company. If this candidate is as interested in the company as she claims to be, it wouldn't take too long to get to know the employer and what problems they're facing. Perhaps the applicant could connect through a blog or at an industry event. Maybe they'd make a note about something that might be helpful: "Hey Sally, nice to meet you! I remember you were looking for new type foundries—here's a link that might help." I'm scratching the surface here, but you see what I'm getting at.

Doing this requires an investment. Where one applicant's colleagues might apply for hundreds of jobs a day, the smart one would take extra time to research the company and make a meaningful connection. To cut through the noise, you have to give your audience a reason to believe. That takes more than telling us you're the greatest thing since sliced bread. I'm not suggesting any of this will be easy. Of course, establishing a meaningful relationship hardly ever is.

How did it get so bad?

Most of us think it's better to blend in than stand out. So a lot of people find out what everyone else is doing and copy. We often reason that others must be doing it right, and this keeps us from thinking for ourselves. Much marketing starts with a few people who speak loudly and exaggerate frequently. The next group discovers this pattern and mimics it. Subsequently we're left with a whole bunch of groups screaming lies about themselves. Surprise, surprise—most of us stop paying attention.

Some people work around this. For example, I've been around a few who speak very quietly amongst others. Almost every time, the sound level drops so others can hear what this person has to say. Not all are as prepared to change their tone.

Some get frustrated that they can't break through the noise, and instead of changing how they communicate, they start looking to gimmicks and novel delivery mechanisms. As a result, advertising becomes prescriptive: marketers create lists of items to add to their plan, hoping that one might do the trick. They create new email newsletters, print glossy mailers, and buy a few ads on the radio. All of these things are added, without much thought regarding what they're intended to do, other than some vague notion of "creating awareness." Then along come the web and social media, and these poor, overworked souls are left trying to do even more.

Lies, noise, and "stabs in the dark" comprise the core components of how many organizations approach their marketing. They thrash about wildly, trying anything that might hit paydirt. Thing is, few of us are in the gold mining business—we're just trying to establish relationships. To do this you need to concentrate on what you want to say and proceed methodically. It also doesn't hurt to give these efforts a little time to grow. Although we love the idea of instant relationships, they are pretty much unheard of.

Who are you talking to anyway?

It seems to me that marketing often struggles with intention. Just look at how companies speak. The clumsiest ones talk about themselves or their products, but only in glowing terms: "We do this, we do that, yadda yadda yadda." Ask yourself, if you were on a date with someone who only spoke about himself, would you want to meet him again? Didn't think so.

On the other hand, some get lost in "you." One marketer I'm familiar with suggests that we skew our language to use pronouns like "you" instead of "we." Fine enough and point taken, but try actually doing this and see what you're left with. It's really frightful—kind of like someone playing a trick or trying too hard to impress you. "Oh you, you, you, you. You're great! You're special! Everyone loves you!

You should buy some of our stuff. Did we just say 'our'? Sorry about that! We should have said 'you.' Oh, you!"

Faking interest in your audience is as bad as talking only about yourself. Don't bother—people can almost always tell, and it makes them feel like they're being patronized. There are all kinds of other similarly weird messages, like talking about "us" as though we're "all in it together." This leads to ads about hopes, dreams, and equally vague nonsense. I ask if the problem with all of these examples is a lack of sincere interest in the actual audience.

Mostly we're left with companies that talk about themselves: a few that try to woo us, and others that attempt to bamboozle with some kind of vague promise. What if it doesn't need to be so tricky? What if we just have to look at marketing as a way to erase the gap between our companies and the people who want our stuff?

Marketing is really important

Just because a great deal of marketing is crap, doesn't mean it's without purpose. Fact is, you need customers to know about what you do. This is easier if you can get a few people to love your company. Doing so isn't complex or even that difficult. Getting people to love your company is similar to getting people to like you as a person. But I'm jumping ahead of myself. We have a few things to cover before we get to making people know and love our companies.

With how I've carried on—and I know I do—you might think I don't like marketing, but that isn't the case. Some see marketing as a manipulative pursuit, but I think that's an overly cynical perspective. Marketing is largely about communication. I'm fascinated by it, and I think you should be, too.

Most of us offer something of great value, but many fail just because they can't articulate and share their purpose compellingly. I know great artists whom you'll never meet; your life is less colorful as a result. I've been to restaurants with unbelievable cuisine, but you'll never taste it, because they couldn't pay the rent. We've all heard songs that should be enjoyed by everyone but won't because something was just a degree off. (I can't tell you how many Canadians are frustrated that The Tragically Hip still hasn't "broken" stateside.)

We'd like to think the world is fair, hard work pays off, and good products find an audience in spite of limited resources. In actuality, lots of great products never get into the hands of people who would love them just because the marketing was off message, poorly executed, or resources ran short. While it's the product that we may love, it's marketing that often alerts us to pay attention.

Some who work in marketing have spent so much time lying that they don't even realize they're doing it. Perversely, telling the truth has become hard to do. It's time to go "cold turkey" and start telling it like it is. Besides, it's easier this way.

Get straight

Most marketing is bullshit. That only gets us so far, though. We still have to figure out how to get our messages out there. That's the whole point of this book, and it comes down to just a couple of things: 1. Begin by understanding what you have to offer and who you are (be it good or bad). 2. Spread this message to people who care.

To do these things, you will have to let go of "me too" advertising. Most market by looking at what others do and replicating it. Sort of like saying, "my neighbor drives a Volvo, so I should drive a Volvo.", "My boss likes bratwurst, so I should like bratwurst.", "The kid in shop class stuck his tongue to an icy pole…" You see where this leads. Little good can come from blindly following what others are doing. I ask you to step back and think about who you are. Is there something about your company that's memorable and true, even if it's not necessarily something others would think to promote?

A Canadian cough syrup company called Buckley's serves as a fine example of this. For me, the name of their cough syrup actually comes to mind after their memorable tagline: "It Tastes Awful. And It Works." I don't have to tell you how rare it is to hear a message like this. Most companies don't like to admit their flaws, but Buckley's does. As a result, we take notice. Conversations start because of this tagline, and belief forms as a result. Besides, most of us are more willing to believe something is good once we're aware of the bad parts.

Your company probably has more in common with its competitors than it doesn't. So you have to move past talking about having "great quality, service, and price" and find something that's actually notable. This may require you to openly admit what you don't do, aren't good at, or perhaps what you are obsessive about. Good things rarely start by misleading your partners. The strange part is that so many companies miss out on connecting with us because they don't see opportunity in their *real* stories.

Tell me that you're awful!

Most of us see honesty as a baseline. Someone saying, "I'm a really honest person" only leads us to wonder why they felt the need to make such a claim.

Companies often twist messages in their favor and then think they can turn around and build some kind of trust. (Try doing the same with your spouse and see what happens.) Trust doesn't happen when it's built on partial truths. Nope, you're going to have to embrace your flaws, mistakes, and shortcomings to build real trust. Don't worry—it's not as scary as it sounds.

Building trust is actually easy. Just start by telling the truth, and then do as you promised. Really—how bad are the very worst things about you and your company? Are you part of the mob? Do you have bodies concealed in your trunk of your car? Is your product poorly made? Does it cause cancer? Any of these would probably be good reason to hide. My bet, is that the things you're uncomfortable with aren't quite so bad. Actually, I think there's opportunity to be found in things that might be mistaken for flaws.

McDonalds' reputation has been tarnished in recent years, in part because they haven't been honest with us. While burgers and fries were for so long a staple of our culture, a shift in public interest towards healthier options led McDonald's to try and be "that too." They've introduced a number of initiatives like the Lighter Choices Menu and the Go Active program, ostensibly intended to make us see the company in a more healthy light. Few of us bought this story, and once information on the actual calorie counts of these options came to light, McDonald's faced a mess. Headlines noting that their salads are more fattening than their burger probably weren't part of the plan: "A chicken Caesar salad with dressing and croutons contains 425 calories and 21.4g of fat, compared with 253 calories and 7.7g of fat in a standard hamburger. Add a portion of fries to your burger and the calorie count climbs to 459, but is still less fatty than the salad at 16.7g."[28]

Calories and fat aren't actually the problem for McDonald's. What chips away at their brand is that they pretend to be healthy. We all know better. Whether they like it or not, McDonald's isn't about health—it's about great tasting junk food. I have to ask why they would give up on this position. Why not own, love, and celebrate it?

The heart attack burger

For many years, I've been saying this is the way McDonald's should go: own their legacy of tasty, but not-so-healthy, burgers. Many of us need an indulgence every once in a while, and there's little wrong with that, so long as we don't overdo it. Recently I learned of a place that has outdone even what I might have suggested for McDonald's.

Dr. Jon Basso makes believe that he's a doctor, but he doesn't pretend his restaurant is healthy—actually, quite to the contrary. At his restaurant there isn't a vegetarian option, nor is there a Lighter Choices Menu. Instead, this hospital themed restaurant features scantily clad nurses (waitresses), who serve up single, double, triple, and quadruple "Bypass" burgers that reach up to around 8,000 calories (that's a lot). Their "Flatliner Fries" are cooked in pure lard, and they offer a selection of other health-hating options: unfiltered cigarettes, liquor, Jolt Cola, and more. With The Heart Attack Grill, we find a company that's positioned itself quite effectively by being bad… really, really bad.[29]

I don't personally like the Heart Attack Grill and what it represents. What I do admire is how they're positioned around this idea. Additionally, they are in many ways more truthful than other fast food chains, but I suppose this is a little like applauding a crack dealer for telling his clients that his stuff will kill them.

The best marketing is done by the audience

If you ever find yourself in Chandler, Arizona, I bet you'll take a drive by the Heart Attack Grill. You might walk in or you might not, but you're likely to remember it. Why? Did Jon Basso send you a brochure that you've been holding on to? No. Maybe his company advertised on your local radio station? Not that either, eh? I've got it! He sent you an email about the company and a coupon for 10 percent off! Strike three? Darn… I thought I was good at this stuff.

Kidding aside, the reason you know about the Heart Attack Grill, and may tell a few friends about it, is that it's not like most other places out there. In fact, it's what all the other restaurants don't want to admit to being. The Heart Attack Grill takes a position that most would see as corporate suicide and turns it into a memorable story. They court controversy and do some things I wouldn't, but they get us talking. People talking about your stuff is a really good thing. (It's also harder to make happen than many of us would like to admit.)

Wouldn't it be lovely if people found what you did and just loved it? Perhaps they'd tell 10 friends, and those friends would tell 10 others, and soon everything would be perfect. Ooh… I'm excited about this already! While we're waiting for this to happen, let's just suppose that getting others to pay attention might require you to get the ball rolling first.

Don't bug people

Later in this book I'll talk about all of the excitement surrounding social media. If I may plant one early seed, it would be to not get overly bogged down by what others do and the delivery devices they use. Marketers are often stymied by which tools to use—and especially by the idea that you have to bug people in order to build awareness. Before executing on any marketing piece, simply ask yourself, "Will the recipient get something out of this message?"

Determine what you have to say and ensure that it matters. From there you just have to connect with people who are interested in your message, and are willing to help you tell your story clearly. I believe most companies would substantially strengthen their marketing by doing this alone. It's all about building good relationships. Before we talk more about that, let's look at the failings of advertising.

CHAPTER 5

The Problem
With Advertising

It's awfully easy to whine about bad marketing, but that's a little like faulting the vodka for your hangover. Alcohol is inert; blaming it is silliness. Sometimes we just make bad choices. Marketing is a part of life, and the reason it so often fails relates to who does it and for what reasons.

We're all in it for ourselves

Ineffective marketing is often the result of poorly-aligned motivations. It would be easier to succeed if everyone involved was shooting for the same goal, but often we play altogether different games.

Let's suppose that your goal is to get people to love your brand. Consider some of the players and what their objectives might be. You, as the owner of the company (assuming you are this person) likely care the most about succeeding. Of all those involved, you have the most to gain but you're likely distracted by a number of things. Perhaps you're concerned about not going over budget. Maybe you have doubts about the ideas presented and want to hold on to the idea your husband suggested. Alternately, you could be fighting with a supplier and finding it difficult to concentrate on any of this.

Your internal marketing team is doing its best to stay the course, but they're exhausted. The project is turning out to be much harder than they initially expected. With numerous programs to run, calls to respond to, emails to address, and a few fires to put out, they really just want to go home for the weekend.

Your agency wants to make you happy and knows it's important to keep clients like you. But no matter how much they do for you, they have other clients who also need support. (If they only serviced your company they wouldn't stay in business very long.) The ad agency has many motivations. Their principals are in a position similar to yours: just trying to keep all those balls in the air.

Those within the organization have lives of their own to consider. Some want to build their portfolios and move into better positions. A few are happy to work in a fun place but not that interested in the work itself. Add office politics, economic pressures, and the egos that can be found within the industry, and it becomes rather amazing that anything ever gets done.

Ad agencies are great... if you're already famous

The advertising and marketing world is typically focused on the big guys and for good reason. They have the most to spend, and their dollars are highly coveted by agencies vying for their business. The problem is that most of us aren't multinationals and few of us have budgets like theirs to devote to marketing our companies.

When you're big, though, marketing is a bit of a different game. Big players have something I think of as social currency. Patagonia, for example, has a fair amount of this. Most of us know the company and its ethics; some of us can even picture the logo when we hear the name. Similarly, everyone knows about Apple, its ethos and its aesthetic. It's hard to think of another company that commands as much social currency as Apple. Many simply want to know what they're up to, as is evidenced by all the blogs that speculate on the future of the company and its products.

You, on the other hand, probably have very little social currency. When mentioning your company to an outsider, you likely have to explain what you do. Famous brands like Coke, Snickers, and BMW are simply ahead of you on this level. They're known, and in business being known is often the most important thing. Advertising helps established players like these reinforce and defend their brands. You might run some ads and perhaps even do so effectively, but the sheer cost of entry makes doing so prohibitive. There are always exceptions, but I'd encourage most small companies to find other ways of building their brands than paying for ads.

It's a changed game

Although the people in ad agencies are mostly nice and well intentioned, a large number of them are doing just what the rest of us are: selling enough stuff to get by. This is actually turning out to be much harder for big ad agencies as of late. The landscape is changing, and many of the rules these people know are being challenged by the decentralization of media.

You could compare these changes to the one faced by horse drawn buggy manufacturers at the dawn of the automobile era. Some of them probably made great buggies, but that really wasn't the issue, nor was the reliability, comfort, or aesthetics of their product. All that mattered was that the buggy was a dead technology. Most people in this position don't like to admit this sort of thing, no matter how true it may be. I can almost imagine the argument: "Horseless carriage? It'll never catch on! People like buggies! They believe in buggies! You just watch; the whole thing will turn out to be a fad!"

In hindsight, of course, it's easy to mock others for their lack of awareness regarding the changes afoot. It isn't altogether that different these days, though. A few scant years ago, I remember hearing top-level ad agency folks muttering that the internet was a passing fad. Most of those same people are now aggressively purchasing interactive shops or building teams to make web services part of their core offering. Ad agencies will be here for a long time; that doesn't change how baffled many of them are by the new landscape. After years of complete control and a fixed supply of media, they're facing a world in which little is in their control and the supply of media is infinite.

It used to be different

Perhaps I'm getting ahead of myself here. Let me back up and provide a little perspective. It used to be easier for ad agencies. Until more recently, the ways to spread your company's message were limited and expensive. There were ads on television, in newspapers, and on the radio; there were billboards, flyers, and plenty of general marketing collateral. With time, the notion of sponsored events, product placement, naming rights for arenas, and the like, also came to light. All of this was centered on the same general principle: interruption.

Ads were intrusive and thrived on the notion of frequency. Advertisers believed if they put a message in your face a sufficient number of times, you'd become familiar with their stuff and eventually buy some. (Admittedly, I'm oversimplifying here.)

This practice worked very well for big companies that had enough money to make a suitable number of impressions. Just go to the websites of companies like Procter and Gamble or Unilever and see how many of their brands have become household names. This was accomplished through well crafted strategies and millions of advertising dollars aimed at building mindshare. The problem was that it didn't work quite so well for everyone else.

Put simply: The little companies found themselves sort of screwed. Most had limited options for advertising due to budgetary restrictions. Actually, most of them would have done better by avoiding advertising altogether, but we were so fixed on an "advertising lens" that we couldn't imagine doing anything else.

While working at a newspaper in the mid-1990s. I watched tiny Mom & Pops buy an ad every few months. Typically they opted for the smallest space available, and it was crammed next to a dozen other similar ads. These companies usually filled every bit of the purchased ad space in order to get good "value."

Selling these ads always seemed a little questionable to me. The ads didn't appear to accomplish much, but the customer's money was taken anyway. I suppose the newspaper had to stay afloat, but I never really thought a business should be built like this. These sales didn't seem to have much value for the client. In my mind this represents a missed opportunity. We could have talked the client into a small but highly-targeted campaign. Or we could have urged the client to hold off on advertising until the budget was adequate. Instead they ran some ads, likely saw little return on their investment, and in the long run probably spent less money on advertising.

I like to think that forgoing a sale today can be an amazing sales strategy. If it shows that you are really looking after your client's best interests, it can build loyalty and substantially better long-term gains. I digress, however.

I suppose you could look at advertising as a pyramid. It's awesome for the people at the top. For the rest of us it just doesn't deliver the same value. That doesn't stop advertising from being one of the primary methods people use to build interest in their companies, products, and services. When you ask most people how they could increase awareness for their company, many will shrug their shoulders and say, "Uh, I don't know... Maybe we could try advertising?"

The times they are a changing

Many of the people in advertising are interesting, well read, and worldly. That's part of why some advertising transcends its initial purpose and becomes part of our culture. People who make culture tend to be tapped into what's happening. These people are well aware of changes in communication enabled by the web, and many have quite significant and informed opinions on the topic.

One thing that can't be said, is that any of this is getting easier. Just imagine if your company needed to work with a new set of tools every day. Today's advertisers and agencies have all kinds of new avenues available to them. As a result, connecting with buyers seems ever more complicated. That doesn't stop most agencies, and many are left adding new services whether they like it or not.

While agencies have always had to understand customers, culture, humor, psychology, media, and entertainment, they're now tasked with even more. Today's full service agency needs to have offerings in spaces including: digital, social media, design, environments, naming, events... *oh, the list goes on.* And as we all know, doing an increasing number of things rarely makes you better at any individual one.

Not this too!

I'm assuming you're part of a small to medium-sized company;

there's little reason to read this book if you're in a large one. So I'm going to keep presenting notions as though large companies are the enemy. In a lot of cases they probably aren't, but it's sometimes useful to have someone in your sights. It can help you stay sharp and focused. I always find that we move more efficiently when we know who we're "against," as this motivates us to "up" our game. (We don't really dislike the big guys; this is just a trick to spark our competitive characteristics.)

Here's a little insight that might give you a leg up: Social media is an utter pain in the ass for big companies. First of all, most of the people in these companies are just as confused as you are about it. They had decades to figure out press releases, ad campaigns, systems for tracking customers, trade shows, and all of that other (not necessarily easy) stuff. Now they have to do all of that *and* much more.

Let's pretend you're the head of marketing for a company with 500 employees in 12 offices across 7 countries. In the past, you fought just to keep people from using the logo incorrectly or sending out a press release with unverified information. Now the floodgates have really opened. Everyone has the potential to communicate directly with your customers, and they may say things you don't want them to. They could be rude, post inaccurate information about your company, or present themselves inappropriately.

Consider the actions of Kristy Hammonds and Michael Setzer: a couple of Domino's Pizza workers who have since been dismissed. Hammonds recorded a video of Setzer spraying snot on sandwiches during their preparation, sticking cheese from them into his nose, and finally farting on them. They then uploaded the video to YouTube, after which it was viewed by a great number of people. As Domino's spokesman Tim McIntyre remarked, "That's the challenge of the web world. Any two idiots with a video camera and a dumb idea can damage the reputation of a 50-year-old brand."[30] Domino's responded actively and dealt with the situation well, but it certainly shows how vulnerable we all are.

Add to this the distraction that comes from everyone wanting to play with sites like Facebook. Do you accept this as a cost of business and encourage everyone to play? Doing so might result in your staff gaining insight, and establishing better relations with customers. Or is it simply a waste of time? Should you deem it unnecessary and restrict access to such sites on company time? I'd have a hard time coming up with a steadfast plan for this sort of thing, and I certainly don't envy those who have to make these decisions. *It's a mess.*

If you're the person who has to help a large company answer these questions, you have your work cut out for you. Not only do you have to take on all of these new tools, you have to figure out what it all stands for in your organization.

Whose message is it anyway?

I don't envy a large company having to deal with all of the tools available to them. It's a tough spot, and I can understand why they look for partners who they can unload these tasks on. Still, I'm not convinced that having someone communicate for a company by proxy is the best thing either.

A few years ago we hired a publicist to work with us. We were swamped and offloading some work seemed like a good idea. We interviewed a few people and found one who was sharp, focused, and direct. I liked her, but that didn't change the fact that working with her was sometimes cumbersome. (To her credit, I think we were a very difficult company to work for.) We wanted to give her what she needed, and she did try to help us. Some things just got lost in translation. It turned out that no matter how hard we all tried, it was simply easier for us to talk about what we do than it was to ask someone else to do so for us.

I think some of our clients must feel similarly. It's our job to dive deep enough to understand their companies and needs, in order to craft an effective strategy. Most times this works reasonably well, and our outside perspective is useful to them. Additionally, we try to outfit them with the right tools and ask them to do most of the actual speaking. This helps ensure it doesn't sound as if someone's doing the speaking for them.

As a result of our blog, I'm regularly contacted by publicists who want us to write about a particular product, company, technology, or author. On almost every occasion they send a boilerplate press release that has little actual relevance to my readership. (I've learned to hit the delete button quickly.) The thing is, it's not like these are bad people; it's just that they confuse quantity with quality. Publicists are likely being asked to make more calls; in doing so, they can't possibly get to know everyone they reach out to.

If you, as the owner of the company, aren't directly involved with your messaging, you're in big trouble. The days of putting layers between you and your customers have long passed. If you employ outside help, you might opt to bring in professionals to set up the framework and strategy for your messaging and interaction with clients. In this arrangement, you'd harness their advice, take an active role in the execution and delivery, and then bring them in when you needed to tap their expertise again.

If you want to unload more of your work, you'll have to build a closer relationship with these people. They'll need access, knowledge, and latitude. If these folks are to speak for you, they'd better know you and what you do, as well as if it were their own company.

Ads work

With the critical things I say about advertising, some might start to think that I don't see any reason to use it. Such a notion would be wrong. I don't question for a moment that advertising works—even for small companies. The reason I sound out against it so vocally simply relates to how ad-centric many of us have become. After so many years of things working in the same fashion, most don't ask if there might be a better way. In my experience, there increasingly is.

I do think some small companies are wise to run ads. In doing so, I just ask you to carefully consider if this really is the best method for building awareness for your brand. If it is—perfect! If not—then it's time to go back to looking at your other available options. In using advertising to spread your message, you simply have to be smart and selective. It's a costly method, so you need to be shrewd about how you go about it.

The best way to save money in your ad buy is to know exactly what you are saying, and to whom. Reducing the number of variables involved can make a massive difference in both the effectiveness of your advertising and the size of cavity it leaves in your pocketbook.

My continual reminder of just how effective advertising can be comes down to a local realtor who has invested intelligently. My wife and I have been searching for a new home for our family. We're particularly interested in a part of Burnaby called Forest Hills. As we've looked at houses in this area, one realtor's name has come up time and again. This fellow seems to concentrate all of his ad buys in this one specific area. He has his ads on what seems like every bus shelter, street bench and any other available space here. Additionally, he aggressively markets himself with direct mail in this area.

Were he to advertise all across the city, he'd likely find his message spread overly thin, but by going narrow like this, he's able to get substantial bang for his buck.

While some over-rely on advertising, I probably lean towards the other end of the spectrum. I simply believe that it's just one method of reaching people, amongst many others. If it works for you, great! Just be sure that you know your market, clarify your message, monitor your success, and have defined objectives from the get-go. Just like any other marketing initiative.

Advertising for some, a different path for the rest

If you're a big company that needs to reinforce a message to a broad audience, it may be prudent to keep advertising, and continue working with a big ad agency. Your objectives are likely focused on defending your brand's position. Agencies are very good at this and have a wealth of domain knowledge that would be difficult for smaller marketing and design companies to compete with.

If you're small, you're playing a different game. You still need to communicate but won't have the same resources to do so. You'll also have to develop a unique strategy, as yours is a battle of *creating* awareness amongst key people. It would be difficult for you to do this entirely on your own; you'll need to connect with an individual or team with expertise in this area that can help you develop a strategy and plan for execution. (It's up to you to determine how much help you need in this capacity.)

The important part is that you remember to keep your company's focus on the goals you initially outlined. Little of this should be about being clever or trying to push boundaries, unless that actually meets a directive you've established. Many confuse marketing a company with doing fun and creative things. Although this may sometimes be the case, it surely isn't always. The point is that you find a way to converse appropriately with your audience.

CHAPTER 6

You're the One to Market Your Company

I DON'T TRUST FINANCIAL ADVISORS. It's not that I see them as inherently bad people; I just don't think anyone will care as much about my money as I do. Similarly, no one has as much at stake in marketing your company as you do. Your reputation, livelihood, and prosperity are on the line with every move you make. Your name is on the lease and line of credit; mess up and your kids will likely have to work at Burger King to cover college tuition.

It's your baby

Once the ad guy from the local radio station sells you a spot, he's gone. My guess is he's not coming back until he thinks he can do the same again. This is fair, as he has his own livelihood to think about; nevertheless, you need to remind yourself that you're the only one who really pays the price if the ad doesn't work. There are plenty of people, ready to promise big, who won't lose a wink of sleep if the ad returns nothing. So I ask, if you aren't willing to take the lead on this, do you think they really will?

A few things can be secondary in your company, but your message and how you are perceived should never be. So I'm asking you to push past all of the people who want a piece of your marketing budget. I want you to take the wheel and hold it firmly. I'm certainly not suggesting that you do it all by yourself, but I do think someone needs to lead this thing. And who's more suited for it that than you?

You're at the heart of your company and know more about it than anyone else. My bet is you bore your spouse by obsessing over all kinds of obscure details. Perhaps you even look upon your business as an extension of yourself. If there's anyone that I, as a customer, want to talk with about your company, it's probably you. So, you'd better be the person who shapes its messaging.

Show us the love

Love is easy to say, but it's a misused term when it comes to marketing. Consider a few of the "lovey" taglines corporations use:

"Love it for life."—Dannon Yogurt
"You'll love the way we fly."—Delta Airlines
"Sanka—everything you love about coffee."—Sanka

Buy any of that? Me neither. I don't love yogurt, I can't imagine feeling affection for someone's manner of flying, and associating love with Sanka seems a little like using silver polish on a plastic cup. Statements like these have as much to do with love as porn has to do with sex: an interesting fantasy, but not close to reality.

Why don't we believe these statements? Is it just that they're complete bullshit? That's certainly part of it, but what else is common in all of these statements? Right—they're pushing it on us. They want us to love their thing, but I have to wonder if even they feel that way. Do the people at Sanka (sorry to pick on you guys so much) love their coffee, or do they just want us to love it?

It's one thing to say you love something, but faking love is kind of hard to do. Love isn't just said; it's shown through how we talk and act around the objects of our affection. If you want them to love your company, you had better love it, and there's little use pretending. People can smell a fraud very quickly, so you'd best be the "real deal" or nothing at all. Problem is, most marketers are faking it.

As I said earlier, I'm quite enamored with espresso and think myself well versed on the drink. Recently I was proven a rank amateur. It all started with a visit to Genius Coffee & Espresso Equipment, which is close to our apartment. I've grown tired of having to leave the house every time I want an espresso, and reasoned it was time to buy a machine for the house (mine currently lives at our office). The fellow I met at Genius (whom I surmised to be the owner) was an espresso guru from a whole other coffee-centric galaxy.

He first explained every model in my price range and the differences between each machine. Around this time he realized my son needed some distraction, so he brewed up a hot chocolate to keep Oscar happy. Then he discussed how certain materials in the machine make a significant difference in the resulting beverage. He finally pulled a shot so I could taste it for myself. It was beautiful.

He continued by discussing his travels to Italy and the qualities of the coffees they were bringing in. He detailed the best methods for storing coffee beans, noting that a sealed bag with a pin prick at the bottom was optimal, as it avoided oxidization of the beans while allowing them to breathe just enough. I could continue, but I think you catch my drift. This guy doesn't just want to sell machines—his passion *is* coffee.

You can advertise anything and speak about it in whichever manner you'd like. You can make truthful claims, misleading ones, or just outright lie. No one will take the time to stop you from doing any of this. What you can't do as readily is make us love you, or even get us to believe that you love your product. The fellow at Genius, however, did exactly that. This wasn't because of a claim, but rather, by being incredibly passionate about espresso.

I can't guarantee Genius will make it. The premium price of their machines is aimed at those who are serious about coffee. I think that's going to make it harder for them to sell a lot of volume. Still, I think that this guy showed me something Sanka's ads simply can't. Now he just has to show a few of the right people the same passion he showed me.

Why you might trip yourself up

Although I sincerely believe that you need to be the person who "drives," owners of companies can be a pain in the ass when it comes to marketing. It's not that they don't care; in fact, it's quite the opposite. They care so much their fear can get in the way. Many owners are so petrified of making a misstep that they suffocate campaigns before they even get out of the gates. I've seen it happen on numerous occasions: Clients once thrilled by the possibility of doing something sensible and effective start to fall apart as the launch date nears.

This happens in different ways. Mostly it's the result of introducing unindoctrinated parties to the discussion. When you buy a new pen, you know what you're looking for and how they generally work. There's little reason to ask others for opinions on such a purchase. With most messaging related projects, though, there's a deep desire to have one's decisions validated by peers. Sometimes this is useful when relying on those who are fully briefed on the effort. Sadly, many seek feedback from people unfamiliar with the project goals and strategy. As a result these people tend to make uninformed and therefore less relevant observations.

Being asked for one's opinion can feel strange. Few like to admit that they don't have a clear opinion on a given topic—perhaps for fear of seeming unhelpful should they give no response. This kind of "say anything" reaction can be crippling. Feedback from those who haven't considered the overarching objectives is bound to dwell on the wrong points. One of our clients changed the marketing direction for their highly technical offering as a result of a ten-year-old son's feedback. They later admitted this to be a mistake, but at the time, this youngster's opinion actually affected the presentation of the company.

This is precisely why you must establish lucid goals and strategy before beginning any messaging or brand related exercise... and involve *only* key parties from the very beginning. If your direction isn't rock solid, it gets too easy to become sidetracked and make decisions based on misplaced emotion. We all want people to respond favorably to what we put out there, but not all feedback is equal. Choose your timing, questions, and those you ask them of, carefully.

Bringing in objective counsel

While you probably know more about your company than anyone else, there are times this can prove a liability. Have you ever asked a programmer about the problems you're having with a system they've developed, only to be met with a befuddled "don't you understand?" expression? You might be just like that programmer when it comes to your company. You're so close to what you do that you know every aspect of it. This might blind you to things that would be obvious to an outsider.

We worked closely with a lighting company called illumivision in early 2008. They manufacture industrial lighting systems—the kind you see used on impressive buildings and public monuments. Before we started working with them, all of their marketing materials concentrated on the hardware they manufacture, with the visual impact of their offering almost entirely neglected. What would have been obvious to an outsider had evaded them. Their audience, while sometimes needing technical specifications, probably wasn't going to be sold on such details. So we asked them to seduce potential customers with images of the end result: beautiful buildings, instead of just engineered casings. The magic is in the gorgeous structures that come to life as a result of illumivision's systems.

Within 6 months of this change, the people at illumivision told us their international sales had increased by 225 percent, and they could directly tie this shift to their slightly-adjusted messaging. We hadn't done anything that spectacular; we just brought a fresh set of eyes to their business. Often, a shift like this is all you really need.

Although I'm asking you to lead, I think wise leaders have to step aside from time to time and let others take the helm when it's appropriate to do so. Establish clear goals, hire smart people, and listen to their input. At any time, it's fair to ask your people—regardless of how impressive their credentials may be—to articulate the rationale behind their choices. Most will do so happily, as it shows that instead of just reacting, you want to understand their logic. It's always fair to question a direction. Just ensure that you do so sensibly, having equally explicable motivation behind your decisions.

The time is right

As a marketing space, the web isn't really as game-changing for established brands as it is for smaller organizations. The advantage that brand stables like Procter and Gamble, Johnson & Johnson, and Unilever had prior to this time was massive. The barrier to entry in a broadcast media setting was colossal; smaller brands aiming to build awareness and loyalty with the audience were left to accomplish a Herculean feat. Sometime in the mid-'90s, the seeds of change were planted. Although established brands may always maintain an advantage over small up-and-comers, the assuredness of this is less certain with every passing day.

Each and every vertical that an established brand operates within can be attacked faster and more effectively by a small company than ever before. Social media and the web in general are not native to multinationals. If these e-media favor anyone, it would be smaller, more nimble organizations that can take risks, disrupt the ecosystem, iterate and adapt rapidly, and build one-on-one relations with their audiences. It's a good time for "little guys" like us to be in business—perhaps better than ever. Now it's just a matter of getting down to work.

The process I suggest comes down to a few core steps. First, you'll need to solidify who you are and what you offer—subsequently you'll need to give people a reason to believe in what you do. (In *Part Two* of the book we'll concentrate specifically on this.) After that we'll look at how you can spread your message using both word of mouth and some of the web-enabled methods of communication that have more recently emerged. From there you'll need to act consistently and adapt as necessary.

First things first: let's look at brands.

PART TWO

FINDING YOUR VOICE

---

*What's your company about, and why should customers
care? To answer that question we need to look at brands
and what they mean to your company—from the basics to
the cardinal rules. You'll also learn how differentiation can
help you uncover your "one thing," and why high school
gets in the way of marketing success. We'll explore the
amazing power of storytelling, and how you can craft ones
that customers will love. Additionally, we'll discuss the risks
associated with losing your authenticity. (I'll even tell you
why McDonald's couldn't make pizza work.)*

CHAPTER 7

WHAT A BRAND IS

OVER THE PAST DECADE, we've heard an awful lot about brands. In spite of how we've been inundated, the notion of a brand is important to contemplate, clarify, and revisit as you build your company and spread your message. Some equate brands with a sort of plot to manipulate people and do ill. Others see branding as just another business trend that will soon pass. I don't blame anyone for such feelings; branding is such a broad topic that it leads to some confusion.

My problem with the term "brand" is that it's often used quite differently from what it actually represents. All that really matters for now, is that we establish a straightforward and reasonable definition of what we're talking about when we use the words brand and branding. Let's start with this: branding is the process of understanding and articulating who you are—both for yourself and to the outside world. That's it. Easy, right? I think Amazon's Jeff Bezos describes the term "brand" best. He explains, "A brand for a company is like a reputation for a person. You earn reputation by trying to do hard things well."[31]

The brand as a person

For years I've endeavored to write a particular blog article but have had little success in doing so. It starts as a great little metaphor, but along the way I find it ties me up in knots. Today I'll play with the same notion yet again. My hope is that you'll be lenient with me should the comparison not be entirely bulletproof.

I argue that we've all come to look upon businesses as something mystical. We abstract what business is with ideas like stocks, shareholders, boards, indexes, and other seemingly convoluted language. I think business is fundamentally simple and that brands are really an awful lot like people. Actually, in the eyes of the law, corporations are seen as individual entities. Companies, like people, need food (money and some other resources), shelter (a place to live, even if it's on the web), security, community, purpose, and a raft of other things.

Thinking about companies like this makes them easier to understand. If a company doesn't eat (make money), it will die, and without security (regular cash flow) it will struggle to act consistently; similarly, without purpose it will likely flounder. Each of us is unique; likewise, our companies are all one of a kind, even if only minutely so.

We should all have a reason for what we do

Most of us have dreams and a sense of purpose. For a company, we call that "vision." Throughout our lives, our dreams and purpose sometimes change. In high school we want to look cool and go to fun parties; as young parents we want stability and safety for our kids. Similarly, a startup often moves recklessly, coming close to the edge as it works to gain footing and build awareness.

Once a company begins to grow, it often has to act more carefully. With a greater number of employees, the sales cycle needs to remain consistent, ensuring that cash flow and jobs aren't compromised. Amidst such change, a sense of purpose is increasingly important. Without motivation, we turn into that 40 year old "man-boy" who laments "not knowing what to do with his life." There are plenty of companies with workable storefronts, identity systems, advertising campaigns, and display signage. Yet those without a sense of purpose tend to make erratic moves. Sometimes these swings reflect the emotional state of the primary decision-maker: brave and adventurous on some days, reserved and seemingly pragmatic on others.

Companies that do this tend to feel a little "bipolar" to their clients: hot at times and cold at others. This leaves customers bewildered and unsure of how they can mentally classify these businesses. Every day for the past year, I have walked by a shop that lacks direction. For a while they were in the embroidery business; later, they added large format printing. They also sell team uniforms, signs, promotional products, vehicle lettering, screen printing, floor mats, and gifts. Yesterday I walked by to find that they now sell brand name clothing as well. What's next? Tacos? Elevator supplies? Prophylactics?

While they stumble about without a clear sense of purpose, they lose the mindshare and momentum that would have been gained by maintaining focus. When it comes to brands and marketing, confusion is rarely an emotion one should seek to elicit. Although some companies may change course along the way, a clear and unified purpose is key to informing effective messages and actions.

How your company dresses

You might compare an identity system to one's wardrobe. Although we can choose to wear anything, most of us dress to represent who we think we are or how we want to be perceived. This is why kids who skateboard choose street wear, and why it's rare to find executives in such attire. Part of this comes down to identification: Most Goths want to get some attention and be perceived as standing apart from the mainstream. Most high-school teachers probably don't want to be confused as students so they choose their dress accordingly. Uniforms are everywhere, regardless of whether we are cognizant of them.

Some people suffer as a result of their choices in clothing. Perhaps it's because they don't have the time or capacity to select something that accurately conveys who they are. This is understandable; most of us are busy and not interested in pondering what suits us best. Like it or not, customers make all kinds of decisions based on what their eyes tell them.

Unfortunate as it may be, we treat beautiful people better than those who are less attractive. Similarly, we spend more on products that are designed to seem of a higher quality, whether they actually are or are not. We place an undeserved amount of trust in the information our eyes feed us. Think about the language we employ: "I wouldn't have believed it if I hadn't seen it with my own two eyes!"— as though our eyes provide an indisputable measure of truth. Our eyes lie to us all the time. We've all seen optical illusions that show how inaccurate our visual judgments can be. Even when we know this to be the case, we still make countless choices using our eyes to determine what's beautiful or ugly, good or bad, safe or dangerous.

The decision for companies then is whether they want to control (or influence) how they are perceived by their audience. This is why we have designers. The good ones can help style an identity around a company just as a tailor would fit a suit to one's body. The great ones get to know you and what you're about, subsequently suggesting things that match your personality and desires.

Some think of a brand identity as an unnecessary extravagance. Smart companies have learned that having a few core elements that "fit well" offer greater value than random impulse driven purchases. Crafting an identity is an investment that saves resources in the long-term. Not having a suitable identity is akin to wearing sweatpants and hoping that your date will look past them and see the "real you."

Mutes, loudmouths, weirdos, and buddies

Advertising is the one marketing related pursuit that most managers seem comfortable with. It's often misunderstood as a direct path to customers, which results in many shouting out whatever comes to mind. As with anything, it's important to understand context, tone, and reputation when we start to speak with the people around us. In the "brand as a person" metaphor, advertising is your mouth.

All of us have mouths and each of us uses ours differently. Some don't say too much, while others are always talking. Similarly, there are companies who never tell us anything about what they're doing, while others bombard us with so many messages that we stop listening altogether. Most in the latter category have deep pockets and would argue that being ever-present affords them brand awareness.

We also know people who say things that are weird, boring, safe, funny, sensible, and pretty much everything in between. Each of these has an advertising equivalent: Ricola's ads are weird, IBM's are boring, Gap's are safe, Budweiser's are (sometimes) funny. We get to know about these companies because of what they say about themselves and how they speak to us.

An advertisement or ad campaign is in no way a brand. In fact, ads sometimes get in the way of brands. Just think of the odd Seinfeld/Gates campaign devised by the ad agency Crispin Porter + Bogusky (CP+B) for Microsoft. In the first of the two, they bump into one another at the mall, after which Seinfeld assists Gates in selecting shoes.[32] The commercial is long, clocking in at a minute and a half. During the spot, they discuss showering while dressed, the fact that the Conquistador (some kind of a shoe) "runs tight," and Shoe Circus Clown Club memberships. The ad was later followed by another spot (almost three times as long) in which the magnate and the comedian move in with a suburban family.

Although the ads resulted in a great deal of discussion, they seemed a bit out of character. CP+B is sort of the toast of the town in advertising, in part because of their clever and off-the-wall campaigns. Personally, I love some of the things they've come up with. That doesn't mean these approaches always work for their clients.

Microsoft (like every other company) has a brand, but theirs isn't one that most people fall in love with. They're like a big utility provider. Many of us rely on their services, but we often feel as though we do so more out of necessity than choice. Plus, they're so gargantuan and multifaceted that it's really hard for them to focus on saying any single thing.

The Seinfeld/Gates ads grab our attention a little like a cracker-white middle-aged suburban dad dressing like Snoop Dogg. We're left thinking, "OK… that's weird, but why are you doing that?" Their ad agency created something memorable, but I have to wonder if they might have failed to address the most important question: Does the message spoken fit the entity it's coming from? Microsoft is many things, but it doesn't seem particularly quirky. It's worth noting that these ads went away rather quickly. A few months later, that same "mouth" was saying quite different things.

As a result, we're left with a number of questions: Who are you, Microsoft? What do you want us to know? Why should we *love* you? We don't have to like what they're saying, but these ads might do worse: they confuse us. We're left to ask, "Why do you want to confuse us, Microsoft?"

I should note that the Seinfeld/Gates ads were highly amusing, and that I have blogged from a very different standpoint in the past, emphatically calling the campaign a success. My argument here isn't focused on the campaign in isolation, but instead, how it relates to the brand and the larger picture.

I do _____, for _____, in _____

The larger the organization, the harder it is to be just one thing; and, when you're many "things" it's particularly challenging to say anything clearly. (In advertising it's generally good to say one thing and then repeat it.) The challenge for companies like Microsoft is that they do so many things, it's hard for them to know what to even say any longer. Should they market software, music players, game machines, multi-touch technologies, online portals, advertising services, search, or one of the other things they do? Microsoft's size and success is a bit of an Achilles heel: it keeps them from positioning effectively.

Positioning for a company is a little like specialization in one's career. It allows you to get really good at something and as a result, thin the competition. As of September 2009, there were an estimated 6,790,062,216 people on the planet; there are also many different and highly complex disciplines and careers.[33] Certain factors beyond our control determine the opportunities that are available to us, and which opportunities we're able to pursue.

Being one of 6.79 billion people can make anyone feel a little insignificant. How do you stand out amongst all of those people? How do you earn a living? Odds are that you can't be as good as everyone else at absolutely everything, so most tend to specialize in one way or another. Let's take the case of Susan: earth resident number 6,790,062,217.

Being born to a middle class family in the First World narrows the field for her substantially. Displaying an early proficiency in certain subjects leads her to go to university, which narrows the field yet again. She majors in Philosophy; field narrows. From there she attends law school; field narrows. After a few years of practicing law, she decides that intellectual property really interests her, so she learns more about this specific practice and starts to specialize in it. She then decides to focus specifically on IP law as it relates to the internet. She gets particularly interested in issues related to traditional books being showcased online without the authors' consent. While there may be a few other people interested in this area of law, Susan has certainly has cut her competition drastically from the 6.79 billion people who were at the starting line with her.

It stands to reason that certain opportunities will be available to her that wouldn't be to others just because she's positioned so specifically. If Google, for example, need an attorney to represent their Books division, Susan's going to look like a solid choice. (We can also surmise that she'd command a premium salary, given her knowledge in this highly specialized area.) *This is positioning.*[34]

As a small company, positioning is critical. It allows you to occupy a unique space and gain specific expertise and knowledge in that particular area. You often—but not always—limit your serviceable client base, but that isn't necessarily a problem. You simply need to choose a position that is lucrative enough to sustain your company. A restaurant in Albuquerque that specializes in organic vegan food for albino schnauzers weighing between 26 and 28.5 pounds is a clear position, but there may not be a sufficient number of those socially conscious little doggies to keep that business profitable.

On the other end of the spectrum, choosing to start a general design business today can be pretty harrowing. Everyone with a computer thinks they are a designer, which makes it a tough racket if you aren't willing to differentiate. A friend of mine runs a studio that concentrates on creative services for law firms. As an ex-lawyer, he's well suited for this kind of work. Additionally, most law firms need help with their marketing and design, even though some aren't that excited to take on such work. Doug and his company are, so they've established a name for themselves in this sector.

Are they the best creative services company in the world? Not even close—but that doesn't matter. They offer a reliable service and have an intimate understanding of their clients' businesses. There are plenty of law firms who need marketing help, have sufficient funds to invest, and aren't all that attractive to Doug's competitors. My bet is that this position pays off well for Doug and his colleagues in a few years time.

As you get more focused, it's typically easier to spread your message and make decisions on how to do so. This isn't easy, and a lot of us dance around such discussions for years. Choosing a sound career/position early on and sticking to it can help you springboard past those who dabble in a little of this and a little of that.

A brief tangent…

Do you know the sound of fingernails on a chalkboard? Multiply that by 10, and you'll have an idea of what designers experience when a client asks them to "make the logo bigger." It's actually a not-so-secret in-joke amongst designers that has resulted in a satirical song by the fictitious band "Burnback."[35] There are many other playful takes on this request, including a site that allows clients to buy "Make My Logo Bigger!!!" Cream, which removes pesky whitespace and promises to provide full value from that logo you paid so much for.[36]

Objections to increasing a logo's size can sometimes be plain silliness on behalf of the designer. Young ones sometimes have a tendency to make logos microscopic, which can be a problem. Still, most designers have faced this request more times than they care to recount. I've put some thought into why "logo bigger" syndrome seems so universal. Mostly I wonder if logos are simply the most misunderstood elements in marketing.

This realization finally came to me when we worked on a specific website project. The client is a good one and they gave us plenty of latitude in the strategy and resulting design solution. All went swimmingly until we unveiled the finished site to the board of directors. One of the board members wanted to… wait for it… make the logo bigger. At this point, the logo already occupied a larger than average area in the top left quadrant of the website. Still, it wasn't enough… he wanted bigger! He thought it would be great if the logo took up the entire width of the screen. The committee started to rumble, with another noting, "I'd like that too! You know, the logo really needs to be focal!"

I treat such situations with care, as they can backfire if not addressed delicately. I explained that although a 25 percent increase in size could be accommodated, more than that would be problematic. This logo appeared on every page of the website. Enlarging it as much as they wanted would result in the logo taking up half of the monitor for some visitors. Still, their position was set. The fellow vying for the change noted, "We need to build our brand!" "Ah-ha!" I thought, "We've found the culprit!" The logo was being confused for a brand. It's not like everything was easy from that point on, but at least I could understand why he wanted to see the logo bigger. He thought that the logo was what the site's visitors would build a relationship with; this *never* happens.

Think of the Nike swoosh: in itself this shape says and does very little. Actually, it's really just a rounded check mark. It strikes an emotional chord as it has been built into a powerful symbol, but that one word is pivotal: *built*. The Nike swoosh was not inherently more beautiful, sporty, fast, or "Nike-esque" form than the many other ones out there; no, it was built to represent all of those things.

Nike's ubiquitous swoosh is the "Paris Hilton" of logos: the lucky winner of the genetic lottery, beneficiary of billions,[37] but otherwise unremarkable. Decades of investment in persistent and well executed advertising, brand building, and marketing efforts are why we see so much in the Nike logo. It's that collective set of marketing efforts and engineered touchpoints that inform how we see the logo. I argue that all of these references associated with a logo can result in a conditional reflex. After seeing thousands of sporty images next to the logo, we imbue certain characteristics on that brand identifier.

On the opposite side of the spectrum, we have the swastika. Although identified by most as a symbol of genocide and Nazi brutality, the symbol has a history much further reaching than most are aware. The form is one of the earliest known symbols and was long used as a decorative pattern and religious symbol.[38] The hideous acts of the Nazis burdened this symbol with a legacy that has little to do with those two squiggly lines.

A logo or mark of some sort is typically necessary, but we tend to overvalue its actual carrying capacity. It simply identifies and represents a group; and that's all. The company and its marketing inform the logo—not the other way around. Few like to believe this but your logo has more in common with a name tag than your actual brand. If you don't have few hundred million to invest in associated marketing efforts, you'll probably never get to where the Nike swoosh is. (The nice part is that it doesn't really matter that much.)

Are you your hat, hair, shoes, or cell phone?

When considering elements in isolation, it's easy to become confused about what a brand is. Because people know logos and see them everywhere, they start to think that logos *are* brands. This is a little like thinking that a hood ornament is a car. Some get past this and decide that the collection of visual treatments around a company make the brand. This is also incorrect—like thinking that a paint job is a car. A brand is all of these things and more. If it were one single part of a person, I'd like to think of it as a soul, but I think there's even more to it than that. A brand is all aspects of the organization; it's the body, mind, spirit, character, sounds, smells, and feelings we have for them. A lot, right? No wonder we have such a hard time wrapping our minds around what a brand is.

My business partner is a great guy. I've known him for years, and I trust him implicitly. My sense of him isn't solely based on what he wears, says, does, or believes; yet, all of those (and many other) things make up the whole: the "brand." In the same sense, my perception of the Coca-Cola brand isn't limited to a wordmark, Pantone color, or ad campaign. It's also not their tagline, the crisp "snap" upon cracking a can open, the bubbly carbonated dance on my tongue, or the caramel aftertaste. It's all of these things and more. It's an idea, a belief, and a feeling. It is organic and transforms daily. It is a part of our individual personal histories whether we like it or not.

CHAPTER 8

Brand Commandments

THERE ARE A NUMBER OF CONSISTENT TRAPS that cause brands to fumble. Most of these are avoidable, and remaining mindful of the following cautions can help temper the pains faced in building a strong brand. Let us begin:

One: You shall be yourself.

Fools try to be something they are not, or to mask their true character. The best companies align their appearance, interactions, and voice with the values, motivations, and the spirit of their organizations. You shall do this as well. The key to your brand is in aligning how you present yourself with your passions. Done effectively, you can connect with those who are looking for a company just like yours.

Your voice may be defined by concentrating on something that's already there and amplifying your passion for others to see. Or, it could be a simple matter of editing—you might just have to cut some of the "clutter" so that people can better understand who you are. Before you concern yourself with any marketing, you need to know exactly who you are and what you love doing. In doing exactly this, many brands have found a way to be unique. As a result, they stand out from their competitors.

Two: You shall not imitate a smorgasbord.

We commonly take on more than we should and this comes back to haunt us. Many reason that, "If we add another thing, we'll do more business." In actuality, each addition multiplies the complexity of their messaging and operations exponentially. Imagine being a veterinarian who also dabbles in civil engineering, product design, and international relations. In each area there is opportunity. Together they become a mess.

Instead of going all "smorgasbord" on us, refine your offering and elevate the level at which you operate. By doing so, you might pinpoint an opportunity that can make you truly spectacular. The band AC/DC ultimately performs the same song ad infinitum; they make lots of money for doing so. Subaru doesn't offer a lot of cars, but if you want one with all-wheel drive, you're likely to think of them. Sandra Wilson's company Robeez, which started in her basement, only makes shoes for toddlers. (She sold her company for $27.5 million USD in September 2006.)[39]

All of these groups could do more, offering a greater number of products, variations, or features. This would likely be easy for them, and they'd probably have good reason to do so. Instead they've suppressed the desire to be all things. That's why we know exactly who they are and don't get confused when we encounter their brands.

Three: You shall not take your true value in vain.

Some companies look only to price as their key point of differentiation. I think this is a foolish misstep. Although you can buy an inexpensive knockoff, most would prefer an authentic Louis Vuitton handbag—even with a cost of many hundreds of dollars. Similarly, no-name pharmaceuticals (often materially identical to their branded counterparts) can be had for a fraction of the cost. Still, you probably buy NyQuil when you have a really bad cold.

It's not that price is inconsequential, but it shouldn't be the only consideration. While many say that price singularly informs their purchases, consumers actually tend to act quite differently. Sure, you can differentiate on price, but you might also create an idea or proposition that is more valuable and defensible. In these situations, a higher price can even become necessary.

Four: Remember your purpose, to keep it holy.

Plans are easily made but harder to stick with. Many seek to redefine their purpose at the first sign of hardship. I don't propose maintaining a fruitless course of action, but I do believe that the impetus to change purpose should be contemplated carefully before acting upon. When you change direction, you lose momentum and have to rebuild it all over again. This is costly, and it can become a pattern. Those who hit "reset" every time the path gets rough find it awfully tempting to repeat this action indefinitely.

It tends to take time and careful contemplation to determine what it is that we want to do most. Some find their calling early, but such luck is hardly the rule. Often we find ourselves doing something out of happenstance and simply dealing with whatever circumstances come our way. Fledgling brands have limited resources and as such must be of clear mind in order to have a fighting chance. You can accomplish almost anything; you just can't do everything.

If your purpose isn't crystal clear, you need to stop immediately and determine what it is that matters to you—and where you're going. This will be your rock when you're bombarded with requests to do things outside of your capacity; similarly, when business is slow and you're tempted by divergent opportunities, this purpose will help you concentrate on what really matters.

Five: Honor your brand.

I used to go to an upscale Italian restaurant with killer risotto. At around the same time, I would spend Friday nights with friends at nightclubs and bars. After one evening out, we decided to grab a slice of pizza at a generic franchise. While seated I noticed a familiar face; the maître d' from that great eatery was ending his night here with some greasy low-grade pizza. Even with his access to great foods, he had opted for a fast food imitation. I was left to wonder why he would do so.

If you make cars, drive the ones you make. If you sell marketing services, you'd best market your company using the same methods you espouse. And if you sell fine Italian food, don't be caught dead at the generic pizza shack. We all know people who sell one thing and buy another. This is a sure sign of a doomed company. If you won't use it, why would anyone else? On the flip side, just because you do, doesn't mean that others will. In any event, your "subscription" is the baseline. If you haven't bought into what you're offering, it's time to reconsider your plan, and ask whether it's worth continuing. If you don't believe, no one else will.

Six: You shall be honest.

Every day we find countless opportunities to embellish, misrepresent, or entirely fake what we do. As we all know, such a charade becomes difficult to maintain, and a single disgruntled customer can quickly pop our little bubble.

We have to build trust with our patrons. The only way to do so with lasting effect is to behave in an ethical and transparent manner at all times. While some truths may not always endear us to others, speaking mistruths can prove doubly damaging. It's easier to just tell it like it is, particularly as your organization grows and you need to ask others to speak for your company. It's hard to get one message across effectively; it's made infinitely more so when you have to keep all of your corporate lies straight.

This honesty should move beyond your marketing and become a core element of how you operate. Slogans are easy to write, but rarely mean much to anyone. To achieve meaningful communication we have to get the mess out of the way and face brutal facts. If you're bullshitting your clients, you're clouding your own vision too.

Seven: You shall not confuse a logo for brand.

The lines between design, brands, and marketing are fuzzy, so it's understandable that we sometimes get confused. A logo is not and never will be a brand. It is simply an icon. An identity is just a system used to lend a clear and consistent voice for your organization. It doesn't change who you are; it just augments how you are perceived by others.

A brand is a bigger and vaguer sort of thing. Largely, it's the overall perception of your company. Some refer to it as being what others feel or say about your organization, which is partially accurate. It's a number of other things as well. I like to think that it ties into the soul of your company. What's most important to remember about a brand is that although you can shape it, you can't entirely control it. You can only control your half of the equation; the audience will determine the rest.

Brands and identities are not specifically "marketing" but that doesn't make them any less necessary. Your identity and brand help people understand who you are and what you offer. When you market, you're creating awareness by spreading your message. I'm of the mind that your marketing is found in every interaction you have with others. I also like to think that it has as much to do with how you deal with customer complaints as it does your ad campaigns.

Eight: You shall not overuse superlatives.

Adjectives, adverbs, and descriptive terms flow freely when we market our companies. It's all too easy to casually toss superlatives around and feel like we've clarified our position. Descriptive terms don't necessarily change how you are perceived; just like a new paint job on an old El Camino won't turn it into a BMW.

Ask for a stout and I think Guinness. Say "vacation" and I think Hawaii. Mention heavy metal and my brain goes to Metallica. Safe car? I'll think you're talking about a Volvo. All of these brands have had competitors and new challenges to contend with. Somehow, they tend to occupy space in our minds without saying things like, "the loudest, heaviest, coolest heavy metal band" or "the warmest, nicest, friendliest, tropical islands." Superlatives are hard to remember but positions are hard to shake.

The thing is, if you don't position you're left to play the superlative game. Think: "We weren't the first ones to build a brand around it, but you know Jerry, maybe we should market ours as the *tastiest* stout!" In actuality the only word we hear in all of that is "stout" and that just makes us think Guinness. You can add all the superlatives you'd like in such a case; it will still be an ad for your competitor.

Nine: You shall not make it unnecessarily complicated.

Don't expect your audience to give your product even a moment of thought. We're all too busy for that. Instead, go the other way: limit what you say to one spectacular thing about what you offer. (This of course, necessitates doing something spectacularly.) If you need more than a sentence to do this, you might be in trouble. Smart people can make complex things seem simple—it goes the other way too.

When you make things complicated, you scare people away. The best plans and brands can be explained quickly without added verbiage, complexity, or defense.

Ten: You shall not covet your neighbor's brand, nor his ox, nor his donkey.

We humans are predisposed to following. Even when given the choice between a busy lane of traffic and an empty one, we tend to choose the more congested option, reasoning that there must be a cause for the increased activity. In wanting to learn how to ski, most of us don't just start skiing. We take lessons and mimic someone who's more skilled than we are. In a room full of strangers, we survey the situation and try to match the tone and subject matter of conversations in progress.

In part, this is just sensible behavior. We seek out functioning models and mimic them in order to benefit from others' experience. Why invent something when the knowledge, skills, and habits have already been established?

Brands that follow others start to look like copycats and most people would rather have an original than a fake. In branding, imitation rarely brings any good with it. This doesn't preclude you from learning from others' brands. Perhaps you'll look at a popular category or brand, assess what they are doing, and ask, "what could we do to be the exact opposite of everyone else here?" This might lead to some keen insight or discovery.

Be mindful: anything you learn from this should solely inform your research process, and *not* become a template to follow. Besides, they might be operating in fruitless territory. You'll probably do better by moving someplace altogether your own.

CHAPTER 9

Focus and Differentiation

EARLY IN THE BOOK, I DISCUSSED a few of the key issues that our studio has helped companies sort out over the years. Two of the most important points (touched upon in *Brand Commandments*) deserve extra attention. Long before a website, brochure, or ad campaign is contemplated, your company needs to *focus* and *differentiate* from others in the marketplace. Failing to do these two things is quite possibly the greatest reason that marketing fails.

Do you share your full mailing address on a first date?

First dates are weird. Each individual tries to present their best characteristics. In doing so they edit what they say, in order to hit the high points and not overwhelm the other. This is common sense, right? You just don't share every tiny detail about your life during an introduction, do you? Well then… tell me why the majority of companies' website home pages are cluttered with text and information that just doesn't matter.

Many of us act like a frantic person who has to point out every imaginable detail. "We do this, we do that. Want our blog? Sure! Need a site map? We have one of those too! How about a search? We can help you do that! Here's our support section, but don't forget our news area. Oh right, these are the most popular downloads from our site. Hey, wait a second… Did we show you these photos from our staff Christmas party? Oh! Oh! Oh! Here are some testimonials, and a few of the things we do. We do other stuff too—just ask! Whatever you want, we can probably do. And we'll do it better than the other guys. We don't know who they are, but we're better... honest!"

This sort of mess is by no means limited to websites. It goes right down to the core of many businesses that lack focus and therefore stumble in presenting themselves. When your organization lacks focus, it is reflected in every aspect of your messaging. So let's step back for a moment and look at the big picture. To do this, we'll bring in our old pal, Jack Palance.

Curly has "one thing"

Remember the movie *City Slickers*? It was a corny 1991 comedy that somehow generated around 124 million dollars. The movie is about a few men who go on a cattle drive and learn some life lessons along the way. One of these lessons is something I think about when we help companies determine what they want to center their brand around.

In the film, Billy Crystal's character, Mitch Robbins, experiences a midlife crisis. He and Curly, the trail boss played by Jack Palance, initially find themselves at odds with one another. They later connect, in part as a result of Curly's insights. At one point, Curly asks if Mitch wants to know the "secret to life." He then holds up his finger stating, "One thing... just one thing." He concludes, "You stick to that one thing and everything else don't mean shit."[40] Bear with me here—I promise there's something useful to take from all of this.

The challenge we often face is that with so many possibilities for things we could do, we often fail to ask which ones we actually should. In our businesses, we start working on one thing. If it doesn't immediately prove fruitful, some are quick to leap to another approach. This leaves us in what business consultant and author Jim Collins refers to as "The Doom Loop": a seemingly endless pursuit of new directions that rarely lead to success.[41] Similarly, many find it difficult to say "no" to work, which leads them to take on things that can be managed but are perhaps not the company's forte. Mitch then asks, "That's great, but what's the one thing?" to which Curly responds, "That's what you've got to figure out." This is precisely what you have to determine: what is your company's one thing?

Perhaps I shouldn't be relying on pop wisdom presented in a movie to tell my story, but ask yourself: what is your company's one thing? My guess is that you likely do a few different things, and don't feel quite ready to concentrate a single one. It is, after all, unnerving to think about dropping any potential sales.

Once you do something well...

I like noodling about on the guitar but I can't actually play a whole song. I enjoy running in races, but limited time keeps me from training sufficiently. On some weekends I find interesting recipes and cook, but the results are spotty due to infrequent practice. Every year I promise to go snowboarding but most winters pass without me having done so. Over the years I've also owned a punching bag, weight set, bass guitar, medium format camera, and the list goes on.

My bet is that you know this feeling too. Although many of these pursuits seem exciting, there just isn't enough time to learn them all. So we tend to find a few things we really love, and just concentrate on those. This can lead to a cycle in which we get more practice, are subsequently praised or rewarded, and therefore are even more compelled to work at it.

The same basic principle holds true for your company. By concentrating on one thing, you find all kinds of little advantages that you didn't anticipate. First of all, training time for new staff is reduced as you'll better systematize and document processes. Ordering will be simplified, as the variety of inventory will be reduced. Better yet, by buying larger volumes of specific things, you might manage to negotiate better rates on the ones you do order. The point is that by doing fewer things, you will be much better at them.

I should also note that some choose to position around one thing without completely suspending their other activities. This doesn't help simplify organizational processes, but it can help a company get known for something. Often the company's choice is to be known for one thing, or unknown for many.

Pizza at McDonald's

When McDonald's first opened in San Bernardino, they served hamburgers, milkshakes, and fries. In the years that have followed, they have experimented with a number of different products including: deli-style sandwiches, McLobsters, poutine, McRibs, chicken fajitas, hotcakes, Spam, pies, smoothies, and many more.[42] Testing so many of these different options gives McDonald's something to advertise. People like new things, and you can only advertise the same burger as "new" so many times. Additionally, their presence in international locations gives good reason to explore more regionally appropriate options.

The one tangent that sticks in my mind is the McDonald's pizza. Although they toyed with the idea twenty years earlier, McDonald's finally introduced family and personal-sized pizzas in the early 1990s. The ads were brilliant, featuring the word "Pizza" in white on a bold red backdrop. The "z"s were replaced with two sets of golden arches, and it took just one quick glance to catch the message.[43] Nevertheless, you can no longer buy pizza at McDonald's. Why?

Some cite the challenges found in the time required to heat the pizza, while others criticized the flavor. I'm more inclined to think the whole mess related to a focus problem. We'll allow most companies some latitude when it comes to their offering. We accept a chicken sandwich at burger shops as it seems closely related to what they do. Similarly, curly fries and onion rings fit. Pizza, however, doesn't play nice with burgers. Both are foods, but from different "families." This leads us to ask, "Why would I go to a burger place for a pizza, when I could go to a pizza place for one?" Let's put this another way: How would you feel about buying your condoms... at a bakery?

Just before McDonald's launched its new product, a *New York Times* article by Eben Shapiro discussed the industry as being worth $21 billion and detailed how McDonald's had put several years of R&D into perfecting the technology and offering.[44] This process included widening drive-through windows so the pizza boxes could be passed through them, not to mention the remodeling of kitchens to accommodate the required ovens and warming bins. McDonald's believed that adding this item would strengthen their dinnertime business, and one can certainly appreciate their desire to do so. Yet, the research and development, massive advertising budgets, and all the other reasons they had simply didn't change one simple fact: people don't buy pizza at burger joints.

What you get for going tight

Think about the frustration of being a McDonald's franchisee and learning you needed to pay for these changes and equipment. You'd also have to train a batch of teenagers a new set of processes and find a place to store all of the uncooked pizzas and boxes. These are the kind of problems you experience when you take on things that aren't part of your core offering. You're forced to do too many things, and it can make you crazy!

McDonald's reasons for this new thing blinded them to the facts. They didn't accept that their pizza simply wasn't as good as that of established pizzerias. They also didn't offer delivery, which is a service typically seen as standard when it comes to pizza. Likewise, the options to customize one's pizza simply weren't to be found, given the logistics of offering pizza in a burger shop. For McDonald's to have made their pizza a viable offering, they would have needed to give us a big reason to choose them over a neighborhood pizza place. They had none. It was a "me too" effort, and it died as such.

For you, pizza may be a fine business, but you'll need to focus in order to get people to talk. I already have Marcello's where I can find authentic brick oven roasted pizzas; Panago fits the bill when I need something quickly; and Flying Wedge helps with of my craving for interesting, deep-dish styled pizza. I have the über-cheap 99 cent slices across the street from the apartment, the Pizza Hut for all you can eat at lunch, and the place across town that makes delectable flatbreads. Still, somewhere in there is room to stand out. The important part is to figure out how, and then maintain your focus.

A little risk is required

Innovation, and subsequently differentiation, can only be achieved by people willing to do unconventional and maybe even risky things.

This can be frightening, and sometimes the results are hard to measure. Again, when most of us try to innovate, we look to our peers and work to understand what they are doing successfully. This is a valid approach—surveying the marketplace is certainly worthwhile. This is where our interest in others' actions must end, though. Once we understand the competitive landscape we have to suppress any urge to imitate or replicate what others have done.

Have you ever noticed how any small innovation quickly ripples through an industry? Let's consider something as inconsequential as the notion of "bottomless" soft drinks. For the first restaurant that offered this, it was probably a great little perk. Others quickly followed suit, and soon this didn't make anyone seem notable. If you choose to differentiate, you might be wise to think about defensibility. Any computer manufacturer can replicate Apple's aesthetics and innovations. That will just result in pale imitation. Few have a culture of design and innovation like Apple. Some will pilfer ideas and cheaply copy them. Apple will still be a year (or more) ahead of the pack, doing their own thing.

Living with PHSSD

I remember adolescence as an exercise in conformity. (I suspect this is still the case.) Although there were ways to differentiate a little, these methods were kind of "regulated" with tribes (i.e., nerds, headbangers, jocks), which formed to establish a kind of safety in numbers. Truly differentiating oneself in adolescence came with the risk of being ostracized by one's peers, or "looking stupid." With all of this risk, many chose to lay low and not do anything too unique.

Ten or twenty years pass, and some of us find ourselves marketing a company. This is where Post High School Stress Disorder or PHSSD (a term I've completely fabricated) rears its ugly head. Here, at a moment with great opportunity and a blank canvas, we find ourselves unable to do anything but follow. So we look at every other company that's similar to ours and "try on what they're wearing." As I've noted before, doing what others are *seems* sensible, but it might not actually be working for them. Also, marketing successes aren't transferable. (We'll get into that in a moment.)

Most times we find ourselves left with a few options:
1. Copy someone else.
2. Do something boring but safe.
3. Be different.

The choice seems like a no-brainer. The first option should be "out," given that we'd be labeled copycats and have to adopt the limitations of our neighbor's campaign. Number two just seems foolish; boring marketing is about as sensible as ordering flavorless food. The third one? There might something there. Perhaps this is an opportunity to break through the noise and say something contrarian, exciting, scary, wild, cheeky, poignant, or even memorable! Yet, this almost never happens, due to our cunning nemesis: PHSSD.

Sure, we may flirt with some of these exciting possibilities, but at some point, we're struck with a paralyzing fear of making a blunder, getting fired, or "looking stupid." I bet I don't have to tell you how badly we don't want to look stupid! So instead we fall back on either option 1 or 2, and are then left to wonder why our marketing isn't performing as we'd like. At least we didn't get beat up by our boss. Whew—dodged a bullet there! (Now if only we could find someone to take to the prom!)

A fruit company?

In 1985, I was at the height of my personal "dork-dom." I read books about ninjas, played Dungeons and Dragons, and drew pictures of naked women. (I typically focused on breasts.) My brother and I watched movies like *Revenge of the Nerds* and *Weird Science* not just for entertainment, but instead as life manuals of sorts. These movies illustrated just how we might rise above our lot in life by starting a fraternity of dweebs, or by engineering a woman with our own home computer. We really wanted a computer.

For obvious reasons, I don't often think back upon this time, but a memory of the *1985 Computer Buying Guide* is lodged firmly in my psyche. I have my dad to thank for seeing the importance of a computer in our lives and anteing up for the purchase. He didn't do so haphazardly; a computer at that time cost several thousand dollars. And keep in mind, those are "1980s" dollars, which made it a substantial purchase. No, my dad first bought the *1985 Computer Buying Guide,* in order to make an informed decision. At the same time, I put down my drawings of breasts for a short while, and studied that book from cover to cover.

At a time when terms like "operating system" sounded unfamiliar, these guides helped people understand and compare the available options. I have to say, it was an awfully crowded market! There were many computer makers (some you know, some you don't) trying to grab a piece of the market. Some were industry leaders like Xerox, Sony, and even AT&T. Others like Microdigital, Robotron, and Merlin are names most have long forgotten. A few had truly bold monikers like MSX, ICL, NCR, SMT, NEC, IMCE, and CCD.[45]

In light of this, it's understandable why the people at ACT chose to try a different name. Sure, they could have gone back to their full name, "Applied Computer Technologies" but that probably seemed a little long. No, here was a chance to do something different: not a meaningless acronym or some long-winded name. They could come up with something unique that wasn't even related to computers— something that would stick with you just for how unexpected it was. And they almost did, with their newly chosen name: Apricot. Hey… wait a second! Isn't there another computer company named after fruit? Hmmm… that's weird! What a coincidence!

I still remember the Apricot name from that *1985 Computer Buying Guide* not for their innovation (apparently they were a highly innovative company) but rather as "the one that changed its name to sound like Apple." My guess is that someone at ACT reasoned, "It worked for those guys; why can't it work for us?" Unfortunately, that logic doesn't hold when it comes to branding. As a result, you've probably never even heard of the company.

In case you're wondering what ever happened: Apricot was later acquired by Mitsubishi to help them compete with Japanese PC makers. Although they continued to innovate, their approach was slow and resulted in an inability to compete with faster moving rivals. The company closed and their remaining assets were sold in 1999.[46] Since then they have re-emerged as a maker of netbooks. Curiously, the photo showcased on their homepage is of a new Apricot netbook with Apple wallpaper on it.[47] (Some people never learn.)

"We have this product, and, well, it could be good… but (minor issue) one of the original founders is, well, sort of involved in some… well… um… genocide. Any ideas?"

Advertising agencies often talk about "big ideas" and that's because the right ones can be incredibly powerful. With one particular project the odds were very much stacked against the agency. Today, our perception of the Volkswagen brand relates to a personable car that's fun to drive. In the late 1950s when the ad agency DDB (Doyle Dane Bernbach) was first presented with the assignment, things were quite different.

The 1973 oil crisis was years away and Americans loved their cars. They favored ones like the Chevrolet Impala, which could be outfitted with a 348 cubic inch (5.7 L) W-series Turbo Thrust V8. This was the kind of car that people wanted to drive. So if you were marketing cars in 1959, you'd probably talk about the driving advantage of wide track wheels, fuel injection offering huge horsepower, and "striking show-car styling." Volkswagen wasn't selling cars like this.

Created with a very different notion in mind, the Volkswagen was intended to be the "People's Car."[48] In contrast to the big and showy nature of what was in vogue stateside, they concentrated on creating a more economy-focused vehicle with better reliability and increased ease of use. Oh yes… I should also note that the Volkswagen Bug was the result of collaboration between Ferdinand Porsche, and a rather angry little man named Adolf Hitler.

By the end of the Second World War, the Volkswagen factory was heavily bombed, only really surviving as a result of Ivan Hirst, a British Army major, taking interest in the company.[49] It sputtered along for years, almost having its factory moved to Britain in the process.[50] In 1949 the company came under the control of the West German government and became representative of the country's regeneration. In 1955 Volkswagen of America was formed, and the Beetle was on its way to becoming one of the most recognizable and revered cars in history.[51]

Ask yourself: left with the challenge of marketing this car, what would you have done?

1. Copy someone else.
2. Do something boring but safe.
3. Be different.

I think most would have gone with the second option. They would have looked at the market, determined what was popular, and tried to appeal to the supposed interests of consumers. If the Impala was roomy, the Beetle could be made roomier! If it was powerful, perhaps the engines in the Beetle could be souped up! If the trim was popular on the Impala, why not add something like that to the Beetle? Really... how hard could it be?

But the folks at DDB didn't suggest any attempt to mimic the competition. Instead, they looked at what the car truly was and from this built one of the most famous marketing propositions in history. They asked car buyers to "Think Small"[52] and consider the economy of "using five pints of oil instead of five quarts," of "never needing anti-freeze," and of "racking up 40,000 miles on a set of tires." This understated ad copy was coupled with clean, minimal layouts, and witty headlines. As a result, the Beetle didn't need to compete directly with cars like the Impala. Instead, it started its own race. The car's simple, reliable, sensible, and *different* presentation made it something of its own.

In light of today's oil prices and concern regarding climate change this campaign might seem almost passé. In the late 1950s, however, this was radical differentiation. It took the domestic car companies decades to catch up—if you believe they ever really did. Fifty years later, and that campaign still holds its own. It occupies first place in *Advertising Age's* list of Top 100 Advertising Campaigns; moreover, it serves to inform the company's brand values to this very day.[53] They travelled less familiar ground, and doing so changed the future of that car company, and advertising itself. Differentiation works. As Bill Bernbach (legendary ad-guy and partner in the agency DDB) himself said: "Rules are what the artist breaks; the memorable never emerged from a formula."[54]

Differentiation has to be woven into your company's soul

Once you stop following others, your direction can truly be your own. I could carry on about all of the companies that have differentiated effectively, but I don't really need to. You know them already. You know that Marilyn Manson is a weird, semi-alien seeming guy who likes to yell and shock. You know that FedEx is overnight and that The Body Shop is natural. Similarly, we all think the Nintendo Wii is fun, Google is search, and that Jeep is off-road. By clearly differentiating at some point, each of these brands has become remarkable, and therefore memorable to us.

But, you counter, it was easier for these people to differentiate: they had more money. I argue that some of them have money now, *because* they chose to focus and differentiate. All of these companies could likely do many more things than what they're known for. By exercising restraint and fighting the desire to fit in, they succeeded where others have failed.

CHAPTER 10

STORYTELLING

THE WORD "STORYTELLING" CAN SEEM VAGUE and overly grandiose. It's the kind of term that might seem more at home in a first-year liberal arts class than in marketing. Thinking of it so would be a mistake, though, and it's too important to not give due attention. Choosing to ignore it is just what makes so many marketing efforts flop. Many concentrate on the notion of selling, when they could harness the power of "tell me more."

Are you *too* safe?

Middle managers are a core ingredient of big companies and they tend to be known for making safe, reliable choices and running proven methods. When you need to have your staff arrive on-time, stay until the end of their shift, or ensure that the project is completed on schedule, these folks are perfect! A lot of them do even better yet with the best bringing a team to life and boosting morale. These are very important people, but I ask if their skills just aren't suited for every role.

These people are hired for their consistency, but that belies what's sometimes needed in order to market a company effectively. We rely so heavily on middle managers to be safe that they sometimes can't see anything else. They often lean towards brand attributes and marketing campaigns that concentrate only on clichés because these seem to be more practical approaches. They can do "25% off" ads, direct mail pieces, or pop-up ads touting features because these all appear to be sensible things to do. When it comes to connecting with your audience, there's more to the picture than just being sensible. Although risk should always be weighed carefully, it's sometimes necessary to uncover something amazing.

Control is a brake pedal

We love to claim that we measure results, act on data, and apply "best practices" when it comes to marketing, but most of this is a fantasy held in place by just doing what others have done before. Meanwhile, middle-managers are so concerned with being safe and practical that they don't find much room (or reason) for being messy, sexy, dirty, noisy, or "in-love."

We people are wired differently. We like all of the stuff that doesn't fit nicely on a balance sheet. We like the grease, gossip, and tawdry details. We can't resist the cover of *People Magazine* that promises a glimpse at celebrities without their makeup. We want to read about a company's stumbles on their way to success. Similarly, at the scene of an accident, we turn and look—no matter how little we want to admit doing so.

Control is a tricky construct. Although it lends comfort, it slows us down. It kills messages with politeness, politicking, and predictability. Most middle managers don't particularly mind this. In my experience, most would rather keep a foot planted firmly on that brake pedal than even take a small chance. No one's getting fired for hiring IBM, but they might if they make the company look silly.

Here's why you, as a small company, can clinch this marketing thing: you aren't trying so hard to cover your ass. All you have to do is make sure that people buy your stuff. So what if you look a little silly from time to time? What's the problem if you stumble occasionally? You are likely free of shareholders, boards of directors, and investors who might chastise you for such a slip. You just have to choose between massive opportunity and politely blending in.

I say you grasp hold of the wheel, take a chance, and give people a reason to listen.

What happened next?

Stories are amazing. J.J. Abrams talks about this, and the power of mystery, in his presentation at the TED conference.[55] He references how stories like the one told in the first *Star Wars* pull us in by tapping our curiosity until we're invested. (I'm paraphrasing liberally here; go to the TED website for the real deal.) What's important is that even the simplest stories, told well, have the potential to sweep us off our feet and make us concentrate. Marketing is largely about just that: getting people to pay attention.

Most marketing doesn't give the audience any reason to listen. It's knee-jerk messaging that concentrates more on the speaker than the audience. This is where things fall apart. For the most part, I don't care about your company; I care about me. Your claims of great service aren't about me; they're just there to persuade me to buy your stuff. Frankly, "great service" is pretty-much the worst story ever told in marketing—because everyone else says exactly the same thing!

Last week I drove to Seattle with my wife Amea and our kids. Along the I5—somewhere around Skagit—I spotted a government-issue sign that lists local businesses of interest to motorists. I rarely pay attention to such signs. One restaurant I'd never before heard of, hacked their sign by telling a good story. (By "hack" I mean: using a system in a way unintended by its creator to one's advantage.)

The sign read: "Iron Skillet—great food, lousy service." I thought it to be a misprint, or a victim of vandalism. I looked again, smiled, and proceeded to talk about it with my wife. This is storytelling with just six words… and they hooked me with only one! Instead of saying the same thing as everyone else, they grabbed me with the question of why they'd admit to bad service, followed by the inevitable, "How good does their food have to be in order to willingly make such an admission?"

I don't know that I'll ever stop at the Iron Skillet near Skagit, but I'm awfully tempted.

Even free isn't good enough

Twenty years ago an ad selling on price alone could break through that noise; today you'd have to drop that price to zero in order to even budge the needle.

When I was in fourth grade, a department store in our city had a giveaway. They advertised a coloring contest, with all the kids who entered eligible to receive a free toy. This was the talk of the school-ground, with all of us thinking we'd get Transformers for our hard efforts. (Instead we got skipping ropes that didn't work very well.) Nevertheless, we all had our parents driving to the store two weeks before Christmas, just so we could get our free toys.

It's somewhat different these days, isn't it? Put "free" in front of most things and few of us pay any attention. Free is all over the place. It doesn't matter, and even when it does, it probably hurts you more than it's worth. We all learned that free rarely comes without some caveat, so we just stopped paying attention. "Great, a free phone—pity that the monthly subscription is $60. Free… right."

Deals only get you so far. Stories—real stories—are different.

There are good stories to be found in truth

My greatest aversion to the word "storytelling" is that it brings with it epic connotations, when it's actually far simpler than this. For the most part, we aren't talking about Homer's *Odyssey* when we reference this term. (Frankly, I could never understand that stuff anyway.) Most of the time, it just comes down to giving the listener a reason to pay attention. In my mind, storytelling is a way to move past plain facts in order to wrap others up in the sound, smell, taste, and spirit of the moment. These are the parts that we actually care about.

When we started our company, I likened "selling" to telling people nice things about our company and how we could help them. I now see these first meetings as an opportunity to test how compatible we might be, and to determine if they're excited about the same things we are. Although I used to have a nearly canned "pitch," I now tell stories. Few of them are fanciful or rely on hyperbole—some are downright embarrassing. One that I tell often relates to a past client who's likely still angry with me. He's a particularly smart guy, whose company does forensic science. This means that they investigate mishaps and such, and serve as "expert witnesses" in certain legal cases.

Our work with this client was exciting. They came to us as a result of past successes we'd had and really opened themselves up to our process. As we worked together, we devised an identity system that I am still proud of. Each element involved a sense of mystery and discovery. On the surface, everything was professional and safe, but upon looking closer, there was always more to the story.

The project moved along well. Our primary contact there was rational, articulate, and fun to work with. Our last in-person meeting involved him giving us a thumbs up, noting that it was "just right" for them, and very "smart" (his words). We were happy about this and built the files out to completion as we had been instructed to do. Then things got weird.

Months passed with no response to our emails, and we found ourselves rather perplexed. Early in the new year, we learned of a delay due to a new office; two months later, the project was mothballed. Everyone in their marketing department had apparently been replaced, and the new hires were unconvinced of the direction we had provided.

This same client who had once been so very satisfied became upset, even demanding a refund. I explained that the allotted hours and more had been worked. We could step back in the process, but would have to charge for doing so. To make this less painful I offered a reduced rate and to carry forth some hours to a new project. None of this seemed enough. Ultimately, I could do nothing to bring resolution to the situation. All of his rational insights and sensibilities seemed replaced by blind emotion. He then threatened to share his dissatisfaction with others he knew in business if I didn't refund him. This led him to shout even more and finally hang the phone up on me. That identity system (which I still feel to be some of our best work) never saw the light of day. I regret how that project ended.

I continue to tell this story when we meet with potential clients. Why? First, I think it helps us break through the noise. If a company meets with ten different agencies, they'll find ten slick but largely identical pitches. I want our presentation to stand out, and in part I make that happen by breaking the pattern. I think such truthful recollections illustrate that even with the best intentions, things can go awry; additionally, what better way to lend credibility to our claims than to acknowledge such a mess?

I also think this is a sound way to show potential clients that we really think about the work we do and push to do remarkable things. We've screwed up, but each time we learn from our fumbles. Little has been irreparable, and I believe that a willingness to fail opens us up to the possibility of achieving something great. For the record, I believe that system *was* a success; my inability to get them to commit, however, marks it a failure. Some don't like to hear this sort of thing; others do. These are the people we want to work with. They also tend to retell our stories, and we really like it when people do that.

Why listen if it isn't interesting?

One morning last winter a contact called to ask about the cost of creating a blog for his company. We spoke for a while and I explained that the cost and requirements of a blog can be deceptive. The design needn't be costly and the software isn't either. My comment was that people don't visit blogs for the design or technology—they read them because of the stories. You can have an ugly blog without any features, plug-ins, or widgets and still command an enormous following. What you *must* do is compellingly present information on topics that people care about—that's it.

The prospective blogger then explained, "I think Rob will write the posts. He'll probably do it once a month, but… he's not much of a writer. I don't know how I'll even get him to write that often." We then discussed some of the dynamics related to blogging and delivering compelling content. I urged him to establish a mandate, find a voice, and write good articles. I asked him to consider telling stories they were uncomfortable sharing—perhaps the kind of insights that their competition would kill for. In my mind, this is just the kind of thing that will attract a large following (and buzz).

He noted that this was a possibility, but quite unlikely, as they only really wanted to use the blog for SEO (search engine optimization) that would bring link-strength to their corporate website. You tell me: what kind of a blog would this be? One with boring stories, written infrequently, by someone who doesn't want to write… Hmmm… would you read it?

We never did win that contract. What I proposed didn't jibe with them. It was too costly, risky, and time-consuming. They were looking for something cheap, safe, and fast that would build their business. Aren't we all? I later looked back on the blog. Not one post had received a single comment. (I sure hope it helped on an SEO basis.)

You're more interesting than you think

It's easy to toss about terms like storytelling, but many are confounded by the question of how to start and what story to tell. Let's eliminate this fear right now; good stories are everywhere. They're in the weird guy on the bus this morning; the hardest project you ever worked on; and, what your kids said at dinner last night. Stories are around us even at the most banal seeming moments. So why do we find ourselves stymied when it comes to telling our business' stories?

My opinion is that it all relates to how we put layers between ourselves and the truth. Perhaps these are helpful in insulating oneself, but they get in the way when it's time to tell a story. They lead us to edit when we really need to concentrate on just communicating. We start to ask questions like: Are we being too personal? Will we sound unprofessional? Is this too much information? (All valid questions, but they're often asked at the wrong time.) So we find ourselves verbally constipated.

The next time you're stuck, I suggest you just start. Get it out first and *edit later*. By simply putting something down, you build a little inertia and ideas will feel less evasive. I think we all have stories worth telling, but see them as unremarkable because we've lived with them for too long. This leads us to toss great stories in the waste-bin, thinking they're boring. You have to dig up those stories, dust them off, and see how they look in fresh light. Once told, we're often surprised to learn that there's more to them than we had once thought.

Personally, I think our most interesting stories are the ones we hesitate to share. "Nerdiness" for example, is something we often cover up to shield ourselves from what we believe to be the wrong kind of attention. Doing so allows us to maintain an illusion of safety, but it also keeps us from tapping great stories.

Nerdy people

I'm a nerd. As a kid I loved drawing, comic books, talking too much, computers, weird printing techniques, over-the-top heavy metal, and countless other things. These, alongside my social awkwardness, kept me from being invited to most high school parties. I also had a really bad haircut. To the point, though, all of those nerdy interests are to credit for the interesting things I do today.

My love of drawing led me to design, in which communication (and sometimes talking a lot) is vital. My interest in computers helped me embrace technology and understand its paradigms. Those capabilities in part lead some to seek out our firm's expertise in these areas. Of course, there's more to who I am than the aforementioned points, but they do comprise an important part. Neglecting them would have resulted in a career as an accountant. For me that would have been a grave mistake.

The fact is, you're a nerd. Somewhere inside you is one who can recount every passage from *This is Spinal Tap*; or, perhaps you can provide a detailed summary of every Stanley Cup playoff over the past decade. Maybe you can disassemble and reassemble a motorcycle without breaking a sweat; or, you might know volumes about Argentinian wine. I don't know what you're nerdy at, but I'd be surprised if there wasn't a nerd just a scratch beneath the surface.

This obsessive nature is a result of love, and something that many find compelling. When we're wildly excited about a topic, we speak differently. We light up and become enthusiastic; we make wild hand gestures and race to get our point across. A few might roll their eyes and claim boredom at such obsession, but let's not worry about these people. If they don't want to dive in, there's little you can do to convert them, but there are probably many others who share your passion, or will at least find it somehow compelling.

We're fascinated by those who follow their bliss

Look back at a few of the documentaries that have stuck with us over recent years. Many of them feature people who have gone far past what the rest of us would consider normal. This is ostensibly because they felt some burning need to do so. *Go Further* brought us into Woody Harrelson's world of obsessively healthy living, raw food, and closer connections with the planet. In it, Woody and his friends get on a bus and drive down the West Coast, teaching others how to live differently while sharing their stories along the way.[56]

In *Surfwise* we meet the Paskowitz family. Their domineering patriarch "Doc" forsakes a career as a doctor, embracing a life of adventure and hardship. Their family of eleven spends decades in a small camper subsisting on a meager diet, while observing a seemingly dogmatic commitment to surfing.[57] Gary Hustwit's *Helvetica* spends 80 minutes involving us in the world of designers who passionately verbalize their love, or hatred, for the ubiquitous typeface. It tracks the type family through its past and ever-present use today.[58]

In each of these cases, we find ourselves transfixed. In part, we're just captivated by those so fanatical about what they love. Few of us will become vegans, sell our worldly possessions in order to surf, or be able to discern the difference between Helvetica and Arial. That doesn't matter; what does is that for a moment we stopped what we were doing and paid attention to these stories. This isn't something we'd do as readily for less-nerdy folks. So many stories out of Hollywood are based on obsessive behavior of some sort. Ask yourself: what are you obsessive or nerdy about? Somewhere in there is a great story waiting to be told.

Just under his sleeve

Unique stories, characteristics, and obsessions are just as common in companies. Sure, some may be cubicle-farms without character, love, or personality, but let's be honest: the people in those aren't reading a book like this. (If they are, it may be time to shake things up or find a new place to work.) It's hard to find a company that didn't start from some kind of love. This passion doesn't necessarily have to make sense to others. What matters is that you remember why you started and that you stay connected with those feelings. Once you're there, it's easy to embrace your company's inner-nerd.

A few years ago, we worked with an arena that housed anything from concerts to sporting events and trade shows. It was a strange process, as the number of stakeholders involved made the process cumbersome. There were a number of disparate interests at work, requiring us to merge two distinct identity systems into one overarching solution. Additionally, the facility wasn't particularly beautiful.

The discovery stage started unremarkably, with a number of predictable responses to our questions. Things changed half-way through the meeting when a seemingly shy fellow rolled up his sleeve. He operated an ice-cleaning machine called a Zamboni and was so proud of his role, that he had an image of the machine tattooed on his arm. Upon sharing this, the rest of the group opened up and started to add their personal stories. All of them loved to put on a good show for attendees and took enormous pride in doing so. We had found the story to tie the brand together.

I've used this example on numerous occasions since that meeting. The interesting note is that this insight didn't come from those one might have expected. The leaders, managers, and executives all contributed to the process and had things to say, but their responses sounded practiced. They were saying exactly what one would expect them to. The story that made the difference came from a guy who didn't even want to be at the meeting. He just loved his job.

Nerdy companies

The Moleskine is a simple notebook housed in an oilcloth-wrapped cardboard cover. It is held closed with a soft, fabric-based elastic band and has rounded corners. Aside from this, it's in no way remarkable. On the other hand, their story is. Moleskine claims to be "the" notebook of Picasso, Matisse, and Hemingway. While this story is contested by some as not being wholly accurate, it creates a wonderful mythology.[59] The company uses this as part of their culture, championing notions of exploration, discovery, and self-expression. They don't promote any other products. They're obsessed with the magic of a simple notebook.

Most of us use Google services. Their offering rarely seems as visually polished as that of their peers, but most of us appreciate the utility and ease found in their products. Designing user interfaces to be this intuitive isn't easy. One team at Google was so obsessed about making a product perform best that it tested 41 shades of blue just to determine which proved most usable.[60] Google is nerdy about analysis and function—so much so that many of their products become category killers.

One of the designers who worked at our studio told me the story of Nudie Jeans. This company, based in Sweden, is obsessive about denim. In their website they propose that, "Jeans share the same soul and attitude as music."[61] Additionally, they claim that denim should be looked upon as a naked material that transforms to become a second skin for the wearer, becoming increasingly beautiful with time. You aren't supposed to wash Nudie jeans for the first six months, to maintain the intensity and character of the denim. Nudie Jeans are considerably more expensive than most standard brands; they also have a compelling story and start a surprising number of discussions. I initially found the whole notion absurd—now they're the only jeans I want to own.

Everyone's got something

None of the stories contained in the provided examples are particularly earth-shattering. There is no swordplay, bank heist, or car-chase even remotely associated with these examples. By many standards, I've actually talked about rather mundane things: a blank notebook, some web-based software, and a brand of jeans. Does that matter? We all like to get excited about things. We want a reason to believe in what we do, say, and buy. I even argue that we enjoy how some of these banal things delight us and provide stories to recount. I'd bet that if you dig a little, you'll find some stories of obsession in your company too.

Perhaps you want to serve the best seafood in the city, and have established relationships with local fishermen to get the first pick of their daily catch. You might be the kind of company that takes broken iPods and refurbishes them with bigger hard-drives, enabling people to take their entire music collections on their players.[62] Maybe you're a florist who only uses local flora in your arrangements as you care deeply about sustainability. (I haven't ever heard of anyone doing this last thing, but if I did, I'd frequent that shop regularly.)

Our company is nerdy too. We have long discussions around se-mantics, debate the perfect amount of spacing between glyphs in a wordmark, and even argue whether the "Cancel" or the "OK" button should be placed on the right. (I've learned to not share these stories at dinnertime, as I all too clearly remember the blank expressions when I did.) Although it's not necessarily captivating subject matter to all, for those looking to hire a design agency, these discussions are probably compelling evidence of our commitment to our craft.

Before I opened the box, I had little idea...

I made a presentation at an event last fall. As a thank-you to the speakers, the event organizers graciously packed some gifts for us. Being rather exhausted, I initially paid little attention to the contents of the package—not even the box of chocolates it contained.

The next morning I passed the chocolates around the office. One-by-one, each of us responded with amazement. Shinya seemed to melt; Devin's eyes opened wide; I exclaimed, "holy crap that's good!" Shelkie (our resident "chocoholic") simply sat back in his chair and said, "That puts a Hershey bar to shame, doesn't it?" I think our col-lective idea of what constituted chocolate changed at that moment. What was their secret? How did they do it? The investigator in me had to know, and I took to the web for a little sleuth-work.

Cocoa West is a small chocolatier on Bowen Island—approxi-mately 5 kilometers from Vancouver. Here, Joanne Mogridge and her husband Carlos Vela-Martinez make their delicious chocolates and truffles from organic and locally sourced ingredients. On their website, they talk about the exotic spices, garden herbs, local fruit and cream, and Canadian maple syrup that they bring together with organic European chocolate.[63] Their boxes contain small quantities of chocolates and are marked with an expiry date, given that no pre-servatives are used in their creations. Those who feel so inclined can even stay at the couple's "Bed & Chocolate"—a B&B-like place in which guests can indulge their chocolate cravings on-site.

This is a simple story but one that many of us can identify with. Who wouldn't love to replace their desk job for island-life? This story is made remarkable by the mouth-watering delights they serve up.

Their obsession with, and capacity for, crafting remarkably good chocolate, coupled with their unique location, makes it an easy story to tell: "You have to try this chocolate! It's made on Bowen Island, and it's amazing!"

Boring them to death

The problem that most companies face in telling their stories has little to do with production value or their chosen delivery channel. It's typically boils down to a simple reality: they're telling boring stories.

I know a guy who does this. He's well dressed, successful (bewilderingly), and quite possibly the first walking, talking, human sedative. It wouldn't even help if he was wearing a suit made from flashing-lights or sported a strap-on dildo as a hat. He's boring, and his stories are equally so. I don't listen, and I probably never will. If I ever have to sit with him again, I'll crack my skull open and scoop out my brain with the first available utensil. Really… seriously… no joke—I'll do this! The unfortunate part is that your company might suffer from the same affliction.

The problem for the aforementioned fellow is that he's so in love with his own drivel that he doesn't ever stop to ask if anyone else cares. (My hunch is that if he had to listen to his own stories, he'd likely join me in my "brain-scooping" expedition.) But he doesn't, so he won't. He'll just keep talking and people will keep snoring. In thirty years he might figure out that he's a boring twat who's been spewing out platitudes and buzzwords for his entire life.

As a business owner, you don't need thirty years to figure out if you've been blowing smoke. As you know, most companies only have a few ways to succeed. Some have gobs of cash, which gives them the freedom to do anything until the money runs out. The rest of us have to make great stuff and give people a good reason to care. Failing to do so will simply result in us euthanizing our own companies.

A story worth telling

Great advantage can be had by giving people a reason to pay attention. Part of this comes down to telling a good story. Determining which stories meet this criteria is easy. Do the following:

1. Pick up the phone.
2. Call a friend (the kind who would tell you if you smell).
3. Read your story (brochure copy, website text, ad script) as it's currently written.
4. Keep reading until you feel uncomfortable.
5. If you don't reach this point, wait to see if they stop you.

If, at the end of your call, you're still talking and they're still listening you might be on the right track. You could do the same with almost any piece of literature for most Fortune 500 companies without success. Typically these stories sound like a sack of lies or the awkward love child of the legal and marketing teams.

Going unnoticed is worse than ruffling some feathers

People get scared when it comes to the possibility of upsetting others. This is a shame, as some deserve to be poked and cajoled. It's all too easy to claim that nothing's exciting and then do little to change things. You and I will say some things that others might not, in order to ensure that we've got the audience's attention.

Take the passage a moment ago. It's sort of mean to make fun of my dull colleague as I have. Some who read it might have stopped out of pure disgust at my abrasive tone. You're still here, and that's the important part. Whenever you say or do something that isn't safe and nice, you run the risk of losing a few.

I am of the mind that this risk isn't nearly as great as the one associated with going unnoticed. The jackass doing the funky chicken on the dance floor won't have women swooning, but he might get a few laughs and strike up a conversation or two. The wallflower remains unnoticed.

Take the pain out of brainstorming

I write, give examples, and carry on, but at some point you're going to need to tell your own stories. Perhaps you'll hire someone like me to help determine which stories you should be telling, and how you might go about doing so. If not, you may find yourself looking at a blank page unsure of what to do next. In later chapters, I'll talk about methods of executing on your plans. For now, I want to share the question that makes brainstorming easy. It is simply: "Wouldn't it be cool if?"

Coming up with ideas is easy. It's so easy that in doing so we often find ourselves dumbfounded. So we make it harder: we doubt, criticize, and edit too early. In short order we find ourselves pulling out our hair or trying to throw computers out of closed windows. That one question though? It's magic! The reason it's so powerful is that it opens us up to wonder. It gives us a chance to dream of things that might blow us away. Resist the urge to edit yourself prematurely, as doing so can put a damper on your "wouldn't it be cool if?" party. Let's open this thing up by pretending that we're a company that makes low cost pocket-sized video cameras.

Wouldn't it be cool if we...
- Sponsored our own mini-film festival, showing the best ones on the web?
- Had everyone in the company document a year of their life?
- Held a free summer-camp, teaching kids how to make movies?
- Gave cameras to world travelers and asked them to share their experiences?
- Devoted 20 percent of our time to making videos that tell socially relevant stories?

I'm unclear of the logistics found in doing all of these things, and perhaps they would be deemed impractical upon further inspection. That's OK—we don't need the perfect idea. The sole point of such an exercise is to break away from writing a spec-sheet and attaching a corny marketing slogan to it. Besides, I don't mind having a thousand lousy ideas if they get me closer to the one that gets people talking.

My one caveat with the "wouldn't it be cool if?" question, is to avoid thinking solely from the company/marketer/designer's perspective. Most times these people have different motivations than those who use the thing we're selling. So they come up with things that are boring and sound like ads. No—if we want to truly connect, we have to momentarily forget about selling product. The story that connects with your audience might not be the one you want to tell—but, it might be more important to engage them than "sell" them. We need to dig deeper, get closer, and pull out the things that people really want to see, hear, do, and feel.

Give good value

37signals is a small operation that creates software largely centered on simplifying tasks, notes, collaboration, and project management. Some swear by their software while others criticize them as inflexible and overly dogmatic.[64] Either way, they've established a respectable presence, largely through storytelling. The first way that 37signals seemed to connect with people was through their blog *Signal vs. Noise* in which they share opinions on "design, business, experience, simplicity, the web, culture, and more."[65] They're good writers and have built a substantial following by using this platform to discuss things they care about.

They often espouse doing less, and a powerful mythology has formed around this belief. Their ethos is at the core of their brand's philosophy: creating software and services free of the complexity and bloat seen in enterprise solutions. They even created a manifesto of sorts, called *Getting Real*, which espouses the values that they develop software around. They claim to have sold over 30,000 copies of the PDF alone, and many know of them because they're such strong advocates of agile development. The particularly interesting part, in my mind, is that they've made "doing less" a virtue. How many other companies use that as a selling feature?

Whether you agree or disagree with the methods that 37signals promotes, it's difficult to find fault with the quality of the content they share. They do market themselves, but they don't send a high ratio of sales pieces or get overly aggressive in their marketing. Instead, they've built a community by sharing the processes that helped them ship a number of successful products.

Lots of people get excited by new technology and think that it will do all the work for them. I argue that this is why so many Hollywood blockbusters turn out to be disastrous heaps of turd. No amount spent on special effects will get you past a bad movie—just consider a few of the more recent *Star Wars* flicks. Don't worry about using every gimmick, tool, or form of social media; just start by making something good.

Mythology

I briefly touched upon the notion of mythology in my ruminations regarding 37signals. When I use the word mythology in this context, I'm referring to a set of stories and ideas surrounding a particular entity. Some of these are crafted, while others come to life in a more organic fashion. Either way, they tend to be present in many of the brands that we hold close to our hearts.

In some ways, this is rather slippery territory, as corporate mythology and brands are rather similar. My personal feeling is that mythology taps into a deeper kind of storytelling than brands. For example, I know that the Xerox brand is synonymous with making copies, but that doesn't necessarily give me a story to buy into. Ubiquity may very well be the pinnacle of brand success but mythology can lead to achieving that. Although, it can probably be found in any book relating to brands or marketing, I'd like to talk briefly about Harley-Davidson. Not referencing their coup would be foolish, given what a great example it is.

Harley-Davidson was in dire straits. Since its acquisition by AMF in 1969, quality had gone down as a result of a reduced workforce and more streamlined production. At the time, some also associated their brand with a criminal element. (Some of us remember when the terms Harley-Davidson and Hells Angels seemed closely related.) Alongside competition from Japanese motorcycle manufacturers the company was nearly bankrupt when a new set of investors took over in 1981.[66]

At a time like this, many businesses would choose to follow the trend set by the dominant imported motorcycles. Instead, Harley-

Davidson made a bold move: they started a "revival" in which they mined and embraced the more unique historic characteristics of their company; began a campaign to re-connect with riders; and, fused their brand with Americana.[67] Harley-Davidson didn't chase the other guys. They amplified their own story and built a mythology. We all know how well this decision has served them. Incidentally, the Harley-Davidson brand recently ranked 73rd in Interbrand's 2009 Best Global Brands scorecard.[68]

Stories aren't in limited supply

You'd think that with all of the people out there with something to say, we'd have told just about every story possible. In fact, there are an endless number of twists, turns, and variations to keep all of us in stories worth sharing. Perhaps you'll surprise your audience or include them in a personal tale. Some will connect fans with a universal truth or purpose that they can all rally around. Others may entertain and amuse, and a few will craft a mystery that gets people guessing. None of these are inherently better than any of the others. The approach you take is really dependent upon who you are and what you want to achieve. It's OK if it's messy and it's OK if you fail—just give us a reason to pay attention.

CHAPTER 11

Authenticity and
The Zellers Paradox

I'd like to point out an irony in this book. Let's suppose that you apply the suggestions made and they help you reach your goals. In doing so, you may find yourself at odds with the same things that once gave you an advantage. Perhaps you'll transform from a passionate, hands-on company with a staff of six, into a cross-country franchise. This may leave you hard-pressed to maintain the same attributes that got people to love you in the first place.

While I'd like to write a tell-all passage relating to how one might address just that, I think the task may be too great. The one thing I will contemplate is this slippery topic of authenticity. It's a tough perception to achieve, maintain, and in some ways even understand.

Everything in the marketplace is fabricated

Many answers for your brand can be found by reflecting candidly on whom you are; likewise, I think the best method of ensuring consistent relations with your customers is to act ethically. On the other hand, I do struggle around these notions of truth and authenticity. Some great businesses are good at just *seeming* authentic.

Häagen-Dazs, for example, elicits sensations of a hundred-year-old Scandinavian ice-cream maker with a long legacy of craft. Their product occupies the "super-premium" category and is available in 50 countries worldwide. While few dispute the quality of the product, the associations suggested in its evocative name, are more exotic than their actual roots. Häagen-Dazs is in fact an American brand founded in the Bronx in 1961 by Reuben and Rose Mattus. The name came to be as a result of Reuben "riffing" on the Duncan Hines name in faux-Danish.[69] Yet, the moniker has become legendary and this conceivably helps justify the premium pricing, given that it appears to be an "imported" product. Incidentally, Häagen-Dazs is now owned by The Pillsbury Company.

Similarly, the Burberry fashion brand could easily be perceived as being born of luxury. They are positioned amongst other luxury brands and rely on advertising that suggests they represent a modern day aristocracy of sorts. (Seemingly this new upper class is largely comprised of waif-like men and women with highly pronounced cheekbones.) This defies the company's more utilitarian beginnings.

Thomas Burberry did invent gabardine, but it was intended as a hardy fabric for outdoor wear. His trench coat was actually fashioned for military use. In contrast to the high-wheeling lifestyle currently portrayed by the brand, Burberry himself was an anti-alcohol crusader with modest interests. His obituary in the *Daily News* read, "Mr. Burberry cared for little outside his business except temperance, religion and agriculture, and he never read novels."[70] Hardly a description fit for the high-flying founder we might have imagined.

Or consider Captain Morgan Spiced Rum: the seventh largest brand of spirits worldwide, recognized for its tagline, "Got a little Captain in You?" This mascot crafted for the brand seems jolly and fun, in spite of its mildly sinister expression. Few of us would have likely chosen to hang out with the "Captain". The brand took its moniker from Welshman Henry Morgan, a privateer (pirate) known for "bloodthirsty" attacks in the Caribbean.[71] Although the man was real, he had little to do with the company, which was originally a distillery called Long Pond that was purchased from the Jamaican government by Seagram Company in 1944. It's hypothesized that the real Captain died from liver failure due to his enjoyment of "the sauce."

Does it matter?

I question if we might all confuse the notion of authenticity and that of originality. While originality relates to the beginning of something, authenticity is a characteristic of something that is true to its origins and sincere. The issue then comes down to which origins we remain true to.

Just think of those things that we hold up as American icons. What's more American than Budweiser, the "King of Beers"? Actually a fair number of things. The Budweiser name actually means "From Budweis," with Budweis being a city in Bohemia (now called České Budějovice). The ownership of Budweiser? Belgian—they're a part of Anheuser-Busch. It doesn't end there. Church's Chicken is owned by Bahrainis, 7-Eleven by the Japanese, and The Chicago Skyway by an Australian-Spanish consortium.[72] Hate to break it to you, but even "as American as apple pie" is a bit of a myth. This icon's recipe dates back to 14th Century England.[73] Apple trees weren't even to be found in the Americas until the early 1600s.

Does knowing this make apple pie feel any less American? Do the not-so-exotic origins of the Häagen-Dazs' name result in their ice-cream tasting any less delicious? Should the pious nature of Burberry's founder make their current fashions seem any less luxurious? Probably not, and I believe there are two reasons for this. First, by crafting and repeating these myths, we've come to believe in them. It seems that even belief proven to be ill informed is hard to shake. Once those neural pathways are formed, it's very hard to rewire these associations. Secondly, it can be argued that a brand, expression or idea really only needs to be true to itself.

Authentic mashups

Consider Andy Warhol's silk-screened paintings of Campell's soup cans. Warhol didn't invent the soup can, and he certainly wasn't creating these images for the soup company. No, he re-imagined a banal household item as a work of high art. Although Warhol begins with a commercial representation, the end product is something altogether different from that which first informed his work. The soup can paintings, car crash representations, and posterized images of celebrities all became part of what Warhol was. He didn't need to replicate, or be true to, the subject matter he started from in any subsequent work (i.e., the soup cans or Brillo boxes). He just needed to be authentically "Warhol."

DJ Z-Trip and DJ P are the respective monikers of mashup artists Zach Sciacca and Danny J. Phillips. Mashups are new creations (art, music, videos, software) comprised of two or more existing works. Their collaboration *Uneasy Listening, Vol. 1* was released in short supply in 2001 and went on to critical acclaim from the likes of Rolling Stone, Spin, URB and the New York Times.[74] You can hear it for yourself on DJ Z-Trip's website: www.djztrip.com.

As you listen to it—and you should—you'll hear something quite unique from anything you've ever heard before. Seamlessly, they bring together diverse and seemingly unrelated sounds, artists, and songs. For example, Glen Campbell's *Rhinestone Cowboy* stitches together with Pink Floyd's *Run Like Hell*. Dialogue from *Star Wars* leads to Tears for Fears' *Woman in Chains*. Along the way, we hear the Macintosh system voice, The Beastie Boys, Pat Benetar, Martin Luther King, Jr., and Ratt. It's a rather weird experience, as you find yourself drawn in to familiar melodies, completely reinterpreted.

Listening to this "construction" is a little like traveling through a musical stream of consciousness. There are mellow passages, energetic ones, and a few points that are simply unexpected. Sampling from so many artists results in a completely new work. Do DJ Z-Trip and DJ P "owe" their new creation to these ingredients? Most wouldn't think so; we've come to believe that such works constitute wholly new creations. From an authenticity standpoint then, are DJ Z-Trip and DJ P limited to using the same samples indefinitely? Hardly! They can take inspiration from wherever they wish. Their creation is of their own devising and, once again, they only need to remain authentic to themselves.

The perception of their authenticity could be shaken should one of them choose to write bubblegum pop songs for Top 40 radio. That wouldn't seem like the DJ Z-Trip and DJ P we've come to know. Similarly, by having their music tied to commercials for a brand like Puppy Chow, they might risk coming under scrutiny. Listeners aren't as concerned with their influences as they are in receiving what the artists have promised. This kind of promise isn't necessarily a verbal one, but instead the result of a relationship formed over years. With each creation and element of communication, a dialogue is established; breaking from this could cause loyalists to feel as though the group's authenticity has been compromised.

Can we bring this discussion back to the topic of brands, please?

Let's apply this same train of thought to a company like Starbucks. When Howard Schultz took his sojourn in Italy and saw how the coffee bars were a culture unto themselves, he saw an opportunity for America. It's unlikely that he believed he'd create exactly this experience back home, but he was clearly influenced by what he saw. This is comparable to how Warhol was informed by popular culture. From that day in April 1984, when Starbucks first started publicly experimenting with the sale of coffee beverages, they began a dialogue and made certain promises to each of their customers.

Few would criticize Starbucks for losing its connection to the Italian coffee bar, just like few would call out DJ Z-Trip and DJ P if they never included another '80s sample in a collaboration. The work these artists created was something unto itself just like Starbucks is. Most people probably aren't even aware of Schultz's travels in Italy and his enamorment with espresso culture; so, why would they disapprove of how inaccurately it is reflected? Nevertheless, Starbucks has struggled with authenticity.

I suspect that you love the smell of freshly brewed coffee as much as I do. In the fall of 2006, customers walked into Starbucks to find this seductive aroma overpowered by the displeasing smell of the company's new breakfast sandwiches. Many voiced their disapproval of the addition quite loudly.[75] (Later the recipe was changed to reduce said smelliness.) Off-brand additions like these chip away at Starbucks' authenticity to itself. When Schultz once again took the role of President and CEO in January 2008 his effort to regain the romance they once had afforded customers had everything to do with the Starbucks they *had* once been. Authenticity isn't limited to what influenced you, but instead relates to who you promised to be.

What should be worrisome to Starbucks is not what first informed them, but rather the promise made to patrons. Growing too fast by seemingly infecting every suburban mini-mall has compromised what the brand seemed to once stand for. As Bill Breen notes, "Playing the authenticity game in a sophisticated way has become a requirement for every marketer, because the opposite of real isn't fake—it's cynicism. When a brand asserts authenticity in a clumsy way, it quickly breeds distrust or, at the very least, disinterest."[76]

Perpetuating the myths

A company's actions and voice create a mythology of sorts. We associate stories with organizations. These become powerful and difficult to change. It's important that your organization speaks and acts in a fashion that is consistent and appropriate. You can brand yourself in almost any way you'd like, but when customers receive signals that don't harmonize with the brand, they start to question the brand's authenticity. Think of a well groomed fellow walking into your office in an Armani suit, cuff links, elegant shirt and tie… and a pair of grubby, stained sneakers. It wouldn't matter that everything else was perfect; we'd only see those sneakers, and they'd shake our perception of this individual.

When McDonald's starts to sell salads, they don't immediately transform into a "healthy" restaurant. That message feels wrong and is off-brand. Actually, it's worse than that as doing so leads us to ask how bad their other foods are. We all suspect that eating there isn't good for us. Therefore, most of us limit how much we go. McDonald's shouldn't try to be something it isn't. It just has to be an authentic indulgence. Lots of us have the occasional scotch, vodka, or gin, full well knowing that we're not drinking wheatgrass. That doesn't mean that Johnnie Walker should create a "Healthy Choices" scotch.

Brands that deviate from the dialogue they've established with followers, loyalists, and customers risk alienating those who've helped them maintain their mythology. This is worrisome, as it can happen quickly and be very damaging. If you're skilled—and lucky—enough to get people to care about your brand, you'll find yourself with a great responsibility on your hands. You'll need to ensure that you keep the contract you've made with these people. Not doing so could cost you all the loyalty you've worked so hard to build.

The Zellers Paradox

For a short period in the late '80s, I became rather enamored with skateboarding. It only took a couple of hard falls for me to rethink this fantasy. At the time, though, I'd thumb through magazines like *Transworld Skateboarding* and *Thrasher*, examining a culture that was foreign to me. I particularly remember the irreverent and sometimes cryptic ads from brands like No Fear, Vans, and Airwalk. They were so different from what I'd seen before that I didn't know how to interpret them. It was clearly a culture of its own, and I admired that.

Airwalk shoe designs were playful, featuring wild patterns and bold colors. While most teenagers were wearing high tops, Airwalks were mostly worn by those in the skate/surf community. By the mid-'90s—long after I had abandoned skateboarding—I noticed a proliferation of Airwalk shoes and garments appearing in the mainstream. Even though I had never really been a part of skate culture this seemed odd to me.

As skateboard culture moved into the mainstream, they expanded beyond skate shoes and made their products available in chain stores like Zellers: a bargain department store in Canada. Shannon McMahon examines the implications of having done so, in her article "Skating to the top." She notes how "...skateboarders shunned the company for dipping too deep into the mainstream."[77] Brand loyalty eroded and the company eventually declared bankruptcy.

By 2004, Airwalk was acquired by Collective Licensing International who purportedly planned to return the brand to its roots. Admirable as that goal may be, it's optimistic. Part of skateboarding's—and ostensibly Airwalk's—original draw related to how it connected with a particular segment of youth counterculture. In once forsaking this to reach a less select market (e.g., suburban kids' soccer moms), the company sacrificed its authenticity. I doubt the Airwalk brand will ever regain the cachet it once had.

Many of us start a company and struggle just to keep it afloat, dreaming of someday (maybe) taking a holiday. We ask our friends to try our products, hound the press for interest, and sometimes even beg for attention. By the time that we reach a modest level of success, most are so tired that it's hard to even feign the love we once had for it. Think pizza: I love pizza and at times have eaten it three times a day. But, if I ran a pizzeria for ten years, I'd probably feel quite differently. Making pizza, talking about pizza, selling pizza, promoting pizza, washing pizza dishes, smelling like pizza… I'd probably never want to touch a slice again.

The customers wouldn't know this. They'd come into the pizzeria loving our market fresh ingredients, unorthodox toppings, clever names, and the vibe of the place. It builds up a following and people start to talk. Some begin to feel like this is their own little place, and we get to know patrons by name. As word spreads we find ourselves able to add a few extra locations.

This gets covered in the local business media, and soon an investor asks to franchise the shop and license the name for a line of frozen pizzas for grocery stores. This proposition might be awfully tempting. Money would help modernize, add better training programs, increase consistency, and even afford funds for advertising. Plus, after so many years of hard work, some money and the possibility of a day off would be nice. Who would say "no"?

Suppose I did accept; things would change. New staff members would be added and probably not remember all of the customers' names. Some special items that regulars loved would be removed from our menu to focus on more popular and profitable ones. Those who thought of this as "their" place might find themselves without a seat on busy nights. The loyalists could very well feel displaced and start looking for a new place to call home. "You know, Eric's was such a great pizzeria, but it's no fun any more. I even saw one in the Dallas airport last week. It's just not the same." This is the Zellers Paradox: small brands that gain mainstream attention often find their authenticity compromised and seemingly impossible to maintain in the eyes of the public.

Everyone wants it first

Many of us like to think of ourselves as modern day explorers of sorts. We revel in the discovery of something new, and even feel a little special when we introduce less-knowing peers to these finds. Brands benefit by having such advocates spread the word for them, but this romance can be short-lived. Few want to be late to the party. This means early adopters are quick to move to another thing, once word travels, and their discovery is relegated to the mainstream.

Few would admit to becoming a fan of the grunge phenomenon Nirvana after the band achieved mass awareness as no one wants to jump on a bandwagon. Many of us got excited about the band some-time around 1991, and they subsequently moved from the fringes to the spotlight. The band shouldn't be blamed for this. They didn't change, or do anything differently after success than before. They were just caught in a wave bigger than themselves.

What did change was how we felt about something we liked be-coming the "flavor of the year." Few want to talk about the same band that their kid brother/sister is raving about. No, we like thinking that we're special, and that sensation is compromised when the masses come knocking. This forms a curious paradox: we find a great band and complain that no one appreciates them, only to have them later gain mass appeal. At this point we find our ownership somehow ne-gated and seek out something that appears less tainted.

When a person champions a product in limited supply, their ex-perience with it is more personal. By investing time, energy, and ef-fort into a brand, they tend to feel like it's theirs. This can result in some becoming evangelists for your offering. Should the same prod-uct become available in bulk at chain stores, a sense of betrayal may arise. Those who invested in the brand early on may feel as though a connection has been eroded, even if you've done nothing to augment this relationship. They may feel a loss of sorts as they witness this personally significant product, service, or place reduced to a com-modity.

Careful what you wish for

Should your small company grow, you will experience this. You'll change and your customers will feel it. No matter how hard you try, people will start to question your authenticity and whether you've changed for the worse. I can't offer a steadfast way to combat this. My one suggestion is that you try to "think small" even as you grow. You can't control how others speak about your company, but you can work to reinforce the values and experience that you promised from the beginning. Do whatever you can to avoid becoming seen as a bland commodity that is available everywhere and to everyone.

PART THREE
FOSTERING RELATIONSHIPS

We all want customers to know and love us, but how do we make that happen? We'll get to that, and share some flirting tips. (Don't worry; it's not as weird as it sounds.) Then we'll talk about how important it is to just be nice, and how hard it is for big companies to do so. We'll end this section by taking the sting out of sales and sharing the two most important words in sales—and the two most damaging words for your brand.

CHAPTER 12

Do They Love You?

It's important we look at how to get people to love our companies. I do believe there's something to this whole "love" thing, but worry that we approach it the wrong way: our actions are like those of a sixteen-year-old with a perpetual boner. He might utter the word "love" ad infinitum. This wouldn't mean that he actually understood what it meant.

What we love about companies

I love a few people but I don't feel that way about the company Shell, and no feel-good ad will ever change that. Still, I think we can associate emotion with our companies. We might not love an office park, stock valuation, or corporate fleet of vehicles, but look more closely, and you'll find things to love about a company. After nine years of building our company (smashLAB) it's something that I feel a fondness for. We've learned a great deal from it and it has become a large part of who we are.

Similarly, I think we can appreciate the hopes and dreams that others invest in their companies. When people care that much, their energy becomes infectious. I also think people love their iPods and it seems that some quite like a pint of their favorite beer after a long day at work. People form bonds with a car that's delightful to drive, clothing that makes them look their best, and meals that consistently make their mouths water.

We may not feel something for a company in itself, but I think we can get close to it. We're moved by those who are passionate about what they do. Similarly, we can develop good feelings around certain products and services, when they bring ample reward with them. If there's a way to build goodwill—and perhaps love—for our companies, where do we start?

Love grows

Earlier in this book, I noted how critical we all are of the many company slogans that make great claims regarding "love." I stand firm on this point—just saying the word doesn't really mean much. That doesn't make it any less important for us to try to connect with our patrons. My position is, we have to do it sincerely, instead of thinking we can get away with using the words void of any real investment.

If we aspire towards having people love our companies, we need to get past the empty platitudes we typically subscribe to, and instead start to think in terms of real relationships. One thing we know about relationships is that good ones don't start out fully formed. Love is generally contingent on time spent together. As commonality is found, bonds can be formed.

You don't plant a seed and stare at the ground until a bud appears. With this in mind, isn't it odd to go into a meeting with a new prospect and say "You're going to love our service!"? That kind of exuberance may be understandable but it's sure strange to hear. My tendency in such situations is to think, "You don't know me, so how can you say that?" In trying to build an emotional bond between your customers and your company, you have to relax and wait for things to develop. There aren't any shortcuts.

I know you

To grow a relationship, we need to build familiarity, establish trust, and simply get to know one another. The first is easy: you just need to be there and keep being there. A person who only shows up when there's something in it for them makes for a lousy friend. A company that only pops up when it can make a buck is about the same.

Companies that are "there" for us (when we need them and when we don't) get stitched into our personal landscape. Let's take the corner store down your street. Although you may think little about it, I bet you know the person who works the counter there. One day you needed milk and visited the shop. The next week you picked up the Sunday paper. Sometimes you even grab ice cream or potato chips to satiate a late night craving. The owner of the shop would be foolish to see you as a single-serving customer; instead, he'd know that you were building a relationship and that with time you'd get to know one another. He might watch your kids grow up, and you might see his do the same.

Writing this passage feels strange. It's so obvious that it shouldn't need to be documented. Yet, on countless occasions I see companies treat their customers poorly, or approach them as a resource to strip mine. It's obvious that this is shortsighted behavior, but it begs to be restated. As Voltaire said, "Common sense is not so common."[78]

When the going gets tough

My wife is a lovely and accepting person; there's little you can do to shock or offend her. I'm rather particular about things and a tad obsessive. I suspect that I'm not quite as easy to be married to. Still, we're decent, caring, and committed partners who love one another. This doesn't exempt us from the same struggles and challenges that other couples work through. What keeps us together—knock on wood—is that we care about one another enough to keep working on things and to persevere through hard moments.

Recently, our son's throat swelled up terribly. (I'm writing this passage in hospital, while waiting for him to recover.) When he went to day care all was fine, but by afternoon he couldn't move his neck and his lymph nodes swelled drastically. By the time we arrived at the hospital he was despondent, blotchy, and not breathing properly.

After a number of tests and many nervous hours of waiting, Oscar was admitted to hospital where they are treating him for an infection of his throat and tonsils. The whole thing really isn't that big of a deal; he'll be fine. Thursday was pretty nerve-wracking, though.

There was swelling near his spine, and the possibility of his airways being blocked. This didn't happen, but for the next few days he had a tough time as he was poked, prodded, and handled. This was a small scare, but it freaked Amea and I out considerably. Oscar is still little and means absolutely everything to us.

Although I never want to repeat this experience, I think it brought us closer together in a way. It was unpleasant, but we've shared an experience and got through it. As we waited for doctors and test results, Oscar and I talked and read a number of books. As he started to feel better, we munched on popsicles and watched cartoons. In a way, we spent a week bonding. Life is full of moments like these: some in our control and others outside of it. Making our way through these things, can strengthen our bonds with one another. Things aren't always smooth in between companies and customers—choosing to "own" those more prickly moments might prove a rewarding strategy.

Sure, we put more effort into our families because these relationships are most important. That doesn't mean the experiences we have with clients aren't important and worth working on. You wouldn't know this by how some companies treat their clients. Your cell phone company promises great options when you sign up, but then imprisons you in a multi-year contract. The coat check drops your hat in beer and then pretends it was water to get out of the dry cleaning bill. The salesperson fawns over you until a local celebrity with walks into the store. Relationships are destroyed at moments like these, or are they?

I say these are the exact times at which we can build love with our clients. Just imagine if that cell phone company eliminated contracts and allowed you the freedom to choose. Or, what if that bistro had the hat cleaned and offered a complimentary meal as an act of apology? Or, how would you feel if that sales-clerk pleasantly acknowledged the high-roller but noted that they'd have to wait while they helped you: one of their most valued customers? Smart businesses show us love when it's inconvenient to do so.

Can we talk about this?

Sandra seemed increasingly reticent over the past few weeks. My hunch was that she was getting blowback from her superiors on the new creative and was starting to question our studio's suggested direction. I didn't really know how to address the situation, so I finally just put it out there: "Sandra, I sort of get the feeling you want to punch me. Am I right?"

At first she laughed and then there was a brief silence; I continued, "I know this is an odd part of the process. Some of our customers get freaked out at this point and I bet you're getting resistance from the folks at your office." I continued, "What I want you to know is that you can speak freely with me. I just want to make sure that you get what you need out of this."

That's all it took to break the deadlock and get things back on track. Just asking a somewhat playful question opened up the possibility of speaking casually, and banished the cloud looming over our heads. Acknowledging our client's fears and assuring her that we'd take care of their needs helped reinforce that we were on same team. "Camps" start to emerge on some projects; it's my job to ensure they don't become destructive. We all need to share the same goals.

My wife and I rarely argue. When there is a problem, though, I find that we tend to clam up until someone's willing to break the silence. I don't understand why, but making that first gesture can feel overwhelming. Yet, once the conversation gets started, common-ground is established and we get things rolling again. This isn't uncommon; of all the conflicts I've experienced, only a few haven't been minimized through simply talking.

Break from the script

There's a restaurant near our office that's housed in an old bank. It's tastefully remodeled and has a good lunch menu. Recently I ordered something new from the menu: a couple of fish tacos that were nicely presented and rather tasty. Yet for a main dish, they seemed poorly portioned. Perhaps the host heard my stomach's growls as he later asked if the helping wasn't enough. I explained it seemed more like an appetizer than a full course. He returned shortly with another helping, noting that they'd change the dish to a larger portion soon. Most wouldn't have done a thing, but he won me over by paying attention, asking questions, and treating my opinions as relevant. I return often and bring friends with me.

You can address situations like these in many different ways but I've found luck in sometimes just breaking away from what's thought of as "professional" behavior. Instead of having a set-protocol or any excuses, I try to treat clients like good friends. Sometimes this means breaking from the script and talking with them candidly. On others, it means writing off some time or reworking a project to make them more comfortable. Mostly, it comes down to ignoring policy and simply trying to understand what's bugging them. We can't make everyone happy. Then of course, there's little reason to not open the lines of communication and try to fix a mess. After all, it's easier to keep an existing client than find a new one.

Move over

We may uphold ideals of selfless love, but most of us are actually quite self-involved. Needless to say, our companies aren't all that different. We start by thinking about what we want and then seek others to further this desire. Think of the language we employ: "I need to hit *my* quota!" "Why won't they just stop tire-kicking and buy the thing?" "This guy keeps calling with stupid questions. I don't have the time for this shit!" "My client keeps asking for pointless changes. You know, if you took the clients out of this, I'd actually like this job."

We sometimes act like jerks because we think life's only about us. (I hate to admit it, but I too suffer from this affliction sometimes.) By only thinking about what we need, we deprive ourselves of fulfilling experiences. There are many great things we can be a part of, but perhaps they don't all start and end with us.

Although I make many suggestions throughout this book, I accept that some of my observations are outright wrong. One thing that I'm convinced of, is that the good stuff in life... the really, really good stuff doesn't come from us but rather is a result of those we're surrounded by.

I'm not a particularly exciting person, and I don't need to be. I'm surrounded by kind, colorful, and interesting people. Each one adds something to my life, and I'm grateful for that. I also accept that these relationships are strong in part because everyone involved benefits equally from them. Be it support, exchange of ideas, sharing of experiences, or just casual talk—there are numerous reasons why these relationships work. None of them are solely about me, though. That wouldn't be a relationship—it would be advertising.

Ask questions

When it comes to interaction with others (be it personal or business) we often open the outgoing valve fully and close off the intake. We're so caught up in what we think we need that we forget to ask who this person in front of us is and what they need. My wife has an interesting kind of interaction with people, and I think it's largely because she asks so many questions.

You see, she's simply interested in others. Amea likes to know where people have come from, what they love, how they are motivated, and what their personal histories are. I should note that she does none of this with any kind of ulterior motive; she's simply curious. As a bit of an introvert, I watch this with amazement. I'm a little nervous when it comes to talking with people and asking personal things. I tend to shy away from doing so until I know people well. Watching Amea do this opens my eyes to the connections that can be formed by doing so.

You likely spend a fair amount of time telling your clients about your company and what you do. Might it be better to instead start by trying to understand their motivations, hopes, fears, and all that other stuff? Companies sometimes act like narcissists; who wants get in a relationship with one of those?

It's just "business"

We're told repeatedly that "business isn't personal," which is in my opinion a complete and utter heap of stinking bullshit. Of course business is personal! When you lose an account, you feel crummy. If you make your client happy, you probably feel good. Should you be promoted or praised by someone you admire, it likely changes how you feel for the rest of the day. The only time that business isn't personal is when it doesn't affect you. Even then, it's probably personal for someone else.

Let's consider the people (or as we say in business: connections) that help spread the word about our companies. Do they do it just because of business, or is it perhaps more personal than that? When you give a pleasant customer a deal, is it only because it's "good business," or is it also because it's enjoyable to do so for nice people? Pretending that business isn't personal is dangerous. Some may feel that I'm falling into hyperbole here, but I believe such thinking to be de-humanizing. It leads companies to make terrible decisions.

We've worked with one customer for several years. Time and again, we've proved our value by performing our job well. Over the years we've also learned about one another. She's shared her excitement about her son flying planes for the Canadian Forces and her daughter getting into college; she's equally interested to hear how my little boys are doing. Our conversations always come back to business, but along the way, we talk about our challenges, successes, careers, moving experiences, real-estate, good wine, and almost everything else. In working together for so long—and not hiding our personal lives—we've built a real relationship.

She's spent hundreds of thousands with our company as she's moved from one organization to the next. I also can't forget the thousands of dollars others have spent with us thanks to her recommendations. I like to think that her support come as a result of the things we've helped her achieve, but I must acknowledge that she probably also chooses us out of comfort. She trusts us, knows us, and we have personal interactions. She cuts us slack when we screw up; additionally, she knows that in a pinch, we'll sort things out for her regardless of the hour or what needs to be done. Many claim that business isn't personal, but our business has benefited a great deal because we are personal.

Trust

In my late twenties I felt like a bust when it came to dating. So I swallowed my pride and decided to take any advice I could get. On a lark, I ordered a book that promised to help one learn how to "date better."

I can't remember the title of that book, but it was well worth than the twenty or thirty dollars I paid for it. The author focused on one simple notion: dating is harder because of the creepy guys out there whose actions put women on guard.

Some companies act like smarmy guys: they talk a good game, but all they really want is a little "action." Once they get some they vanish faster than they first appeared, and give little care as to the impact of their actions. Why else would we need *Consumer Reports*, the Better Business Bureau, or have terms like "buyer beware"? Most of us accept that companies are programmed to exaggerate and over-promise. So the one-in-a-thousand company that actually does as it says is often shot down and forced to go home alone before it has a chance. Advertising has made us cynical and with good reason. With people so disinclined to trust, how do we get anyone to believe those of us who do as we say?

Trust is easy, but it doesn't come quickly. Establishing it requires you to concentrate on helping your customer, even if it means there's no immediate sale in it for you. By doing so you begin to establish trust, but that's just the first step. You confirm your trustworthiness by maintaining consistent and appropriate behavior over time. It's all too easy to over-promise and under-deliver; avoid this common tendency. Try to say less about how great you'll be and just over-deliver. I find myself asking if I shouldn't be writing more on this topic, but ultimately it all comes down to that: do what you promise (maybe more) and always act in your client's best interest.

Bring home flowers

In dating, grand gestures are common. Unfortunately, these niceties tend to occur less frequently as we move along. We grow complacent and too easily take people (and things) for granted. This happens in business just the same. We forget how important a client is to us, and how we once felt like the luckiest person in the world just to have them in our lives.

The person you didn't expect to give you the time of day who eventually married you. The client you dreamed of working with that now relies on you as their primary supplier, or even the house that felt like a mansion on first viewing that now seems like just a roof over your head. We excite quickly and lose sight of how lucky we are. Sometimes I think we need a stern kick to the rump to wake up to what's right in front of us.

Great people leave partners because they no longer get what they deserve. Great customers change suppliers to find the attention your company no longer seem to give. The funny part is that you don't need to do much to remind those people how important they are to you. Often it's the small stuff that adds up to something big. So every once in a while take a moment to remind these people what they mean to you. I find that such gestures are best made at times not marked on a calendar. Gifts at Christmas seem like a duty more than anything, so I tend to avoid them altogether.

A little surprise makes anyone feel special. Done well, these gestures are held onto for a long time. The great thing is that they're also inexpensive. Surprise is remembering a customer's name after only a couple of visits, or, being able to recollect the sandwich they order every time. Surprise is a note in their bag, saying how much you appreciate their business. Surprise is a rebate for always coming back. Surprise is a ticket to a concert that they mentioned in passing. Surprise is locating a copy of something they recently lost or just couldn't find anywhere else. Surprise is a free upgrade that wasn't expected. Surprise is all of these things and thousands more. Sometimes surprise is just a matter of emptying out the dishwasher before heading to work. Surprises are cheap, plentiful, and a nice way to keep the magic alive.

So there you are... the recipe for love

If you do everything noted here, your customers will love you. They'll tell each and every friend about the great person you are, and convince them to buy only from you. Money will overflow from your cash register and you'll never need to put another cent into advertising. The only real problem you'll have will be to find a way to get past the throngs of adoring fans at your doorstep.

OK... so that might not happen; similarly, being a great partner doesn't ensure that your marriage will work out. All you can really be responsible for is how you act. There are (at least) two parties in any relationship. You have to accept that some things are beyond your control. By setting yourself up for good relationships, I believe you stand a better chance of making it work. Love isn't guaranteed, and it doesn't necessarily last forever. When it works, little can beat it.

CHAPTER 13

Do They Know You?

Before love is even remotely possible you need to establish some level of awareness. Most marketers race about madly shouting their taglines, marking territory with their logos, and trying out any device that could possibly raise awareness. While this behavior and its motivations are understandable, it's still flawed. Perhaps we can best contemplate this challenge by looking at our own actions. Let's consider how we become aware of the companies that we eventually buy something from.

How do you find a plumber?

The Yellow Pages has countless listings for plumbers in any city. This can leave us in a rather odd predicament. Imagine that the pipes have burst and someone needs to be called. Who's trustworthy: The one with the big ad? Or the funny name? Or the neat mascot? It's hard to choose, so we do one of two things: we take a random guess or we ask a friend who they suggest. I prefer the second option, as I trust my friends. I also think there are other factors to consider.

One of the most important ways to succeed in life is to simply "be there." For example, of the people I've hired, many had reminded me regularly that they wanted to work for our company. Likewise, I buy from the florist next door, because their location makes them focal. Additionally, I tend to get wine at a shop a block from our apartment out of pure ease. This says little of the brands that are more universally "there" as a result of consistent and repeated messaging: I *Google* when I need to find something, I blow my nose on a *Kleenex*, and I *Xerox* documents.

I admit that these are a somewhat tired set of references. Still, it proves how important it is to just "be there." Additionally, becoming ubiquitous in a given industry is quite viable, if one's determination to do so is strong enough. Some may have to concentrate on servicing and marketing to a specific region, while others may choose to narrow their offering to a particular type of clientele. These are both sensible ways to make becoming top-of-mind less arduous.

Known quantities

This notion of "being there" is really about becoming a known quantity. No matter how adventuresome you are, I bet that you frequent the same few restaurants more than others. Additionally, I'll wager you order the same few things there repeatedly. It stands to reason that their other dishes would be as good—or perhaps better—than what you're comfortable ordering. Similarly, there are likely dozens of other delightful establishments you could try, which you'd enjoy equally so.

Each time we try something different, we run the risk of finding something that we don't like. This desire to remain in one's comfort-zone is really important when we look at brands. In a world containing limitless varieties, most people reach for the same brands (and experiences) time and again. Almost anyone could order crème brûlée and give it a try. They could take in an opera to see what all the fuss is about. Or, they might forsake a year of work to live in a beach-hut in some reasonably-priced tropical climate. Sadly, few do, regardless of means, because doing so involves the possibility of the unknown. Horror films have taught us well that the unknown is where danger resides. So instead, we do our "9 to 5," after which we curl up in front of the television with a bag of Doritos and watch an Adam Sandler movie. Thankfully, those all end exactly the same way—no risk there!

I could carry on regarding what a sad statement this is about the human condition, but that would be off-topic. What's important to take from this is that people crave known quantities. When I see companies trying to do something exciting and different every time they approach their marketing, I worry that they're missing the point. Customers really want to know what you are, and that you'll always deliver on the same promise: "The café with the amazing peach pie!" or "The oil-change shop where you never have to wait." or "The technology company whose stuff always works."

The French painter Matisse once explained he wanted his art to have the effect of a good armchair on a tired businessman.[79] Some will say—particularly in light of new technology—that we should push the boundaries and do only edgy and wildly exciting things when we market our companies. I feel this advice to be flawed, and argue that we should instead create companies that feel like that armchair Matisse spoke of. Our companies should strive to be classified easily by customers and hold this position by maintaining their trust. A customer should feel as safe in calling your company as they would settling into that loyal, old chair that's been in the basement for as long as you can recall.

To do that, we need to first determine why our companies matter, and then craft a message that can be repeated indefinitely.

My "ordinary" mistake

For all of the assistance I give to others, I'm often hamstrung by one of the simplest mistakes. I erroneously think our company needs a massive qualitative advantage when we market our own services. If I say that we create "great" websites, I want to have a method of proving that this is more than just exaggeration. Similarly, as a young fellow trying to meet women, I was often limited by my fear of being overly ordinary. What's problematic here is that so many of us are stuck by these same misconceptions. In ways you are ordinary—as is the person next to you, and the one next to her, and so on and so forth. Your company is likely quite ordinary as well.

I have met with numerous law firms that have sought to differentiate their operations by building a brand identity or website that would show how great they are. One specific website we built years ago is to blame for this. Countless law firms have since called us into their offices and asked us to create the same for them but better. This is typically after the seemingly compulsory discussion about how "different," "out of the box," or "fresh" their firm is compared to all of those other "boring" law firms. (I never have the heart to burst their happy fantasies.)

Most all of these firms were doing fine, being ordinary law firms and doing what I suspect is pretty ordinary "law stuff." This in itself is probably enough to keep clients walking in the door. A few firms might find a competitive advantage by servicing a specific kind of clientele, or differentiating in some way. The unfortunate—and no-table—part is that those who want to market better typically aren't willing to do so. Instead, they just copy their competitors with the intention of being "a little better." This leaves a lot of companies rely-ing on a set of vague superlatives like "fast-acting," "super strength," and "exceptional service." The real issue at hand isn't one of being better. Instead, it's a matter of getting known for one specific thing.

Musical chairs

Advertising has told us that we're all too busy, old, fat, boring, sub-urban, smelly, wrinkly, ordinary... and the list goes on. The implicit message is no matter how good you are, you still haven't arrived—and you should keep on buying something else until you do. This leaves many of us looking at the people around us, asking what we can do to better ourselves—regardless of whether such "betterment" is relevant or necessary. You may think that you're immune to this, but a lifetime of being told that we're not good enough does have an impact. It even skews how we see our companies.

This nonsense leads us to look at our lives—and businesses—and get "change happy." We've had enough of being deficient, and we start to make bold, sweeping changes.* We call in branding firms, ad agencies, change consultants, and designers to "right" every wrong and change everything we can. That classic logo dating back to the start of the company thirty years ago? "Hah! Garbage! We're getting one of those neat 'web 2.0' ones!" The old brochures? "Those will go to the recycling bin—besides they are *so* last year!" Positioning statement? "Do you really have to ask? We're a whole new company. Everything is going to be different. Change is good!"

This seems a little like me deciding to run ultra-marathons, abstain from alcohol completely, and embrace an all raw-food diet. These goals, although admirable, may be too "whole hog." Perhaps I just need to exercise more, limit myself to a glass of wine a day, and go for a balanced-meal instead of a Whopper and fries. It's almost impossible to change our personalities. I ask if the answer might be to steer clear of transformative change, and concentrate on isolating and addressing our real problems.

Please note that "bold sweeping changes" are sometimes necessary—particularly if you make lousy products.

A small twist of the knob

What if the only change your company requires is a small one? Getting a message across in marketing tends to require some deal of repetition. Establish one clear message and avoid deviating from it. This also holds true for your brand. Sure, you can make changes along the way, but haphazard ones can be perilous. Each time you abandon your track and begin anew you lose the inertia you've already established. You are then forced to completely start over.

Bold changes in your marketing direction shouldn't be undertaken without ample consideration. For many, I propose there is little necessity for disruptive change, but rather a need to turn a few knobs. The one that most often needs to be tweaked is labeled "Presence." Quite often companies have a strong value proposition, exemplary service, and effective marketing assets. Yet they fail to act upon them. An analogy for you:

Doug is a nice guy. He's employed, well read, and spends his weekends volunteering; at the same time, he's a little lonely and would like to date more. After work on Fridays he goes for a run, showers, and prepares for a night out. He primps his hair and gets dressed, only to look in the mirror and realize that something's not quite "right." He changes clothes, then changes yet again. Each time his garments look fine, but he can't get past the notion that he could do better. He sneaks in a brief dinner, tries on a few more things, and finally realizes that it's too late to go out. So he sits down on the couch, impeccably groomed and dressed, and watches a movie alone.

Scott's a different sort. He wears out-of-date clothes and ratty t-shirts. His hair is unkempt at the best of times and he has a little dandruff. Sometimes he forgets to put on deodorant and gets a little "aromatic." He's funny and nice, but has a tendency to speak too loudly—sometimes putting off those around him with his bad breath.

Both are decent fellows who are just a twist of a knob away from meeting people. Doug just needs to pick something to wear and get out there. (It doesn't matter how well you're dressed if no one ever sees you.) Scott, on the other hand, has to get some dandruff shampoo, deodorant, a toothbrush, and a clean t-shirt and jeans. These aren't pivotal, life-altering, Tony Robbins' *Personal Power* kinds of changes. We're talking easy stuff.

When I look at small companies who want my business they often fall into one of these categories: well presented "Dougs" who never make themselves known, and "Scotts" who are visible but don't give their presentation a moment's thought. Ask yourself: which one of these are you? I'm betting that we have a lot of "Dougs" out there who do good work, but feel uncomfortable making themselves heard.

By the way, Most large companies are Edgar: He stands at the bar wearing tacky but expensive clothes shouting, "Hey buddy!" to all those around him. We might dislike Edgar, but he still meets lots of people.

Position, refine, speak, repeat

I'm fascinated with the moment of change. What turns a funny ad into a cultural meme? When do loose connections become movements? At which moment do you achieve breakthrough? This is elusive and difficult to pin-down; nevertheless, I believe there's a pattern that can help lead us to this moment. It's not guaranteed, but the architecture for it seems sound.

First, organizations need to know who they are. Without a defined purpose, the company will progress in no clear direction, simply floating about wherever the wind takes them. Second, with a strong position in place, messaging is honed to articulate this proposition. Without it, your message will run long and be incapable of elevating past the noise. Next, this message must be spoken where people can hear it. Failing to do so leaves you with a "Picasso in a vault." Sure, it may be yours, but no one else will ever get to enjoy it.

With all of this in place, we come to repetition. Every brand, tag-line, jingle, logo, icon, and treatment that has become lodged in your mind has done so through repetition. Coca-Cola, IBM, Nokia, Toyota, Intel, Disney, and all those others have done many things well. At some point they clarified their brand proposition and pummeled us with a few core messages and icons until it became virtually impossible for us to forget them.

Remind me you exist

Almost every group that our company has worked with has had something notable—or even remarkable—to offer. For one reason or another, though, they didn't talk about this advantage. Perhaps it seemed too insignificant in their minds. Maybe they didn't even realize they had it, or it could be that they didn't know how to pitch it. Once they had isolated this value, you'd think it would have been easy to move ahead.

A moment ago, a representative from a print shop just down-stairs from our office walked in with some samples. I've seen their logo a thousand times and they're probably worth considering when we need a printer, given how close they are to us. Still, I continue to work with remote suppliers because I'm familiar with them. It's not like I'll redirect all our business to the print shop downstairs through a single personal introduction, but they did remind me that they exist. Heck, I might consider them for our next print project.

When I suggest that you need to spread the word, I don't mean it to be in lieu of everything else you need to do. You can't have bad service, scrimp on your marketing materials, or treat your staff poorly. That's the hard part: you have to do all of these things well *and* you need to get out there to actively spread the word.

Make some action

Maybe you need to devote a fixed amount of time each day to tell people you're available to lend a hand. Perhaps you need to call the people you've previously worked with and ask if they might introduce you to new prospects. You could even have an open house and invite potential clients to meet your staff and try out your products. Without knowing your company, it's hard for me to suggest what will work for you. Regardless of your circumstances, I think it's safe to say that you need to act.

I'm always surprised by the faith put on marketing pieces. Some think that a blog will bring in new sales on its own. Others hope that a presence established through social media will make sales efforts unnecessary. Some go-live with a new website and think that the all work is done.

A few weeks ago I met with a client over drinks, who noted, "I hoped the website you created for us would bring in some new work, but I guess it doesn't work like that." I was somewhat taken aback. This is a highly intelligent and insightful fellow; yet, he seemed under the misconception that the website alone had this sort of power. I felt pretty guilty about this for the rest of the night—as though we hadn't delivered on a promise. I've thought about that conversation and others like it, and found a bit of a pattern. All of these prescriptive notions surrounding marketing have us putting a disproportionate amount of trust in the tools, and this is a problem. Buying a lawn-mower doesn't result in a cut-lawn; it's only the means by which you could cut it. Similarly, a website is a fine way to convey a proposition to interested parties and remove any doubt about your operation. But before that can happen, prospects need to find your website. This requires you to get out there and spread the word.

Marketing collateral, advertisements, and identity materials are important but largely inert—on their own, they do nothing. Printed materials need to be put in people's hands for them to be read. Advertisements must run where customers will see them, to encourage action. The most suitably crafted corporate identity will do little in a documentation booklet; it needs to be implemented and real people need to touch and see these things. Websites and blogs are particularly challenged in this regard. Aside from turning up in search results they are islands. You have to direct people to these properties and cultivate an audience.

No one plants a garden expecting it to take care of itself. You must water, weed, fertilize, and prune; its success depends on constant attention. With marketing, some think that the collateral will magically do the work for us without any intervention. I once spoke with a fellow who was completely frustrated with the poor performance of a campaign. It later turned out that 90 percent of their promotional booklets remained boxed in storage. I suppose the customers should have been delivered to their brochures, instead of the other way around. ;-)

Good habits

Word of mouth is a wonderful phenomenon that we should all seek to harness. In the meantime, we can't expect such buzz to occur spontaneously. We need to be active participants in this process, and the first pushes are often the most difficult. These days it's easy for Apple to get amazing word of mouth, but they spent decades building relationships that allow this to happen. I'm guessing they experienced a few tough days along the way too.

Marketing isn't a sprint; it's a marathon that requires you to simply put one foot in front of the other. It would be odd to think of any one stride being more important than the rest. Similarly, it's unlikely that a single campaign or marketing device will result in an overnight success. Although such miracles make for great headlines, reality tends to be less dramatic.

So keep moving and don't get preoccupied with little slips along the way. Call a few prospects every day to introduce yourself. Send a thank-you to someone who lent a hand. Write a blog post that provides insight for those who are struggling in an area that you are knowledgeable. Check the site statistics to learn who is referring traffic to your site and how you might encourage more. If you want customers to know your company, you'll have to get off the couch... no matter how nice your outfit is.

CHAPTER 14

How to Flirt With Your Customers

A LITTLE SMILE, A CASUAL GLANCE, a few flattering words… It doesn't take much to spread a little love. And let me tell you, we're starved for the stuff. Many throw the word "connection" around pretty liberally. I'm a little cynical. Sure, lots of people are happy to jam a business card in your face, but this in no way represents a real human connection. Many of us are lonely.

Get in a bus accident

Last Wednesday the driver of the 135 seemed to have dozed off, awaking at the last second. He only escaped "creaming" the back of a small sedan by pounding on the brakes and veering wildly. Passengers were tossed about, and a few colorful words of surprise were barked. That's all it took. The person beside me turned and did something rather unbelievable: she started talking. For the next 10 or 12 blocks we chatted about this-and-that. Upon reaching her stop, she noted, "It's weird, people never talk unless something like that happens."

She was right. A number of people on the bus struck up conversations with the people around them. This was different from what one generally finds on public transit. On your average day, you'll see cell phones, iPods, and portable game devices. A few read newspapers and books; others blankly stare out the window. It's incredibly rare for people to speak with one another.

We don't talk to "strangers." No, we sit down, find something to bury our heads in, and keep our mouths shut. You'd think there was some kind of legislation in place, given how obediently we follow this code. Most days, it's rare to even see a smile on the bus. Here we all are texting our friends in order to stay connected; meanwhile, interaction with real people around us seems almost unnatural.

We love moments of connection

That bus serves as a model for today's world. We're all connected but in an abstract way. Many of us have hundreds of "friends" on social networks, but are only connected to a few on a personal level. Some mask what they truly think in an effort to maintain control. We're also going a little bonkers, because words like "friend," "connection," and "network" don't seem to mean that much any longer.

At any moment, we could break through this façade. Little is actually required to make this happen. We don't need a new technology, slick campaign, interactive strategy, scheme, or gimmick. All that's required is a small, simple gesture. We just need to flirt. This isn't particularly difficult; yet, it's amazingly effective because so few do it. We're sheep. We take the path of least resistance and rarely ask whether ours is actually the right approach. Just think about spam in its broadest form: unsolicited telephone calls, direct mail campaigns, and good old email newsletters*. Lots of companies do these sorts of things yet they only work on the rarest of occasions. So why do we do it? Laziness and fear—we just don't have the guts to get out there and flirt.

Some email newsletters are actually quite good. Sadly it's only one in every thousand.

Love through lard

I worked for a short while with the "Master of Flirting". At the time, I was so self-conscious that I could hardly open my mouth—particularly around women. With that in mind, you can likely imagine how amazed I was to witness how easily he could strike up conversations. This was by no means the limit to his flirting; he did it everywhere.

(Even when depositing a check.)

At that time, it wasn't uncommon to have to go into the bank to deposit a check or make a payment. Doing so was a complete and utter drag. Upon arriving, you'd need to fill in a series of stubs for the transactions you wished to make. You'd then stand in a 30 person lineup, while two grumpy tellers slowly worked their way from one to the next. Occasionally you'd be met by a friendly representative, but that was rare. The sheer volume of customers, coupled with how understaffed banks were, resulted in a frustrating experience. The aforementioned Master of Flirting never suffered in such settings. Instead, he got special attention every time.

What was his secret? How did he circumvent all those headaches and instead get special treatment? Did he have someone on the inside? Was he on a costly plan that gained him special access? Nope— he just brought in boxes of donuts at random intervals. That's right; an occasional six dollar investment got him past all the bother. He also said "thanks" a lot. People seemed to like that.

How to flirt

The Master of Flirting wasn't particularly attractive, successful, or wealthy. None of the things I expected to make a difference mattered to him. He just talked to people and made pleasant gestures. By contrast, when I tried to get a date, I'd often come up with an elaborate plan for how to win someone's attention. This hardly ever worked. It took me forever to learn that you don't need to do anything really original to break the ice saying "hi" is often enough.

Acting in this way had a great impact on his life. There was a steady parade of beautiful women who moved through his life, seemingly tripping over one another; likewise, people treated him well in every shop and restaurant we wandered into. From my vantage point, he seemed to be living a charmed life. I did question how sincere his actions were but I couldn't argue that he had uncovered a secret that few others had. It was simple but incredibly powerful. His great, pivotal, game-changing, insight?

People like to feel special.

Simple, right? It's something we all know or should know, but tend to miss entirely. When were you last in a meeting in which someone asked, "How do we make our customers feel special?" Right... I thought so. We get so caught up in what we're thinking, saying, doing, and needing that we miss out on one of the greatest opportunities in marketing.

Think about the people who have immediately made an impression on you—those who you'd like to meet again because they make you feel good around them. How did they do it? I'd guess that they somehow made you feel special. They complimented you on your shirt, told you they loved something you did, or just asked questions about you. This is basic stuff and it works. Flirting starts by establishing the simplest form of interaction and leads to making someone feel special.

I love how flirting is both easy and makes life brighter: A quick email to tell your partner how great you think they are, making note of someone's birthday with a cupcake with a candle, or calling the manager over to tell her that the pasta was remarkable. Try a day of it; you'll be surprised by how hard it is for people to hold back a smile.

This habit of "making people feel special" works as well for companies as it does in personal interaction. It's a secret weapon for the small company. Multinationals are like the high-school prom queen. They don't flirt with anyone because they don't think they have to. Everyone's already looking at them, so they can do whatever they want. This doesn't last forever; the prom ends at some point, as does the reign of any company. Flirting might be the part that eventually turns the tables.

Delightful utility

When we reach for household objects we expect little from them other than that they function. This acceptance of the status quo leads us to overlook the opportunities to redefine otherwise banal experiences as something special. Just think about those companies who have rewritten otherwise "boring" categories by delighting their customers.

Toilet brushes are boring, but Michael Graves' translucent matte plastic version with its elegant form changed all of that, affording a little beauty where it hadn't been expected. Herman Miller's skeletal Aeron chair—that sells for several times more than any other office chair—becomes an icon representative of how much management cares about staff. OXO adds beefy rubber grips to common kitchen utensils and makes them more wieldy, desirable, and profitable.[80]

There are many products that delight us, but I've chosen these examples because they're not altogether that different from their stock counterparts. Graves' toilet brush doesn't clean a toilet differently from a less beautiful one. Few saw the necessity to redesign the office chair, but the Aeron redefined the category. Similarly, OXO Good Grips could have been devised by anyone—but weren't.

I would love to talk more about how we can delight with design but that will have to wait for a future book. Still, I felt I would be negligent to not address this point, even if briefly. The things we make, as much as how we speak and act, help flirt with customers for us.

Less yelling, more seduction

Adam Lowry and Eric Ryan are the duo behind Method: a company that has made something otherwise banal delightful—through good design. Their company makes cleaning products (not something most of us are terribly excited by) and their customers talk an awful lot about them. Method makes cleaning products less harmful by using biodegradable ingredients from natural sources including soy, coconut, and palm oils.[81] They also use recyclable materials in their packaging, offset with renewable energy credits, and avoid testing their products on animals. These are admirable values and they give us good reason to pay attention.

I hardly believe this to be the sole reason we buy Method's products. An informal survey of the cleaning products section at any grocery store presents us with an array of day-glow packages screaming for our attention. A visual pollution of sorts: few of these products consider the user's desire for delightful objects. These are brutish, industrial-looking offerings that do little to engage us. Instead they yell, clamoring to be heard amongst the equally hideous alternatives they share shelf-space with. Method changed all of that.

Designers including Karim Rashid and Joshua Handy were enlisted to sculpt the forms for their packaging; meanwhile, the clean type, reserved color choices and minimal treatments emotionally resonate with buyers. Frankly, the end result shouldn't be so notable; it's just well packaged soap made more sustainably. Given the alternative, though, Method gets a lot of mindshare, praise, and press.

Something has changed, and a walk down that aisle of cleaning products today illustrates how the "prom queens" are quickly following suit. Many copy-cat products now vie for a piece of the action Method has generated. In a 2008 *Fast Company* profile, founder Eric Ryan noted, "When we started this company, we had a saying that we were never going to try to out-Clorox Clorox. We shifted the playing field where now companies are trying to out-Method Method."[82]

Delighting a customer is a little like an unexpectedly fun first-date: it sticks with us for a long time.

Is this really "grand"?

Rise and shine...
　　Rise and shine...
　　　　Rise and shine!!!

(It wasn't until she shouted for the third time that I actually heard.)

This "rise and shine" is how my morning begins at the Grand Hyatt in San Diego. A little fatigued from a day of flying, eating poorly, and not enough sleep, I make my way downstairs to grab some breakfast: nothing fancy, just some eggs. All that I find open is the hotel's coffee garden (there may have been something else—I didn't look that hard). I order a juice, breakfast sandwich, and espresso. I then sit and read my magazine.

Although I provide an appropriate tip, the person at the counter doesn't bother to tell me where I can find my juice; nor, does she walk the ten feet to bring me my meal. Instead, she yells at me until I finally hear. I collect my breakfast: a chewy piece of ham mushed into a rubbery, micro-waved English muffin. There's little "grand" about it; then of course, that adjective seems misused at the Hyatt. As my visit continues, I find myself asking why I feel so cynical about this place—particularly its chosen descriptor.

On first inspection, the lobby is certainly grand. It seems almost opulent, with marble flooring, high-ceilings, and an army of concierges welcoming visitors. It's not like they spared many expenses in creating the space; it's nice in a "look at me" sort of way. One colleague noted that he half-expected Joan Collins to walk out, as the space seemed like something from the television program *Dynasty*. The structure and the chosen treatments don't seem out-of-line with its name; yet, I still feel ill at ease.

Perhaps my misgivings have something to do with the degree of consistency here starting to reach monotony. Upon entering my room I experience a little déjà vu. What I find is almost identical to the one in the Boston Hyatt I visited a year earlier. Same television, same programming, same beds, same layout, same bathroom, same curtains, same, same, same. Consistency is important but this starts to feel bland and flavorless. Worse yet, it seems that there's a charge associated with even the smallest conveniences, and this makes me grumpy. Even if you spend a few hundred dollars for the room, they still "get you" for using the gym, making a local call, or hooking up to a Wi-Fi connection.

Later I start to note that how many similarities the Hyatt has to an amusement park. The veneer is impressive in a way, but upon going to another you realize that each is almost the same as the last. And everywhere you turn, you need to pay for something else. It's awfully difficult to be delighted with something when it feels so much like a collection of toll-booths.

Marta and Troy's wedding

Contrast this with the night that Amea and I spent at the Trickle Inn near Salmon Arm. We were on our way to our friends' wedding and needed a place to stay for the night prior. Marta suggested a little bed and breakfast near the wedding venue. Now, I should probably clarify something right here: I don't much like the idea of bed and breakfasts. Waking up in someone else's house has never turned my crank, and the possibility of it being a "dive" leaves me reluctant to test my luck.

Salmon Arm isn't a big place, and driving after work would get us there quite late; so I acquiesced. Upon arriving, the "design-snob" in me was rudely awakened. I nearly laughed out-loud at the flowery patterns, doilies, and decor—all of which left me feeling quite out of place. The lack of a television was also a disappointment, as I wanted to watch Seinfeld and drink a scotch before retiring for the night. I won't lie to you; the space itself doesn't elicit any fond memory on my part. (Others might have found it homey and comforting.)

We awoke to gorgeous sunshine on the day of the wedding. I was quite ready to bolt and find some breakfast in town, but on our way out we bumped into one of the owners. She was dressed for yard-work and tending to the vegetable garden. Smiling, she asked what we'd like for breakfast. Amea and I were both eager to forge out on our own. Noting our hesitation she filled in, "How about a couple of omelets?" We felt badly about saying "no," so we accepted the offer and made our way to the dining room. Moments later our host appeared in full chef's garb. (I did a double-take as I wasn't sure she was the same person.) Chef's hat and all, she had performed a little transformation. We spoke for a while about the morning, her place, and a number of other things.

She then went about treating us to a breakfast that has become somewhat gilded in my memory. Fresh eggs coupled with basil from the garden, fresh coffee, toast, and so on. This wasn't a remarkable place, but that breakfast was delightful. As a result, that B&B will remain in my mind for years to come. I'll continue to talk about that quaint place with awful decor, where the owner surprised us with an amazing breakfast and some friendly conversation.

It's hard to flirt with everyone

Let's step back a moment and consider the Hyatt any why this doesn't work there. It seems there's little stopping the Hyatt from delighting us like their smaller counterparts; one might even suppose that they'd have a clear advantage in doing so. They have greater resources, more staff members, and better management systems. Given such an advantage, it's hard to imagine why, I find myself smiling about the Trickle Inn but disenfranchised by such a distinguished brand.

Part of the challenge I suspect, is that they've set our expectations so high. At the "Grand" Hyatt, I expect to be amazed by how high they've set the bar. Instead, I feel nickel and dimed every time I try an amenity. Joy quickly erodes when I need to ask how much things cost before considering them. (This isn't particularly conducive to "delight.") A greater challenge yet, is that Hyatt employs 90,000 people.[83] Is it possible for each of those people to make every customer feel special? How would you systematize such behavior? Sure, you can document such protocols in a training manual, but... well... good luck with that.

The breakfast at the B&B was memorable in a way that the Grand Hyatt will never be. Big companies need to be safe and consistent, which isn't a bad thing, but it can make them a little less interesting. This leaves them with fewer opportunities to delight us. It probably doesn't matter, though. The Hyatt surely makes lots of money, and it would be utterly impossible for them to delight everyone. As is also the case with Starbucks, consistency is often what's necessary once an organization reaches ubiquity. There's little wrong with this, but it does give small, smart companies an opportunity to differentiate their offerings. Flirting for companies like yours and mine isn't hard to do well; for those "grand" ones, it can be cumbersome.

Inside access

I think that most companies see their customers as outsiders. These companies spend a lot of time trying to get what they need, but have a hard time doing so because they don't see people; they see wallets. It doesn't have to be this way. What if we invited customers into our worlds and shared our passions with them? This might mean a tour of the kitchen for "foodies" who arrive at our restaurants. It could involve a weekly ride at your bike shop, in which you connect personally with those who've bought from you—and perhaps even those who haven't. You could even write a blog containing insider information that only select clients can access. Just remember to give them the good stuff.

Inclusion like this is great, but it can its lose value if you give it to everyone. If you do something like this, I ask you to concentrate on those who love your brand, patronize your business most, and already spread the word for you. Take that small percentage of customers and ask how you can reward them very, very well. It may be expensive to do so, and perhaps it should be. If these people are good to you, it might be wise to do some heavy-flirting (another completely fabricated term). Get close to them, share something big, and let them know how much they mean to you. After all, does anything make one feel as special as being allowed into another's inner-circle?

Flirting doesn't have to stop

After a couple of years of working closely with one of our favorite clients, I decided to step back a little. I was still directing his projects, but thought one of our designers should take on the core design and production tasks. In my mind, this wasn't a particularly big deal; the assigned designer was seated right beside me, and I kept a close eye on progress. One day our client called, quite frustrated, noting, "Eric, you don't care about me any longer. You pass my calls along to the new guy, and don't even want to talk. What's going on?" In the scramble to keep the job on-track, I hadn't communicated that we were still taking care of him.

I could have made a friendly phone call, introduced the new designer and talked about how the project would proceed. Or, I could have explained that I was directing the project, keeping a close watch, and available anytime to chat. It would have only taken a moment to reassure him of our dedication, and the talent of the designer working on his project. Instead of doing so, I only concentrated on getting the job done… and almost lost our client in the process.

Flirting shouldn't end just because you're in a relationship.

Donuts don't always work

Some of these ideas might not work for you. Although the Master of Flirting did well with donuts, such a thing can become transparent quickly. Like everything else in this book, I can only make general suggestions that you'll need to evaluate and act upon as you see fit.

There's no "right way" and even things that work today may prove to be less effective at other times.

Try to remember that flirting is all about small gestures. This makes it easy to try different things and see what works with your customers. Seek out small things that delight them. These need not be elaborate or complex, but it helps if they're closely connected to your identity and relationship with them. Maybe it's just a matter of making a quick call to ask how they're feeling and remind them that you really want to keep them happy.

In a way, I'm unsure of this word "flirting." It feels too fluffy and perhaps overly cavalier. Some might take it to represent niceties with little actual substance. The tough part is that I can't think of a better word to describe this sort of interaction. For the sake of this discussion, let's work under the auspice that such flirting should only be genuine in nature, with the intention of growing something more substantial in time.

CHAPTER 15

BE NICE TO PEOPLE

GETTING PEOPLE TO KNOW AND LOVE your company is a cloudy process. What works for one group may do little for another. You'll have to sniff about, run some tests, and see what works for you. One thing I've noticed, is that people tend to dislike working with jerks. Sure, we're sometimes forced to do so due to a simple lack of options, but I think that's quickly becoming a thing of the past. It seems to me that we increasingly have more choices regarding who we spend our money with. As this happens, I think most will choose to work with nice people when they can.

Duh!

Again, we're left with the mind-numbingly obvious. "Of course, people prefer to work with nice people. You mean I spent good money to read this sort of drivel?" Nevertheless, if it's so painfully obvious, why is it so excruciatingly rare? Think of the millions that companies put into advertising, only to blow it once we're in the door. My personal example for this is Telus.

Telus is a Canadian telco whose tagline reads, "The Future is Friendly." They spend immense sums advertising around this theme, which is brought to life through playful animals on sparse backdrops. These ads are ever-present in cities like Vancouver. I find them on the bus, billboards, websites, television, and their corporate vans. They have invested heavily in getting us to think they're friendly.

When I call them, I experience something quite different. They appear to have made it deliberately cumbersome to reach a human when problems arise. Should I find a way through their automated maze, their people seem intent on playing "hot potato" with my call. Solving a little problem like double-billing becomes an ordeal. I call them, get transferred, and am accidentally hung up on, until I want to punch someone. So I start to see those ads as a slap in the face. Their future isn't "friendly"—it's mechanical, obtuse, and circuitous. Unless... they want to sell me something or I call to close an account. Either of those change the game completely.

Selling me something (like a bundled service) seems easy enough and they're well-equipped to hook me up. No need to be transferred—just a few clicks and we're done. Similarly, calling to close an account seems to upgrade the importance of my call. Suddenly I'm a "valued customer." Perverse, isn't it? They'll do anything to get a new customer. Ask to leave, and they treat you like family. But as an existing customer, it seems like I'm inconsequential.

I'm going to go out on a limb here, but stick with me. What if... just hypothetically... a company like Telus concentrated less on telling me how great they were, and instead was nice to me? By "nice" I mean that an actual human would answer my calls, that I wouldn't be tricked into a long-term contract, and that I wouldn't find myself extorted upon wanting to cancel something I didn't ask for.

What if the folks at Telus minimized their reliance on clever ads, and became obsessive about servicing their existing customers? Most in their existing markets already know who they are, so awareness isn't the issue. It seems that some others feel like me, and voice their frustrations both in conversation and online. What if Telus re-allocated a few of those millions spent in media buys to just delighting their existing customers? A handful of loyal advocates might just do more than another season of cute ads. Crazy thinking... I know.

The hard part, is that people who aren't nice don't easily recognize this in themselves. Additionally, when they get feedback from others that shines a light on this, they often refuse to believe it. The challenge is to both get accurate feedback, and then act on it. This is exponentially harder for big companies.

Fighting impotency

I don't intend to canonize small companies. Many have abysmal service and act badly, but if motivated they can address such problems rapidly. This isn't as manageable when employees number in the hundreds or thousands. In large organizations you need systems to manage how people interact amongst themselves and with the outside world. Unfortunately these procedures aren't perfect, and some within companies who see the absurdity of a given guideline, find themselves hamstrung by corporate policy.

Sometimes they shrug their shoulders and apologize; at other times I've been told how to get around such nonsense. My question is whether some of the structure and policies we employ are just too rigid. Could we run our companies better by establishing objectives instead of rules? I wonder what might happen if we empowered our people to simply "make customers feel great." There'd be hiccups, as we'd be asking staff to make subjective decisions, but a lot of the current methods certainly aren't working as they should.

The only job I could find after completing art school was at a photo-finishing shop in the mall. I learned something from one of my coworkers who had a nice way with customers. Darrell didn't make a big deal out of things. He wasn't concerned with every detail that had been laid out in the staff manuals. Mostly he just tried to make people happy. One day a customer came in to pick up some photos, presenting me with a coupon that had long since expired. Half-way through my explanation that, "Um... this coupon is sort of..." Darrell walked by and whispered, "Make your life easier—take the coupon."

While I was stuck on an unimportant rule (what's a "limited-time offer," anyway?) Darrell seemed more concerned with the big picture. I think he knew that acting by-the-book would lose a customer and perhaps cause a scene. By being pleasant and just going with the flow, customers came back time and again. People liked Darrell, and we were never worse off for doing any of this. More than that, what should head office be more concerned with: rejecting an outdated coupon or keeping a customer?

What's notable is that Darrell did this sort of thing on his own. I doubt our manager was ever aware of it—she likely would have put a stop to it immediately. By ignoring the more tedious aspects of corporate policy, though, Darrell's actions increased customer loyalty. I have to wonder what kind of response your company would find if you encouraged staff to do the same. To do so you might actually have to rewire your drones to speak "human"—enabling them to get the job done and make customers love you.

A cold-shoulder or a helping-hand?

My brother Mark was on his way from Kitchener-Waterloo to Vancouver for the Christmas break when a massive storm-front took hold in parts of Canada and the United States. He and thousands of others were left stranded in airports unable to make their way home for the holidays. For a few days, Mark was forced to wait at Calgary International Airport while we drank wine and ate nice dinners without him.

There's no good time to be stuck at an airport. Christmas must be the worst, as it's when one would otherwise have an opportunity to share a few precious days off with family. Lots of people were stuck, frustrated, and pissed off. Mark later told me that some Air Canada passengers were highly frustrated. This lead to many negative reviews in the media of the carrier's performance.[84]

Air Canada didn't cause the snowstorm and it would be unreasonable to expect them to cover related costs. What they missed, was one of the best brand building opportunities they'd ever have. You see, the snowstorm wasn't their rival WestJet's problem either. Nevertheless, they took a different approach, making the non-compulsory decision to care for customers, regardless of what it took.

Both Air Canada and WestJet customers were stuck. With their planes grounded, there was little that could be done to change this. Curiously, while Air Canada's customers were left to fend for themselves, WestJet's were taxied, put up in hotels, and given meal vouchers. This was done on WestJet's dime, to the tune of two-million dollars.[85] Each day, passengers shuttled back to the airport in hopes of getting home, but socked in weather and an increasing backlog left many very irritated. Still, WestJet staff put on a brave face, and did things to lighten the mood. They handed out pizza to hungry customers and awarded prizes to those brave enough to sing Christmas carols over the PA system.

Mark has been an admirer of WestJet for some time. What happened in Calgary made him in a dyed-in-the-wool fan who tells the story above to all kinds of people. Ask yourself: if you were in the Air Canada lineup and saw how WestJet took care of their customers, who would you book your next flight with?

"Nice" can be part of your ethos

I flew with Air Canada recently, and was surprised by how much they had changed in the past five or ten years. Everyone was friendly and the flight was enjoyable. Prior to this, I found their staff to sometimes be quite dismissive and snobby.

As much as they work to change their operation, at heart Air Canada is the same company, and this still permeates in the organization today. Booking a flight on their website is unnecessarily arduous, seemingly focused on data collection rather than user ease. What should be a relatively simple process leaves me irritated. Similarly, to the flyer it feels like they take every opportunity to add extra charges. Instead of being able to just choose a destination and time when booking a flight, I have to determine whether I want "Tango," "Tango Plus," "Latitude," "Executive Class Lowest," or "Executive Class Flexible." I don't want to decipher ridiculously named packages. I just want to get somewhere.

WestJet started by doing "less" very well. They've continued to apply this thinking and in doing so their entire process feels like it is built around customer needs first. Air Canada, on the other hand, appears to look for what works best for them. By adding these options they conceivably maximize profit, which was good. Saving two-million dollars on the transport, lodging, and feeding of stranded guests is probably quite fiscally responsible. Yet, in the minds of customers, these things add up. This leaves some feeling that Air Canada is less interested in their customers than the bottom line.

At the writing of this book, Air Canada has just barely staved off a second bankruptcy filing. WestJet on the other hand is adding planes to its fleet and looks stronger than ever. While Air Canada has been a giant in Canadian aviation, WestJet started as a small company just 13 years ago. Over that time it has done everything to act like a little guy. They're nice to customers and service the heck out of them.

Be nice to *all* people

Being nice is sometimes hard: customers can make unreasonable demands; suppliers don't always deliver; and, partners can miss deadlines. A lot of us are hot-headed and react too quickly. I'm one of these people, and I tend to do or say the wrong thing when a situation gets the best of me. Then of course, few of us are Mother Teresa, and from what I hear, even she had moments of doubt.

What we can aim for, is to do our best. We have to look past just the benefits to be had by being nice, and instead form meaningful and sincere relations with those around us. Most do this already. In the rush of a busy day though, we can get lost in the hustle and bustle, only to do damage in ways we didn't intend. Just imagine being greeted by a gracious host upon arriving at a lovely coffee shop. He takes a moment to ask about your day and offers you a slice of their freshly-baked pie. A few moments pass before you momentarily excuse yourself to slip into the restroom. In doing so you pass by this same cordial fellow only to witness him boorishly putting down a staff member. Wouldn't these actions shatter any ideas about the fellow that you first started out with?

The thing is, not being nice has ramifications. When my wife and I walk onto a car lot and the salesman only talks to me, we leave without any intention of returning. Ignoring my partner stops us from buying anything. Did he think there was some kind of camaraderie to be built by talking "man-to-man" about cars? If so, he was sorely mistaken. No, we just walk away, never to come back, and no clever ad will change that. That dullard will likely leave the company someday, and I'll still associate the operation with his poor judgment.

It doesn't stop there. Making rash suppositions based on who you think people are begs for disaster. I've watched as folks have acted condescendingly to the water delivery guy, janitor, or secretary. Don't do this. It only invites people to hate you and your business. Besides, every one of these people could influence a purchase from your company. Some have kids who will grow up to be customers; others have parents who they could convince to buy from you. Everyone deserves respect. It's so easy to lose customers; don't make that any easier.

One other note: If you're one of those brave souls who drives a car with your company's logo on it, always be on your very best behavior. Every time you cut off another driver, run a red light, or fail to give the right-of-way, you risk pissing someone off. Believe me, you don't want their first memory of your company to be the time you nearly ran over their kid. Marketing your company gets more expensive when you act like an asshole.

They need to want it

You can hire the best salesperson in the world, but if you're selling me tickets to the upcoming Yanni concert, you're out of luck. I don't want to hear his music and I probably never will. It won't matter to me that the tickets are front-row, half-price, or that I might even like the show. The fact is, If I don't want it, I won't buy it. I'm not saying that you're a bad person; I'm just not interested.

Branding, marketing, and sales can only get you so far. You just can't make people do something they don't want to do. My suggestion is to be nice to those people anyway. Say "please" and "thank you" and maybe offer to help them find something that they might like— even if you're not the one selling it. By being that rare person who is nice when they don't buy, you make it easier for them to come back. We're emotional creatures and if we think that someone doesn't like us we'll probably just avoid them. Don't make me feel guilty about coming back when I am ready to buy. Just be nice so it's easy for me to do so should the opportunity arise.

Besides… I just walked by a tour bus full of seniors who are dying to see a Yanni show. You never know where the next sale is coming from, right?

When you blow it

In 2002, Capers (an organic food store and restaurant) had an employee become infected with Hepatitis-A. They didn't waste a moment upon learning of this. Regardless of the damage it might do to their brand, they acted responsibly. Within hours they pulled potentially contaminated products from shelves. Then, they alerted media of the concern, asking hundreds of employees and thousands of customers to get immunizations. They even took out ads in the local paper to apologize for the inconvenience. Jim Hoggan (the publicist who helped the company address the situation) later noted, "Their sales were back up to normal within a year and the company resumed growth."[86]

Contrast this with the Mama Panda restaurant back in my home town. *Purportedly* a customer with the stomach flu vomited near the buffet table. This *allegedly* resulted in others also contracting flu-like symptoms. You'll note that although I speak with abandon throughout this book, I've used words like "purportedly" and "allegedly" here. I do so with self-preservation in mind. A journalist (and friend of mine) reported in her piece titled, "Vomit serves up virus at buffet" that necessary steps weren't taken to clean the premises, and this may have caused the spread of the illness. The owners of the restaurant went on to take legal action.[87] Years later they were still fighting a pointless fight; the restaurant was gone, and although I had to look up its real name, the only moniker that sticks with me is "the barf buffet."

Promises are easy to make, but it's our actions that really validate such claims. No matter how hard we try, we will make mistakes. In instances like those noted above, we have a few options. Capers choice was proactive and moral; they have maintained the trust they had worked so hard to build.

Customer loyalty isn't a program

One of my favorite clients is Paul Williams from McInnis. He marks the third generation of the McInnis/Williams family to run their shop, which started way back in 1920. Although McInnis has done a few different things over that time, they've more recently focused on lighting and have done so quite nicely. We had the pleasure of working with Paul on an identity project for his company a few years ago.

Paul is nice without ever being phony or saccharine. He's simply a good guy who treats his customers well. Everyone in his shop knows the products that they sell and readily carry purchases out to customers' cars. Additionally, if you ever have a problem with something you've bought, he simply takes care of it. I find myself perpetually bombarded by big companies wanting to build "customer loyalty" with some kind of card, membership, or vague promise. Paul does none of those things. He just treats customers the way that any of us would like to be.

I learned a few things about business in Prince George. We started our company there, and along the way some people shared their insights with us. I think Paul's stories are the ones I remember best. He had an interesting way of simplifying things in a way that just made sense. He once told me that many of his business insights were informed by his mother, who noted such things as, "you run your business like a household: you don't buy things when you don't have the money to pay for them."

News stories and magazine articles about business often seem to make things more complex than is perhaps necessary. I wonder if we should just try to think of our businesses as extensions of ourselves. This may help us better keep them in-line with the kind of people we are. Few of us act miserably in our personal affairs, so why do businesses sometimes do so?

What you sow

Ever wake up knowing your day is going to be shit? What about the next, when you think everything will be wonderful? Our minds have an amazing power over our perceptions. What we expect to be bad seems to become just that, and vice-versa.

I'd love to believe in the notion of some kind of karma that maintains a measured balance between what we give and receive. I am not that mystic or spiritual, but I do think the way we feel changes how we express ourselves. This in turn informs the experience we can subsequently expect.

Imagine that you're a shop-keeper who decides to assist some teenagers with something they like; let's say you help them find space and free paint to create a local mural. Suppose one of their friends later suggested tagging the side of your shop. Do you think they'd defile your storefront or would they perhaps act differently as a result of your actions? When you're nice, you open up the possibility of others reciprocating. If we're lucky, this results in making a few friends. We all need more of those, because strangers hardly give a moment's thought to whether we fail or succeed.

CHAPTER 16

SELLING
WITHOUT SELLING

ALTHOUGH MANY OF US WANT TO BUY, few of us like being "sold." This proves a strange paradox for a marketer. It shouldn't; it's just that the notion of selling is somewhat misunderstood. Many think that a sale happens when you "close the deal." I argue that this is only a small part of the process, which occurs rather late in the game.

Booty calls

A booty call is an eleventh-hour call for sex. I have firsthand knowledge of this because I was a young, horny idiot. During my early twenties, I'd sometimes find myself on the couch watching a movie, thinking, "she seemed to like me, and she's probably not doing anything… It couldn't hurt to ask." I'd make a phone-call under the guise of, "seeing what you're up to." The nature of these calls was painfully transparent to the recipient, and mostly left me with the sole option of, um, "amusing myself."

The next day I'd awake, embarrassed by my late-night blunder. Worse yet, I was left with the skewed notion that no one was interested in dating me. "No one ever says 'yes'… what's wrong with me?" Sadly, most companies do something quite similar. They treat sales like a booty call, and therefore miss opportunities by fixating on just getting another dollar in the cash register.

In part, I blame the film *Glengarry Glen Ross*, which taught too many over-ambitious young men to "Always Be Closing."[88] More than this, we're all in such a rush that we're willing to sacrifice that which is in our best interests in exchange for short-term gains. Let's start this chapter with one simple agreement: you and I will never make a booty call (professional or otherwise) again. Deal?

"But I'm not good at sales!"

Ask those who run companies about finding good salespeople and you'll get a lot of similar responses. I suspect that 9 out of 10 will say it's the toughest position to fill. Few of these kinds of people have adequate understanding of our offerings and many of those who do, share characteristics with Larry from *Three's Company*. If that reference is unfamiliar, just imagine that stereotypical "used car salesman" we see in the movies and on television.

Although I don't consider myself a salesperson, I've wandered into roles that have required sales efforts of one form or another. Again, this is by no means my vocation, but rather something I've had to do because no one else was willing to. My first experiences of this sort were at age 14, when I started a hand painted t-shirt business. I was so nervous making calls that my voice raised two octaves when I spoke. It wasn't pretty, but I learned one big thing from doing it: *all you have to do is talk*. That's my big sales insight. Sure, there's a little more to it, but if you get this one part right, I don't think you'll ever struggle with sales again. It will also get you past that general feeling of dread you experience when tasked with sales activities.

Shots on goal

Summer jobs were in short supply when I was in college. So I went door-to-door with hundreds of resumes under my arm, willing to take on any job that might be offered. This led to a couple of weeks of treeplanting, and even a short stint in a fast food restaurant. Eventually better things came along. Of all these brief posts, I learned the most from my two summers of selling bottled water subscriptions. Given all that I had done to get a job, I was happy walk around town asking businesses if they might like to buy some bottled water.

I made $7/hr. and an additional $7 for each placement I made. In retrospect, it wasn't particularly easy; I wore a shirt and tie on hot summer days, walked for stretches of up to twelve hours, and a few people were sort of rude. The nice part was that I could make a few extra bucks by putting in some extra effort.

You've likely heard the Wayne Gretzky quote, "You miss 100 percent of the shots you don't take" many times, but it means little until you've experienced it for yourself.[89] In sales I quickly learned that I had to hit a certain number of calls. If I only visited 5 offices a day, I'd be left with minimum wage, or worse yet, get fired. On the other hand, if I managed to reach 200 different businesses, the odds were higher that I'd find someone willing to give us a try. I started to measure the number of calls made on a crude spreadsheet documenting areas, business types, and interest levels in those I met with. I only found one clear (and rather obvious) pattern: the more calls I made, the better my return. It's just simple math and jotting down the number of calls made daily keeps you focused on making these numbers work in your favor.

Gutsy

Around the same time, my dad and I met with a financial planner. I think my dad hoped this experience would rub off on me, and perhaps lead me to start investing at an early age. (It didn't.) The meeting was eye-opening, though, and I'll never forget it. The fellow we met with was well known in our community—first for the media presence he had established through advertising, and later for rumors of some rather dubious personal affairs. Upon arriving at his office, we met the man himself: a boisterous but dim-witted fellow in an ill-fitting suit. I could hardly remember why we had volunteered for this; I suppose it was because he had established "top of mind" awareness, and my dad wanted to hear him out.

After shuffling papers and taking calls that were apparently more important than my father and I, he looked at my dad sternly and said, "Sorry I'm in such a rush—I have to give a talk in an hour and my receptionist is away. Let me put it to you like this: give me ten thousand dollars today and I'll call you when you're rich." I smiled. It was perhaps the gutsiest comment I'd ever heard. All the same, I had to wonder, "Does anyone actually 'buy' a line like that?"

Getting past every jerk in sales

I'm somewhat saddened by the idea that "Mr. Gutsy" probably wrangled a fair amount of business by simply being so confident. At the same time, I suspect this bravery didn't get him far in the long run. Although his audacity was notable, he left me with a dirty feeling. We left his office with little interest in ever seeing that guy again. His wasn't a big company but he allocated great sums in advertising just to get people into his office; yet, he blew his chance to turn us into customers. I suspect he watched *Wall Street* a few thousand times and could recite the *Gordon Gekko* "greed is good" speech on command. Unscrupulous jerks like this have led many to buildup strong armor in order to keep salespeople at bay. This armor has become so strong that it can prove outright intimidating when someone like you wants to talk to people about your offering.

Sweaty and tired on a particularly hot day, I walked into a small refrigeration shop to be met by a rather unhappy receptionist. Within a nanosecond of entering the room she barked, "So what the hell are you selling?" I was feeling beleaguered and had little interest in reciting the "pitch" that had developed over my many days of talking. I halfheartedly responded, "Just water. I don't mean to bug you—look at the brochure and call if you're interested." I started to quietly slip out when something funny happened. My lack of a polished pitch served as a strange sort of "sales kryptonite." Before I could escape, she started a conversation with me. We talked for a while, but not about the product—just talk. Soon we knew a little about one another; moreover, she had a water cooler on order for their office and one for their shop as well. I kept in touch over the summer and she even referred us to a few others.

I can't say doing this will work in all instances, but it is something I've experienced firsthand on many occasions. Just being a decent person can shut down otherwise bulletproof defense mechanisms. The tough part is, you can't fake it. Phony attempts at sincerity stick out like a sore thumb.

The lessons I learned over those summers can be boiled down to two things: numbers and sincerity. I still think they're the most important lessons I've learned about sales. If you don't contact enough people you won't stumble upon opportunities; likewise, if you aren't "yourself," no one will give you the time of day.

"Right, but I still don't know anything about sales"

Many use "not knowing" or "not being good" at sales as an excuse. Make no mistake, it's still just an excuse. You may not be interested in sales, but you sell all the time. We all do, we just don't call it that.

Whether you're trying to get a date, ace a job interview, or persuade your kid to eat their vegetables, you're in sales. What's worth noting is that sales has more to do with attitude than personality. I'm "not any good" at farming, but if there's no food, I'll start planting seeds and watering. If you love your company, you have to sell. You might even ask how you could get everyone else to do it too.

Every staff member needs to understand that without sales, you're dead. With this in mind, I think it's reasonable to ask everyone in your company to take part in sales efforts. Besides, it's really not that difficult. When your fellows spend an extra moment to chat with customers during a delivery, they are selling. Maybe they'll just build rapport and share a laugh; alternately, they might make note of an upcoming sale or new service you offer. None of this should be practiced or insincere. Think of it as connecting with people and reminding them that you're ready to help when they need you. The simple fact is, the livelihood of your organization—and every person within it—is directly related to your ability to persuade people to try you out and stick with you. That sort of thing should be a team effort.

Theirs is a "human-like" machine

I'm perpetually amazed by how willing companies are to sacrifice client relationships by using outsourced call centers. I can't recollect a single good experience I've had with one. On paper, these services must seem irresistible to middle managers. Just think: "we can cut costly local staff, be rid of their idiosyncrasies, and replace them with a low cost team overseas that can work 24/7." Sure, this makes sense on paper, but it belies the importance of human relationships.

I've seen a call center in action; the one I saw was like a machine with human cogs. On outgoing sales calls, the operator consults a sheet of numbers, and works through them one at a time. Rarely do these digits even have a name associated. Instead, they start with a number and move up sequentially. Each card holds dozens of numbers, and the same script is employed each time. The script is actually a highly practiced flow-chart, with clear responses for any objection someone might voice. Organizations like this want to streamline— allowing people to speak freely would put a wrench in the system. It would seem that call centers like this are perhaps the clumsiest ways to initiate a relationship.

Inbound call centers are equally bad, and often seem less interested in resolving our problems than handling a situation. Just for fun, try asking someone from a call-centre for their name. They may share their first, but rarely anything more. What does this say about their brand? This company wants our trust, but their people won't even tell us who they are.

The "anti-call center"

I've expounded on my pure disdain for call centers and how dumb I believe such entities to be. Might companies that spend many millions on advertising be better served by cutting some of those costs and instead servicing their customers? Few do and I propose the notion that by employing call centers, big companies leave you with a huge opportunity. Let them pour their money into billboards and television ads while they starve their customer service departments. Your size allows you to do the complete opposite. You'll get to know your customers and make them love you one-at-a-time. You'll create advocates for your company. You will become the "anti-call centre."

When you make contact (be it on the phone, by email, or on the showroom floor) try to think about how uncomfortable such interactions can be for the other party. Certain things run through their minds, and each one can shut down your "sale" before you even start. Some won't know who you are or if they can trust you. Others will worry that by talking to you, they'll feel somehow obliged to buy something. Additionally, people tend to have things happening in their lives other than your company. Perhaps their cat died or their kid is getting bullied at school, either of which would make your sales call seem awfully unimportant.

Remember, this isn't a booty call and you're not trying to make a quick sale. You're introducing yourself and explaining what you do. No persuasion—just a brief "hello." The sole purpose of this interaction is to let the customer know that you're available when they need you. After you've done that, get out of the way and give them some room to breathe. Maybe ask if you can check back in every once in a while, but don't smother.

If they show interest, I suggest you talk without any rehearsed script and just embrace any mistakes you make. Actually, these can help illustrate that you're a person, not some machine trying to get them to buy. Look at this person like they are a friend of your mom's. Are you really comfortable with what you're saying? Come on… they're going to talk to your mom about this later today. Are you really helping, or just saying what it takes to make a sale?

Repeat: You just want them to know you're ready if they need you.

The two most *damaging* words to your brand

I use profanity around my kids and am not particularly concerned about them eventually picking up some of those words. Sure, there are times when it may be inappropriate for them to do so, but overwhelmingly, the words don't concern me so much as their intent. There are other seemingly innocuous words that offend me far more because of what they actually mean. I'm going to mention two of them; hopefully this will be the last time we ever need to reference them. The words are: "company policy." They basically mean, "Fuck you, we'll do whatever we want." Allow me to share a story that will illustrate how I think words like these killed a small shop.

My mom is great. All kids have to say such things about their moms, but mine is a notably wonderful person. Once, about a decade ago, she thought it would be fun to go shopping on Boxing Day. We had a batch of gift certificates, and she wanted to buy her sons some new clothing.

Before we started, we had to swap some slippers that she had received as a gift. They were a size too small, and we felt it smart to exchange them before the rush. Upon arriving we learned that they didn't have her size and wouldn't receive any for months to come. Given that they were just slippers, she decided to get a refund and buy something similar, elsewhere. The store was empty, aside from three salespeople. There weren't any lineups of crazed Boxing Day shoppers looking to buy arm-loads of slippers; nevertheless, the manager made a grunt of sorts and pointed at a sign that read, "No refunds or exchanges on December 26th."

This seems like a rather silly policy doesn't it? Sure, it might be necessary from a crowd-control perspective, but it sends a terrible message—specifically: "Even though you paid full-price, you matter less to us than bargain hunters." We acknowledged the necessity for such a rule, but noted that it seemed odd, given that no one else was even in the shop. The response was a cold, "company policy" with little other explanation. There was no negotiation or flexibility; the discussion eroded and the sales staff became rude and standoffish.

We returned a week later for the refund and never visited the shop again. Six months later it was gone. I wonder if the phrase "company policy" might bring with it an expiration date for businesses.

The two most *important* words in sales

I make mistakes all the time. These are mostly small blunders but I sometimes screw up spectacularly. All of this is manageable because of two delightful little words: "I'm sorry."

"I'm sorry" comes in a variety of models including: "We're sorry," "I can't believe this happened," "We totally screwed the pooch on this one," and "Oh my God! I'm such complete and utter idiot!" All work similarly, but in the interests of brevity, the first one will probably serve you just fine. These are powerful words. I think that if you take only these from this (most spectacular) book, you've pretty much got your value from it.

The single problem with "sorry" is that people throw it around a little too easily. Think of the brooding teenager who grunts it out to appease a parent, without even a moment's reflection. Being "sorry" is one thing; doing something to correct the oversight is quite another. I think the perfect companion to, "I'm sorry" is a serving of, "Let me fix this for you."

Although many speak excitedly about "service," I think things like call centers are testament to just how feeble such claims are. As the anti-call center I want you to operate with the notion that 99.999 percent of your customers are great people who want to buy more of your stuff. When things go wrong, it's the perfect time to prove that you're worthy of buying from again. On that seemingly unexciting moment when someone calls for support or to complain, I ask you to look at it as the best sales opportunity you'll ever have.

I've found that I'm many times more "wowed" by a company that sincerely apologizes and fixes a problem than I ever am by a clever advertisement aired during the Super Bowl. One of these gets a chuckle; the other keeps a paying customer. It's up to you to decide which one you would prefer.

Removing barriers

As consumers, we often think long and hard about purchases before committing to them. This is good as it helps us reach a more objective state before acting. When you're in sales, though, there does come a time when this process must end so that you can close the deal. Don't get me wrong, I'm not proposing that you push people into doing something they don't want. That would be short-term thinking that would damage your brand in the long run.

I'm talking about the person in your shop who loves that patio furniture (or whatever you're selling) but seems unable to take the next step. In this instance, saying something like "Why not give it a try?" might be necessary. There's nothing pushy about this, just a friendly nudge. If they're already leaning toward buying, this may be all they need: permission to act.

Most purchases aren't "life or death" cases; unless you're buying rattlesnake anti-venom, but really... how often does one really do that? I've witnessed people who clearly wanted what we were selling held-back by only a tiny thread of uncertainty. At these times, I feel that my job is to remove any reservations that don't need to be there. Part of this comes down to reminding them that they're in complete control. Let me share how we do that.

Although I believe our firm offers good value, hiring us generally isn't cheap. I also know there's a lot riding on this purchase in the mind of the buyer. So I remind them that they're "driving" and that the choice to hire us isn't made just now, but all the way through the process. I encourage them to call some folks we've worked with in the past and ask about the service we've provided. I also remind them that they can "fire us" if they are ever unhappy. I'd really like to have a chance to fix the problem, but if this isn't good enough, they can pay out the time worked, and we'll happily go our separate ways.

What's important to remember about these promises, is that if you don't stand behind them, they'll mean nothing. Word travels quickly, and misleading a client will eventually do more damage than if you hadn't made any promises in the first place. I can only speak from my own experience, but when we relax our grip on clients, relationships tend to flourish. Still though, my cell-phone carrier locks me into dodgy contracts that leave me feeling burned.

Sales when no one's buying

Sometimes you can't do anything to make a sale. You've answered all of their questions, built rapport, and prepared the best price possible. Still, they've decided to go elsewhere, or not buy at all. This can be a weird position, particularly if you've put a chunk of time into earning the sale. Early in our operations I met a fellow named David George. He runs a printing and stationery company that's been in his family for decades. One day I confided in him about our frustration in not getting a particular contract. We weren't unqualified for the project—actually we had won the job. A few days after being awarded it, though, the job was cancelled for political reasons, and we sort of got the short end of the stick.

David understood how I felt in part because I think he's a little short-tempered, like me. He said, "Eric, you're always going to have things like this happen. All you can do is smile and tell them that you'll get the contract next time." I haven't spoken with David in a long time, but that piece of advice stuck.

Most prospects won't convert to a sale and you've just got to accept that and take the crunchy with the smooth. Getting emotional or acting like a jerk when things don't pan out doesn't get you anywhere. They might not buy today, but they might tomorrow, or an associate might, or the company they chose for the contract could screw up and they'll need you to come in and save the day.

It's probably better if they want you

The worst handicap in sales is desperation. When we start our companies, though, we're often not far from that emotion. That's why it's so important to keep your operating costs low, so no single sale feels too important.

We were very hungry when we started our company. We worked hard to land new contracts, which wasn't a bad thing. I also think there's something to be said for "going with the flow" at times. I learned this a few years in, when we had a consistent stream of work running through our studio. As we eased off on selling our stuff, people seemed to want to work with us more. It's like they could sense our confidence, and this made them feel comfortable in hiring us. Repeatedly, we've experienced this same counterintuitive pattern. I call it the "nightclub principle." In a nutshell it comes down to this: no one goes into an empty nightclub, but one with a lineup seems to attract hordes.

At these times, when we have many contracts in the queue, more customers seem to come to us without much directly related effort on our behalf. We've seen the same kind of thing happen with our online communities. When one of them sees a little increase in activity, other people (sometimes through no discernible entry point) start using it as well. My mom says, "When it rains, it pours." I just think everyone's looking for the party with the most action.

Selling value

There's a great difference between the terms "price" and "value." In my mind, it's pivotal that those in sales determine how to sell the value of their offering instead of the price. Not doing so leaves a company vulnerable to anyone with ample funds who's willing to wage a battle of attrition. These are bloody things with one clear outcome: the business with the deepest pockets outlives the other.

Unless a product is a pure commodity, most buyers are open to considering its value and weighing it in their decision making process. Just look at Toyota—sure, their cars come with a higher sticker price than many competing domestic brands. Most of us accept this as we think Toyota offers greater overall value. We reason that their better quality and reliability will result in lower operating costs, and command higher resale value. Only a chump buys something cheap today that costs more over its lifetime.

Value comes in many forms. Some buy suits that cost a great deal, but they find value in a garment that fits them well and makes them feel their best. Others will buy a Mac made up of parts very similar to that of a PC, because they appreciate the beauty of an aesthetically refined object, and this makes their time spent on a computer more palatable. Some also find that it makes more sense to pay more at a specialty shop than a box store as doing so gives them access to intelligent suggestions and greater product knowledge.

I was recently confronted by the argument that good software developers write code that is ten-times more efficient than that of their less skilled counterparts. Fred Brooks, author of *The Mythical Man-Month* explains, "Programming managers have long recognized wide productivity variations between good programmers and poor ones. But the actual measured magnitudes have astounded all of us. In one of their studies, Sackman, Erickson, and Grant were measuring performance of a group of experienced programmers. Within just this group the ratios between the best and worst performances averaged about 10:1 on productivity measurements and an amazing 5:1 on program speed and space measurements!"[90]

The curious part is this is that a good developer generally isn't paid ten times more than an average one. Paying twice as much for such a person would be a bargain. So an extra 25 percent should seem like a no-brainer, right? This is a perfect example of how value trumps price so exponentially.

Your job is to clearly articulate the value of your product or service. That shouldn't be too difficult, should it? If it is, you have bigger problems on your hands than sales.

Two dentists

Upon moving, I was tasked with finding a new dentist. Out of simplicity, I called up the practice my wife had been using. Amea noted that her dentist had been great, but was now retired and that a new fellow had taken over his practice. She had yet to visit him, but it seemed like this was as good a place to start as any.

I arrived at a well decorated office with nice views. Everyone was pleasant but perhaps overly so. After completing several pages of forms regarding my health, I met my dentist. He asked, "What would you like to change about your smile?" Given that I had put my modeling career on hold (joke), I was sort of irked by his question. I hadn't scheduled a meeting with a plastic surgeon; yet, his practice seemed geared like one. Screens around me played commercials extolling the virtues of perfectly aligned teeth; likewise, numerous racks of brochures promoted a variety of cosmetic procedures.

By the end of my visit his assistants had me booked for another (that I later cancelled) and I was given an estimate of the dental work that I *needed*. It felt as though I had been fed through some kind of machine, which did everything to separate me from my money, short of shaking me upside down. Although his people called many times over the following few months to schedule appointments for me, I didn't visit a dentist again for nearly two years.

Finally the time had come to get another check up—I could only leave it for so long, after all. A friend of ours suggested that I visit Dr. Kerstin Conn, given the good experience she had found in dealing with her. After months of procrastinating, I booked an appointment. I arrived at Dr. Conn's somewhat bland seeming space, which felt like it had been left largely untouched since the mid-'80s. There were no flat-panel televisions running slick commercials, nor were there any racks containing glossy brochures. No one was overly made up nor were they as eerily shiny as I found in the other practice.

After I was seated, Dr. Conn introduced herself and started to clean my teeth. She explained that she began her career as a dental hygienist, later earning a degree in dentistry. She noted that she liked to clean each patient's teeth personally, as it helped her better "know" their teeth. I was asked about pains or discomfort, and we discussed some of the procedures that had been deemed necessary by my old buddy, "Dr. Shiny." She examined the x-rays, poked about in my mouth a little and finally said, "I'd love to sell you something, but your teeth are great. You don't need anything at all."

I was ready to pay for the procedures I had once been told were necessary. Nevertheless, this dentist did something both ethical and rather smart. As a result of her honesty, she had gained my trust. Next time, she could propose a costly procedure and I wouldn't question it. She gained this by seeing me as a person, instead of just a prospect.

That's selling without selling.

The signature on the dotted line isn't the end

The smart salesperson knows that they continue to sell all the time by taking care of their clients. They understand that it's important to regularly check in with clients and make sure they're doing alright. When someone does buy your stuff, don't just rush-along to the next prospect. Instead, take care of them and ensure that they're still pleased with what your company is providing to them. Take the time to care for those who have already committed to you. Not doing so may leave you cold-calling, and that's truly the most arduous and demoralizing task in sales.

PART FOUR
CONNECTING AND COMMUNICATING

---

*The web makes connecting with customers easier—
particularly for small companies. We'll look at how, and
consider what all of this means for your organization. You'll
learn why the line between people and their companies
is eroding and how you can cultivate the most important
commodity: trust. I'll even provide ten examples of how
different types of companies can use these new tools to make
things happen. Oh, right... you'll also find out why you need
to forget the word "viral."*

CHAPTER 17

NEW TOOLS

IN THIS NEXT PART OF THE BOOK I'll concentrate on how companies can use the web—and particularly social media—to better connect and share their stories with customers. I'm doing so, as I believe that we're undergoing a huge shift in how organizations and individuals communicate with one another. Most will likely agree that this is an exciting time filled with possibility. I'm particularly excited by how game-changing these tools are for small companies.

Being such a new space, it's difficult to offer a clear "one size fits all" solution for how to use these tools in your company's marketing. There are lots of options and equally many thoughts on what might be the best way to go. This becomes more bewildering, given many of the tools seem to mutate and become superseded so quickly. As such, I'll instead look for patterns and try to remain technology "agnostic." My hope is that the principles I suggest will prove more adaptable and long-standing in your efforts.

We all have the keys

When communication channels were limited in number, access was the primary concern for those with something to market. If you had money and a reasonable product, personal relationships with customers weren't quite so critical. Until quite recently, there were few reasons for those in a company to open up to the public. Similarly, there was a clear delineation between most organizations and the outside world. As the methods of communication democratize, everything is flipped upside down. Today, consumers demand interaction, responsiveness, and to know that the companies they choose to frequent operate ethically. Your customers have power and a disgruntled one can damage your brand with the very same tools you use to promote it. The fact of the matter is that the public is taking an interest in how companies act and run.

Although social media is referenced like a tangible and clearly defined kind of thing, it's really just another stage in the organic development of the web. Aspects of it have existed for some time. In the past few years we've just seen it click together in a way that better facilitates—and speeds—interaction. I like to think that the "plumbing" has improved, and this results in a more connected populace. Social networks and voting platforms (like *Digg* and *Reddit*) in particular allow messages to be spread ever-more quickly and with a different kind of credibility. For example, a television ad doesn't hold much credibility as it doesn't come from a trusted source, whereas a suggestion shared by a friend carries a great deal more relevance.

In a way this makes all of us mini-broadcasters of sorts—each holding the potential to spread a message as well as any major brand. Sure, they have greater resources, but these aren't nearly as important as a powerful idea or personal relationship. That's why we see major advertisers awkwardly stumbling in this space, even though they command traditional media so deftly. Whether they like it or not, ideas and connections can't be bought as easily in this setting. This marks an unprecedented opportunity for small companies. It still might not be easy or cheap to share your message, but if it's a really good one and you play your cards right, you can establish connections that are elusive to most large brands.[91]

The pipe

The joy of marketing in a broadcast world was that the viewer didn't really matter that much. If you had enough money to buy the airtime, you could get in the "pipe." There were a few "pipes," including radio, television, publications, direct mail, and billboards, alongside a batch of little "threads." Those threads, like word of mouth and personal contact with customers, may have seemed almost quaint to some and this made the pipe a dream-come-true for big brands.

While personal interaction with customers can be time-consuming, there was little worry of this in the pipe. All that was required was for funds to be inserted then they were free to yell at people until their time was up. It hardly mattered if anyone even cared about the message. So long as the interruptions occurred a sufficient number of times, buyers would become familiar with the company or product. This sort of awareness is, without any question, a very big deal as it helps people feel comfortable about buying stuff. For several decades, advertisers worked hard to find smart and effective ways to interrupt people and repeat a message.

You'd sit on the couch watching *Cheers, Wings*, or something equally captivating, and every few minutes another group would bug you to, "buy this" or "vote for that." The pipe made doing so easy. As advertising matured, brands found progressively better ways to get us to take notice: "Be all that you can be." "I want my MTV." "It takes a licking and keeps on ticking." These phrases became a part of our cultural landscape. If you needed to connect with an audience, you'd go to some clever ad people who'd help you establish such a concept and push it through the pipe.

With so few of these pipes, companies had limited options aside from advertising to a large number of people who didn't care much. Niche-oriented companies found it very difficult to play in this arena. If, for example, you were into performance climbing gear, weird sex toys, or rare recordings of blues legends you probably wouldn't find them in the pipe. This changed a little with the advent of the multi-channel television "universe" and the proliferation of targeted magazines, trade journals, and independent zines. Even a few thousand pipes weren't enough to reach all of the unique folks out there with such varied interests. This left many of us stuck, watching *Murder, She Wrote* and Pepsi ads no matter how little we liked it.

A tangle of wires

With the web, we find ourselves with a whole lot of "digital threads" or perhaps "wires." Most of these are too narrow to be looked upon the same way we did pipes. This results in family websites, ones dedicated to LOL cats, and some resources documenting interesting "after hours" activities. For the big brands and ad agencies this all became rather frustrating. Alongside having to deal with those pipes, they now had to also add a bunch of unpredictable wires to add to the mix.

This proved difficult. First of all, no one knew whether to take them seriously or not. Some even thought it would all be a "flash in the pan." (Hold on for a second… ha, ha, ha, ha, ha, ha, ha, ha… OK… I'm done.) The tougher part was in finding a good place to put the ads. You couldn't jam them in front of people or they'd just leave. Plus, some thought the web should be free of ads altogether. This has sorted out a little since, and most of us accept—or at least "deal with"—selectively placed ads on the web. To the chagrin of advertisers, most of us have learned to ignore these spots.

There are tons of these little wires and they leave big brands trying to decipher how exactly to sell some product. Meanwhile even that good old pipe gets worked over as people figure out ways to skip ads entirely by using their Tivo or PVR, while avoiding print ads by getting their news via RSS (Really Simple Syndication—a web feed format). This gets very frustrating for people who liked the pipe. All kinds of weird things we hadn't imagined start to pop up. Grassroots sites like SuicideGirls.com bring together women who like to share artful photos of their sometimes extensive body modifications. Amazon.com gives us quick access to warehouses of books that were previously only available through excruciatingly slow mail-orders. There's also a rush of almost every tribe, club, and fringe group claiming their own space on the web. This makes advertisers' and agencies' jobs even harder. (It's pretty neat for everyone else, though.)

A few smart advertisers use this to their advantage, seeing that these channels allow them to connect very personally with the right people. We can safely assume that the market for Goth inspired clothing made by a company like Lip Service wouldn't have had many options in a broadcast world. Putting such ads on SuicideGirls.com, though, allows them to connect directly with people who might actually be interested in patterned cross-bone dresses and vinyl garments with prominently featured straps and buckles.

When you think about it, connecting with a few "right" people starts to make an awful lot of sense. Especially as we see some pipes start to burst—most notably those newspapers that once seemed like indelible institutions. We find ourselves facing a very different landscape these days. Some of the people who own those old pipes are freaking out while the rest of us are fascinated and sometimes overwhelmed by all of the newly available options.

Just good stuff

When we step back from the action, it becomes a little less frantic and chaotic seeming. Here, we find that it was actually the era of broadcast media that was the exception. It might one day be considered a short "blip" in the history of media, and that we've ultimately returned to what we had before: simple word of mouth. Sure, this is a little like word of mouth "on speed," but it really isn't altogether so different. People find things they like, tell their friends, and they in turn might do the same. Sometimes companies do things to encourage this but most learn that it only works with people who want to hear what they have to say. Those who interrupt us are labeled "spammers" and quickly find themselves ignored.

Looked at from this perspective, "traditional" media starts to look downright nutty. In what world did it make sense to bug people until they finally bought our stuff? Sure, it still sometimes works, but doesn't it seem like an awfully clumsy way to connect with people?

Many describe the difference between these two ways of communicating as "push versus pull." In a "push" world we shoved things in peoples' faces until they did what we wanted or we ran out of money. In a "pull" world, we try to give those who are interested things they'll actually want, hoping it will lead them to choose our stuff willingly. Some of us think enticing people to ask for our stuff is smarter than just trying to force-feed them gray, over-cooked broccoli.

Word of mouth is generally about people sharing what they like. When we talk about social media and the changes at hand, many can't see where it might work for their company. The subject is hardly worthy of such confusion: Just start by putting aside the technology and first ask who's interested in your stuff and what you might offer them.

The myth of "raising awareness with the general public"

In meeting rooms all around our the world, we find excited people bursting at the seams to say something... really, anything... to anyone. They have nice offices, grand desks, and thick binders full of important graphs, and they're working hard (doing what they do) to "raise general awareness." They don't know with whom, or about what, but galdarnit they'll find a way!

My brother works in corporate communications and the two of us often share a laugh over this: the team leader who enthusiastically decides it's the perfect time to write a press release about something undefined, to "raise awareness" with the "general public." I can't tell you how much I love the "general public"! They're the every-person: ready to listen to our stories, even if these stories hold no actual relevance; yet, we're in communications so someone's got to say something, right? Truth is, there's no such thing as a "general public" awaiting your "awareness raising." The general populace just isn't that interested in you! Even if they're bored, they probably aren't that bored.

I say we grasp our own necks and wrench them back and forth until we manage to regain the ability to focus ourselves once again. In doing so I'd hope we'd come to realize that the only people we should share messages with are those who have something to get out of it. We have to viciously suppress the urge to blather on without purpose, and instead concentrate on saying something meaningful, to people who actually give a shit. That's right, we're going to fixate on talking with interested people and will only utter the term "general public" in reference to the almost forgotten '80s rock band of the same name.

Reduce the distance

When you know who to connect with and what to say, you've already found your way past most companies out there. I remember a money booth on some '70s game show. In it, cash would fall from the ceiling and the person enclosed could keep what they managed to collect. The people in it often became so excited and bewildered by the money floating around that they tried to grab it all, in turn pocketing very little. Companies are sometimes in a similar situation when it comes to marketing. With so many opportunities and prospects, some forsake communicating with those who really matter.

Social media doesn't have to (and probably shouldn't) be concentrated on reaching masses of people. This is why I complain so loudly about all of the weight some place on getting something to go "viral" (messages that spread quickly to a large number of people—hence the name). Instead of trying to reach everyone, we might look at this method of communication as a way to reduce the distance between our companies and those interested in what we have to offer. Seems reasonable enough, doesn't it?

A friend recently recounted to me an experience he'd had with Hayes disc brakes. After making a note on Twitter about buying a set for his bike, Joel Richardson (a product manager at Hayes) reached out to him. Problems later arose with the product so he let Joel know. Within hours a new set had been mailed to him. This isn't "viral," and it's not the kind of thing that will instantly turn your company into a household name, but it's still important. By being so responsive to a customer's needs, they strengthened a relationship. This is how we have to look at building our companies: not an effort to create a quick burst of attention, but rather a perpetual interaction and dialogue. Social media just makes this easier.

Personal connections take more time to establish than putting an ad in the pipe. This can seem frustrating, but as a result of this, they tend to be an awful lot stronger. You can hit me with a thousand ads and they may only make me aware of your company. On the other hand, if you do one small thing to help me out, you can transcend awareness and start to form an actual relationship.

The network effect

Imagine that a frustrated customer called your company with a complaint. You might spend minutes (or even hours) helping them. At the end of that talk you might have remedied the situation, but few would ever know. This interaction might just as well have taken place in an enclosed vault at the bottom of the ocean. No one else heard and even if you went far beyond the call of duty, you'd reap limited rewards. If, on the other hand, you responded the same way on a review site, online help area, or forum, your efforts would be publicly evidenced for all to see and learn from, and remain in perpetuity.

Others fighting similar issues might find your replies and be impressed by your responsiveness. Those comments might even serve to answer their problem, and thus save you from spending added time on the phone. Although you might like talking to clients, I doubt that you enjoy answering the same question repeatedly. I should note that this permanence cuts both ways. Responding in a snarky fashion can damage your company for years to come.

This massive pooling of information brings many potential uses. I've made note of how others can rely on the responses you've provided, but this is just one opportunity. You can also readily tap the collective efforts of others on the web.

Lots of people are "sharing" content online. For some, this might come in the form of a blog containing personal insights; others upload their photos or videos to publicly accessible sites. There are also those who add comments and write reviews, sharing their opinions about places, products, services, experiences, and almost anything else. A lot of these people are happy to have others reference, and perhaps even use, their content. You should check with them before you do so with any of their stuff, but in my experience, many are willing to share. Actually, Creative Commons licensing facilitates just this, establishing more flexible IP standards, better suited to the web.

Let's say you're a travel destination that wants to build a great resource for those who might visit. In the past you would have invested heavily to craft good written content and evocative photographs—perhaps also pleading with past visitors to write reviews. Depending on your skills and budget some of it might not be of the highest quality and photos might look phony or cheap. With all of the sharing that's going on, you might be wise to take a different approach. You could still craft the parts you wanted, but you certainly aren't limited to just that. Perhaps you'd integrate crowdsourced images from photo sharing sites. Then you might work with local bloggers and see if they might allow you to republish their stories on your site. You could even see if a review site had an API (application programming interface) allowing you to pull existing reviews from theirs, directly into your site.

Little of this is hard to do; actually, most of it is quite easy. One suggestion is to credit contributors appropriately. Make sure not to step on anyone's toes. Instead, champion those who lent a hand. Send them a gift and rave about the help they lent—do whatever it takes to keep that relationship strong. Good content is hard to get and typically costly; reward these people accordingly. It doesn't take much to show someone that you admire their talent and appreciate their help.

Beware the scorned customer!

The past was "top-down." People in nice offices crafted marketing messages about new cola flavors or improved toothpaste formulas and dispatched them to the rest of us, regardless of whether we wanted to receive these messages. We're told that because of social media, these brands walk among us. They call this a "flat" world, but I think they've made a mistake. In fact, we, the people have superseded the brands and they now have to play servant to our demands.

Madness you say? Heresy? Nonsense—it's simple fact. I argue that while many rave about the marketing landscape being flat, the whole thing has actually flipped upside down. The brands that lead today are in a way elected by the populace and that same populace has the power to dethrone them at a moment's notice. Brands that do ill, lie to us, or are proven inferior have not a sliver of influence over us. We can remove and replace them whenever we choose.

For a long time companies have acted carefully, knowing that their reputation was linked to success. In the new landscape, cautious behavior is hardly enough. Today's brands need to be decent, moral, and transparent. Not being so can lead to a rather brutal exile.

Ear to the ground

There are a number of companies out there that sell special reports on "consumer insights," which seek to underpin trends and themes amongst certain populations. I pay little attention to such documents, as they're generally not that closely related to what we're working on. I'm also suspicious of the validity of their data, and even offended by their sometimes prohibitive cost. Still, I'm interested—actually, obsessed—with what people are saying about our company and the work we do. I spend time every day trying to determine what the "word on the street" is.

I run searches on our company name and have "bots" working for us. These are (mostly free) services that scour the web and bring back mentions made about us. This allows me to address situations as they arise and remain aware of the feelings regarding what we're doing. In my mind, this stuff is "mission critical." The last thing we need is for a situation to fester unbeknownst to us. The sooner we know of a problem, the faster we can try to fix it. Similarly, if someone loves what we're doing, I like to reach out and say "hello." It's always nice to connect with supporters and like-minded people.

Those consumer insights pieces that I made note of seemed to get old fast. Even if someone could prepare those documents daily, it would still be too slow compared to the feedback we can tap now. With the tools I mention, you can know what people are saying and thinking from one moment to the next.

What do you need?

Focus groups are strange. A bunch of people are brought into a closed space and asked what they think about a few pre-determined things. We then reflect on these findings and potentially use them to shape our course. It's no secret that focus groups have mixed accuracy, perhaps most notably evidenced in the launch of New Coke. Its early testing showed an overwhelmingly positive response in closed settings but in the wild it proved a bust. Past Coca-Cola CEO Roberto C. Goizueta called the experience, "...a blunder and a disaster, and it will forever be."[92]

I'm no expert when it comes to focus groups but the idea behind them seems flawed to me. People react differently when they're being watched. Allowing an unnatural sort of engagement to inform direction seems dicey, as most censor their thoughts when they feel like they're under a microscope. Should we instead conduct research in a setting that reduces such inhibitions? This might assuage the worry some might have of being ridiculed by peers. Additionally, we can harness the speed and ease with which people communicate on the web. I see this as an amazing opportunity to tap real-world customer insight. Here, people tell us what they think—not because they're supposed to, but rather because they want to. This makes a huge difference to the kind of data we can access and learn from.

You might work to diffuse the situations that customers seem most angry about, but I encourage you to take it a step further. I ask you to use these armies of people as your own real-time, real-world focus group. Listen carefully and you could get some feedback that will improve your offering. Should you get really lucky, you might find yourself graced with an angry mob. Most are scared by mobs like this, but they shouldn't be. By actively engaging in their criticisms, you're given access to some of the most valuable data available about your company. These folks aren't getting compensated for their insights; instead, they are people so committed to your product that their entire reward is in influencing an improved version of what you have to offer.

I'm not proposing you do everything these people ask. Actually, I'd caution you against that sort of thing, as it can quickly lead to chasing one's tail—making a change for one person, only to have the next ask you to change it right back. You're not looking for others to lead and their input can't always be definitive. That doesn't make it any less important. You're the leader. It's your job to listen to what's said, measure options, and make the best choice. Still, isn't it nice to gain access to those who care enough to offer their opinions?

What others start with

Ask a few people what they think social media is, and they'll give you some variation of basically the same story. Most will mention things like blogs, forums, content communities, virtual worlds, wikis, social networks, and probably a bunch of other things that I've skipped here. To me, that seems like saying that a car is an alternator, transmission, fuel pump, casing, and so on. This isn't untrue, but perhaps the parts alone aren't the most pivotal part of the story.

Some will likely find flaw with my perspectives, but I still think it's wise to concentrate on the big picture. For the record, I'll share what I think social media represents: a bunch of new and mutating online tools that work together to connect all of us. In a marketing context this is important, as it makes it much easier to connect with the people who are interested in what we're doing.

CHAPTER 18

OUR COMPUTERS, OURSELVES

SOCIAL MEDIA IS BASED ON SIMPLE PRINCIPLES and it actually takes very little to become indoctrinated in it. In fact, for some there's a bit of let-down upon signing up for these services. You know this feeling, don't you? After all of the hype, you finally take the plunge. You fill in your name, get a password, and start adding friends, only to be left wondering, "what's next?" At first I felt like I had just stumbled upon a really big bulletin board and little else.

This is the problem with new tools: we tend to see them as an end in themselves, while instead they are starting points. Pens and paper aren't fundamentally thrilling; it's what you do with them that can be. Social media is much the same, and employing these tools isn't such a big deal—doing something innovative, inclusive, or useful with them is the part worth noting.

Let's take a little time to consider your online persona. I recognize this may seem a bit weird, and you may not think you even have such a thing. Regardless, it's real and it's wise to make conscious choices around it.

References

You found your accountant through a friend, and you've stayed with that accountant for many years. A recommendation for a doctor came to you from a relative. You still go to the same mechanic your dad suggested when you bought your first car. Meanwhile, you happily recommend these service providers to your friends, so long as these companies continue to provide reasonable service.

Welcome to the world of reputation economics, where trust is the currency of choice. Here, the "right person" saying the "right thing" makes a huge impact on your company, and even more so when this person says the "wrong thing" about your company.

Before we talk more about marketing your company online, I'd like to get a little more personal. The curtain has been raised; the mighty voice of Oz is no longer. There's just you. With no layer of corporate protection to hide us, we're left with a strange new reality: we have to put ourselves on the line.

Be yourself

In the early days of the web, everyone was freaked out by the potential loss of privacy. People hid information about themselves, posted anonymously, and some tried to cover their tracks. This perceived cloak allowed some to act like jerks. They'd say things online that they'd never say to someone's face, and this resulted in really ugly "flame wars."

With time, order prevails in even the most chaotic spaces. We've seen this happen on the web; we're also getting comfortable with the idea that a lack of anonymity isn't really such a scary a notion. I also think we're relaxing about the whole notion of privacy. Sure, we're still concerned with protecting our passwords and that sort of thing, but we're not quite so worried about being identifiable in a digital setting. The internet is becoming nicer and more civilized, now that our actions online are getting closer to our real world behavior.

Web-etiquette is still somewhat new. We're using our real identities more online, and we're yielding some of our control regarding privacy, but some of the rules are still a little sketchy. For example: is it wrong to promote your own products on a forum? Can you email potential clients about your services without being perceived as being a spammer? When do you accept/deny a friend request?

Each of these questions leaves one in a gray area, and I can't give you a single clear rule that addresses all of the above, nor the nu-

merous other questions of this sort. You're just going to have to to figure these things out for yourself. I suggest you look around, test the
waters, and perhaps check the depth before you dive in. This might
entail spending a week on a forum, contributing general thoughts,
and getting to know some of the members before mentioning what
you do. It could mean sending out a single email to a potential client
and following up with a phone call, instead of hitting "send" on a
thousand generic messages. It could force you to carefully consider
what that "friend request" means and the kind of online interaction
that seems appropriate for you.

Mostly I'd urge you to start slowly so you can get the lay of the
land. It's fine to get excited about the things you can do with these
tools, but rushing in might make you seem like a bull in a china shop.
Sit back, relax, get to know "what's what," and you'll probably have a
better chance of being seen for who you really are. This is the strongest advice I have regarding web-etiquette: be yourself.

A part of our daily fabric

I ask if we need to look at the web less like a separate thing, and
more like another layer that folds right into the fabric of our daily
lives. Remember those silly movies in the '90s about "cyberspace"?
Filmmakers of the time seemed to like the idea that we'd all go into
these virtual worlds where we'd jump and fly around accompanied
by *Matrix*-like effects. This sometimes made for entertaining movies, and it's not entirely fiction. Environments like SecondLife offer
something like this already. The thing is, there's a lot of ground between reality and a completely immersive virtual world. For most of
us, this is the most relevant space.

This is why so many great little startups have gotten off the
ground in the past few years. It's nice to have sites like Meetup, which
allow us to connect with others who share our interests. It's pretty
convenient to use Evite to quickly set up a party. Facebook is handy
for sharing photos and interacting with our friends. These things
don't replace normal, human interactions; they just make them a
little easier.

As this newfangled stuff ties into our lives, our real personas become more closely tied to our online ones. In time, I don't think we'll even see any delineation between the two. Few of us get excited about adding someone's phone number to our address book; equally so, it will soon be uninteresting to add someone as a friend on a social network. For now though, we're left to determine exactly where the boundaries lie, and what kind of behavior is to be deemed appropriate in such settings.

A good example of a situation that tends to throw people is whether an employer and staff member (or a client and supplier) should be connected on social networks like Facebook. Conventional thinking leads us to believe that separation should be maintained in such a setting. I've heard it a million times before, "No business at the dinner table," "I keep my private life to myself" or, "I don't want the people at work to know too much about me." I'm of the belief that this is outdated thinking and will seem awfully silly in years to come. Such parceling of life-roles is exactly why customers don't care about companies, and why workplace interactions become so awkward. These separations make us act less human in order to seem more "professional." I say: screw professional. It's a phony and unimportant construct. We just need to "get real" with one another.

All just bricks in the wall

What would happen if clients and suppliers, staff and employers broke down these walls? I think they'd start to understand one another better, see what's real, and have a reason to believe more in one another. It could lead to a world in which we weren't worried about getting "snowed" by marketing rhetoric or management double-talk. Wouldn't this be awesome? I don't know about you, but I loathe how predisposed we are to having our defenses up.

While I recognize the utility to be found in hierarchy, social norms, and other customs, I wonder if they perhaps get in the way of other, potentially better ways of interacting. I've employed people who didn't want to tell me how their weekend was. We'd sit next to one another for forty hours a week, without ever having had a single real conversation. I've worked with clients in situations where everyone guarded how they spoke for fear of possibly offending someone.

This is old-world thinking folks—worse yet, it's incredibly limiting. It's time to let it go and move on.

A couple of years ago I made a concerted effort to challenge professionalism. I don't mean that I want to behave poorly or do a bad job of things; I just want to cut out the unnecessary layers between me and the people I work with. Part of this is done by limiting exaggeration. We've been trained to "amplify" reality for so long that most automatically expect that we're all doing so. When someone tells you that they have a "great deal," do you believe them? No way! You expect a catch, if you listen at all.

Advertising has brought us to believe that everything is a pitch, exaggeration, or lie. My goal is to cut through that, so that when I have something to say it will actually be heard. When I note to a client that I've budgeted a project as tight as I can, they know I'm telling the truth. When I explain to a staff member that we really have to buckle down, they don't think that I'm trying to squeeze them and line my pockets.

This is a great position to be in. The only way to it, however, is to invest in the people around you, as you would with friends. This extends to one's digital persona too.

You're building history

Whether online or in real life, it's the history of your actions that lets others know how to categorize you. We all know that Al Pacino is a pretty good actor because he's proven it to us time and again. (Even if he has done so a little less, lately.) How do you think it was for Al early in his career? My guess is that it wasn't quite as easy. Very few really believe us when we tell them what we can do. So we need proof. Winning an Academy Award was probably pretty good proof for Al and I bet all those multi-million dollar box office totals helped too. Gaining such credibility can seem like a massive hump to overcome. On one side few will give you the time of day; on the other it seems like you can do no wrong.

Regardless of what you do in life, you'll need proof in order to get the gig. This means establishing markers of trustworthiness and finding people who'll vouch for you. When you need a new job, colleagues can be proof, helping you make connections. In your organization's sales, a common reference can be proof, allowing you to make contact with someone new and not having them respond with a cagey, "Gee Bob... I'm really busy, can I get back to you?" or "Thank you for contacting ABC Corporation, unfortunately, we have no need for your services at this time."

If you're good at what you do and get enough proof (or references) things will simply occur more easily. They'll come personally, "Oh, you just have to meet my friend Jennifer. She's single too and you guys would really like one another!" They'll also come in a business setting, "If you need search-engine marketing, Roxanne is the only person to talk to. Let me get you her number."

One guy calls me periodically to sell his research services. He calls, asks for my business, gets mad when I don't buy, and then calls again six months later. He spends a lot of time trying to "sell" me, but doesn't care to build any history. On the other hand, Vito at Giuseppe's Bread Deli Da Vito, down the street, is always happy to see Amea, Oscar, Ari, and I. He remembers us and the meals we like. He always takes the time to talk a little, and sometimes even walks our newborn around, so that we can enjoy our lunch. He could be more "professional" with us, but instead he gets to know us, and becomes a part of our lives.

Without history, you're nowhere. Given a choice, everyone would rather buy from someone they know and trust.

What gets in and what doesn't

"OK Eric, OK... I get your point, but how does this relate to how I use social media for my business." I'm getting to that, but I still want to concentrate on "you" a little longer—bear with me, OK? We'll talk about marketing your business with social media soon, but in this context, you—the individual—are more important than ever. This means you have to start by considering yourself first.

In using the web for marketing, I ask if we might be better off to act like people first and corporations second. Personally, I can wrap my brain around human beings but I find it far more difficult to do so with companies. For example, what does Microsoft look like?

How big is it? (Big, I know—but how big?) Do they stand for something? I really don't know.

On the other hand, a person is much easier to build a relationship with. So while I might not believe that Microsoft really cares about much, I get the feeling that Jeff Weir (who works for Microsoft Live Labs) gets excited about what he does. When Jeff makes a note on his blog about something neat that he's working on, I might find myself interested enough to take a look. I bet you know this feeling: even the largest and most impersonal organizations seem a little more approachable when you have a human connection there. The funny part in this instance is that I hardly know Jeff, but even that's enough to make me treat his posts and updates differently from corporate updates.

Part of this relates to how our "filters" are set. When I receive email from people I know, my "ignore" filter is set low. So I read the message. On the other hand, when I get direct mail from companies, my "ignore" filter is set incredibly high. Actually, it's set so high that I tend to not look at all. I throw these things out without a second thought. Looked at this way, bulk-mail seems like a waste of time, doesn't it? Lots of companies still do it, though, and conceivably think that they're marketing effectively.

Why persist given the ostensibly dismal response rate? I don't know. Part of me thinks that it's just because we're used to doing so. Another thought is that it's easy to justify such efforts as a marketing expense, and there's little likelihood of one losing their job as a result of running these. More than that, I think it has something to do with numbers. The idea of building connections with people one at a time seems costly and impractical for many companies. I'm not suggesting that this is inaccurate, but I'd like to look at how this starts to change through social media.

The "bandwidth" for humans just opened up

I often reference social media as plumbing. On its own it's not wholly riveting; nevertheless, it does help some important things to happen. The interactions facilitated by today's tools allow us to scrub that impersonal bulk-messaging approach of old and instead maintain connections with people of all sorts.

This morning I went online to read about a friend going to Disneyland; then, I watched a funny video posted by another friend. I also shared in banter with a designer I've only ever corresponded with online. I also "tweeted" a couple of brief notes of little real consequence. Through these small interactions, I feel like I have a sixth-sense or inside track about my friends' and colleagues' lives.

Do these things add up to much? Maybe not, but I feel as though these brief interactions tend to build dialogue and break down certain layers. The histories we collectively build with one another help us more naturally interact and work with one another. You might even find that looking at your personal interactions like this is more fruitful than the "professional" methods we had grown used to.

Maybe it's been a shitty day

Earlier, I introduced the notion of privacy being out-of-date. This may not be the case in all settings. For example, if you like running sandpaper across your nipples for a thrill, you might be wise to keep that to yourself. Nevertheless, a lot of people are of the mind that many things we were protective of simply aren't a big deal any longer. In the next chapter, I'll look at how we might talk about our companies with this in mind; first, let's consider ourselves: a whole bunch of people just trying to figure out how to act online, and what's appropriate to share.

When we observe how people act online, we find a few different approaches. Many are protective of their interactions; some do wild and crazy things; and a few are just trying to sell themselves and their companies, rarely giving us anything real. This new environment leaves us a little unsure of how to conduct ourselves. I ask if we should simply look to the real world as our model. In "un-wired" life, we edit ourselves but not to the extent that we become phony cardboard cutouts. We may do outlandish things but most pick the time and place for such actions rather selectively. What if we just acted like this online?

I can't say how you should manage your digital presence, but I do think it's an area of importance deserving of careful consideration. The distance between ourselves and the people/companies in our lives is being reduced. You should think about how close you're willing to get.

I'm not suggesting the following for everyone, but I find it easiest to be an open book. I share my thoughts quite publicly, in part out of ease. I don't know entirely where to draw a line, and in many respects, I've found such boundaries to be pointless. Fragmenting my life seems awfully strange, so I don't do it. Additionally, I'll share almost anything online that I would in a physical setting. I tell people when I'm having a crappy day or when things are kind of hard. I also share little breakthroughs and achievements. Sometimes I pass around links that I find useful, and I almost always respond to people who have questions I can help with.

Little of this is uncomfortable, as it's what I'd do anyway. I can't quite imagine how doing so would compromise my work or "personal" life. I moderate my behavior online in almost exactly the same fashion as I would in the real-world. Some get in trouble by posting things on social networks they'd be embarrassed by in a non-digital context. In my mind, the only way to avoid such blunders is to align how you present yourself (and your company) both online and in the physical world.

And, although the temptation to do so is ever-present in social media, I ask you to avoid bragging. Instead, imagine that your best friend is on the other side of the message you're posting. Would they look at you differently if they saw what you're putting out there?

So now you (perhaps) have some new ideas on how to build your online persona and employ social networks for yourself. Let's move on to that business you're running. How can you use these tools to build trust?

CHAPTER 19

Getting to Trust
(and Beyond)

It's one thing to spread a message about your company, but quite another for people to believe it. You can scream it, wrap it beautifully, or get famous people to say it, but you're stuck by the fact that most won't believe you. Everyone else faces the same challenge in trying to sell something: we need to move people from, "Yeah, whatever." to "This thing is actually pretty good!"

Perception and reality

Try this: Go into a shop—any shop—and ask how business is. Odds are that you'll hear responses like "It's great… really great!" or "It's amazing! We're so busy!" My bet is that if you return and ask the same question once a month for a year, you'll never hear much deviation from this. Sometimes this will be the truth and perhaps they're doing quite well. It's also reasonable to assume that this isn't always the case. I think this springs from a fear of truth. More accurately, I believe we're petrified by the possibility of self-fulfilling prophecy. Consider what happens when people start to talk of a slow-down in the economy; almost immediately companies react by freezing spending, reducing marketing, and bracing for a storm. What's the result? Things slow down.

I think this notion scares the shit out of most business owners. The thought process goes like this: "If we tell one person that we're having a slow week, they'll pass that on to their friends. Soon, the story will grow out of proportion and people will think we're in trouble. Then they won't buy anything from us out of fear that we're not stable. Nope—we can't have that! No matter how bad it is, we keep a stiff upper lip, and tell people that we're doing just fine."

In part, I can't argue with this logic. Humans are fickle: A line outside a restaurant attracts others, in part from people thinking that something good must be going on, in order for that many people to be willing to wait. On the flip-side, few wish to be present when the "smell of death" is in the air. I've experienced this first hand. When we're busy, it seems as though new projects simply land in our lap. Yet, when I solicit new work, even our best clients tend to avoid responding to me.

A fresh coat of bullshit

With all of that said, I think there's a flaw in the "everything's great" tone: it loses meaning without context. I have lunch with a certain colleague every few months and, without fail, he recounts his firm's successes and shining prospects. At first I wondered what he had figured out that we hadn't. (Our firm does well, but we're not without our challenges.) Do they afford better value? Are they providing something unique for their clients that we should consider? What's their secret? With time, little cracks around his story appeared, and the accuracy of his observations became questionable.

You can tell a fib every once in a while. The problem is that with each one you compromise the validity of every future claim. Few have unending runs of good-fortune. While one fib attracts little scrutiny, a series of them becomes difficult to maintain. Around the edges inconsistencies do arise, compromising one's story.

The fellow I mention serves as a good example of this. On one occasion—when our firm was particularly slow—he noted that perhaps we should pool our resources. He explained that he simply couldn't handle all of the work that was coming in. This raised my suspicions as we had just spent most of lunch talking about some great people he felt I should hire. If he was so busy, why wasn't he hiring these wonderful people and putting them to work?

A month later the jig was up. We bumped into one another and the look on his face said it all. Things were lean, his staff was unhappy and performing a small exodus; plus, work wasn't nearly as lucrative as had once been suggested. Maintaining an illusion of prosperity can be daunting.

Being transparent

We take a different approach at smashLAB and it may shock you. Most traditional business thinking would suggest it to be insane: we tell the truth.

We tell people when we're slow at the office and don't believe that such admissions have the potential to damage our business. We accept that most people know there are ups-and-downs in any industry. I open my personal life to business colleagues and like the idea that they see me as "human" first and "business-person" second. I tell other studio owners our business "secrets" and believe we have more to gain by sharing knowledge than by being secretive and paranoid. The truth is, few of our secrets are that good anyway. I'd bet that few of yours are either.

We tell the truth for a few reasons. First of all, our moms told us to. I'm not trying to be funny here; that influence is still hard-wired into us. It's also easier. We're not forced to remember which stories we told to which people. We don't have to worry about inconsistencies from exaggerating. Aim for transparency and just put it out there. Edit as little as possible and speak as plainly as you can. You might be surprised by the results.

There's something rotten in here

Acting honestly makes you acutely aware of how easy it is to sniff out bullshit. Liars can't hear truth, because they're surrounded by exaggeration. The rest of us have built-in radars that catch this sort of thing rather quickly. I like to believe that truth builds trust. Admitting it's slow at your operation gives fellow business-owners permission to acknowledge the same. From there you can concentrate on the more important and beneficial aspect of the dialogue, "So what

are you doing about it?" Fear of looking bad only limits these opportunities. Beyond this, you'll find that your "word" starts to mean
more than that of many others. If those around you know you speak
candidly, they're increasingly likely to ask for your counsel. This can
facilitate more meaningful connections with clients, peers, and those
who know of you solely by reputation.

Some people might feel strange about these suggestions. It might
seem as though I'm asking you to put yourself out there for anyone
to look at; in some ways I am. You either have to get over this discomfort or move to a cabin in the woods. Anyone can run a search
and learn a great deal about you. It's up to you to determine whether
others control the resulting perceptions or if you take an active role.
Whether you run a business or work for someone, you'll have to increasingly think about this. Learn to expect that potential clients/em-
ployers are going to learn everything they can about you. Wouldn't
you do the same in their shoes? They may invest substantial trust in
you. It's reasonable for them to do some due-diligence before hand-
ing you the keys.

Just try to remember that very few expect you to be a saint. I
like learning that those I work with are interesting, vibrant, and even
flawed. We all are fallible and had better get it out there from the outset. On the other hand, there's little excuse for poor judgment and
bad behavior online. While you might like to put on pay-per-view
chihuahua death battles *(how avant-garde!)* in your basement, blogging extensively about them will likely be discovered by someone
you'd like to work with. My suggestion is to consider this carefully
and act accordingly.

I've spent a great deal of time here making note of things that are
really little more than sensible behavior. I imagine you're wondering
why I've invested so many words in something seemingly so banal.
I'm getting to that...

Why this matters online

I've alluded to the same notion over and over again throughout this
book; I think it's of particular importance when it comes to your
online persona and your company's. I'm not exaggerating when I

say that there are hucksters on the web calculating how to get ahead through unscrupulous means. There are phishing schemes, theft of content, phony auction items, and countless other rackets. The anonymity and reach of the web makes it easy for people to do things that they shouldn't, and this leaves many of us skeptical about what we find online.

In the past, something published was often taken for fact. This is certainly no longer the case. Publishing tools have become so democratized that the accuracy of media and our faith in it has become compromised. Think about it this way: In a matter of moments you can create a website proclaiming you to be the leading thinker on post-modernism, the CEO of Nike, or even the King of Pupunatuna. (I love Pupunatuna! It's lovely this time of year!) In this setting, reputation becomes a commodity; it may be one of your business' most valuable assets.

Social media is hard to scale

It's interesting to consider how much better social media can work for small companies than their larger counterparts. Let's pretend that you run a micro-brewery and that you have a loyal following of beer-drinkers who think your offering is pretty swell. For you, social media might prove to be quite effective. You'd have limited technology costs, as blogging software is inexpensive (or free) and social networks can be leveraged readily. These methods allow you to "narrowcast" directly to those who love your product.

You could tell them about new beers in development, provide suggestions on pairing certain brews with food, and start to build personal connections with each of these folks. Not only would these connections be fortified through your interactions, you'd also be privy to the good buzz from loyal buyers, increased traffic from higher page-rank, and the opportunity to tap fans for suggestions on how to improve your offering to better suit their desires. With time, this might lead you to write a book, speak at seminars, or perhaps make an appearance on television because you'd be the expert on this particular topic.

What you're probably seeing here is just how important it is to actually live and breathe the product or service you sell. It's your knowledge and passion that attracts a following, and without this, it's unlikely that anyone would frequent your blog—or whatever avenue you chose to employ. Your blog about micro-brewing might not resonate with the masses, but for those who really care—the only people you're likely concerned about reaching anyway—you might find your efforts to be highly effective.

Let's look at why it would be more difficult for a larger competitor to match you in this way. Let's say you own the largest network of breweries in the world: Megabeerco. You're a highly-paid CEO and have decided that although you already sell a lot of beer, you'd like to sell more by employing social media in your marketing. You'd have all the same tools available as the fellow at the microbrewery, and much greater resources. (You are the CEO of Megabeerco, right?) My question is whether anyone would actually care. You're likely missing two things that the little guy has: passion and knowledge.

Well, you aren't really missing these two things; yours just might not be the right kind. Of course, you have passion: you love building a great company, connecting with your staff, and continually improving your operation. The problem is that this might not matter to those who buy your beer. Similarly, you likely have a great deal of knowledge—it's not like you became CEO for no good reason. My guess is that your expertise is more closely related to what you learned through years of managing a large corporation. Sadly, this likely holds little interest to beer fanatics. On top of all of this, you probably don't have much spare time to deal with social media. You have to concentrate on negotiating an expansion, addressing some staff/management conflicts, meeting with screened candidates to determine who's the best fit for your VP of Finance opening, or something else equally important.

"I can delegate!"

Owners of small companies might need to connect directly with fans, but CEOs of multinationals don't. Most are way too busy for that. So instead, they delegate these tasks. They shuffle them to the marketing department: people who are good at marketing, but may have little hands on experience brewing beer—or passion for the topic. "Ah-ha!" you say, "So why not bring in a few people from the company to share their thoughts: perhaps Robert, the brew-master; Tom, that funny guy in accounts, and maybe even Gladys at reception who everyone loves?" You know, that isn't a half-bad idea, but if you do, these people are going to have to put aside their other work to write blog entries or interact with the public. Plus, what happens if they write something that you don't want the public to know? That could be bad.

"Wait a second" you counter, "We can outsource it! We'll hire a PR company—they understand social media and this will ensure that we don't waste any time given that we're already busy." The challenge with a PR firm is that they don't know your company inside and out. They might be good at sending press releases but they probably can't articulate the difference between barley and hops. (For full disclosure, I'll acknowledge that I certainly can't.)

People at PR firms are busy and don't typically have a strong passion for what you do. If they did, they would likely quit their jobs and apply for one at Megabeerco. They're persuasive though, and tell you that they'd love to help you connect with customers. They come up with some fun ideas that might cost a bit. They suggest that you build your own proprietary social network, run some contests, and fly people around in a jet filled with bikini-clad models. (Perhaps it's something a little more sensible than this.) The point is that with each layer of "neat" they dollop on your strategy, they're even further away from building a relationship with the buyer. Meanwhile, the microbrewery guy keeps writing inexpensive posts that reach the people who care, and continues to establish a core group of believers.

I have to take a moment to be extra-clear. I'm not saying that big companies can't use social media—actually, I believe quite the contrary. What I am saying is that the tools aren't skewed in favor of the big guys like traditional advertising was. Social media is harder to employ for a team of twenty marketing experts than it is for one passionate entrepreneur who can put aside an hour a day to write about what they love, and connect with their customers. Plus, social media works better when it's real. I don't want to hear the CEO's story any more than I want to receive a PR firm's crafted press release. I want a real person who loves what they do, to let me in on the inside story.

You might think that I'm exaggerating

Perhaps you work at a PR firm. If this is the case, you're probably about to toss this book out the window. Allow me to apologize; I don't intend to discredit the work you do, and I know there are spots where companies like yours afford enormous value. At the same time, I believe you are experiencing an industry-wide midlife crisis. Allow me to elaborate.

If I arrived at work one day and was told that my keyboard had been reversed for ergonomic reasons, it would likely take me a year before I could type at the same rate I currently do. The tasks that come naturally would feel alien and cumbersome. Methods of working that had become hardwired as motor memory would need to be unlearned and relearned, and I'd be pretty frustrated. I might even continue to do things the way I had originally learned, given that I'd be pissed off that my past proficiency had been rendered out-of-date. I think you're in a similar spot. In fact, I have evidence of it.

Last year I received an email from a PR firm in Phoenix, Arizona. It contained a relatively standard press release, but the sender accidentally started the post with the salutation "Hi <<First Name>>." You guessed it: a bulk email from someone I'd never had contact with.

I won't go into great detail about this (if you want the whole story, you can just read it here: http://www.ideasonideas.com/2008/07/idiots/).In short, for several weeks, I received numerous messages from the same firm, each one nearly identical. I asked them to stop sending these messages but they seemed to think I wasn't worth replying to. With time, this angered me and I wrote the aforementioned blog post. I didn't spare much in my criticism of the firm's methods. The operation's President later wrote to me, noting that she felt my write-up was "nasty."

I can't say that I entirely disagree with her observation; I wasn't pulling any punches. The thing is, her company had been acting in a fashion that most would see as plain bad behavior. The unfortunate part is that my post likely had some negative repercussions for her firm, as it seemed to echo through the blogosphere.

Over the weeks that followed, I received a large number of emails from other PR firms. It seems that my cranky little post had in turn led more PR professionals to my blog. These new messages tended to begin with the semblance of a personal introduction (in the best instances) but would then awkwardly transition into an impersonal press release. It's not that these aren't fine people; it's just that most of them haven't wrapped their heads around the idea that press releases and mass messaging don't work well in this landscape.

PR is still important, and I know there's a place for these people. The feeling I can't shake is that many of these operations need to take a cold, hard look at the new realities of communication and determine how they fit into it. *(Needless to say, some PR firms are clearly ahead of the curve when it comes to embracing more "human" interaction. They can disclude themselves from the above generalizations.)*

This isn't going to be easy

Most of us who use social media in our marketing simply have to get our fingers in the dirt. I'd take this a step further by saying that if you, as the owner of the company, aren't willing to get involved personally in this, it might be worth reconsidering whether to employ these tools altogether. While you can certainly ask for help, I don't think that connecting with your customers can be delegated entirely to external (or less involved) parties. It's your baby; you've got to be there with it!

As seductive as it may be to think so, most good things just don't happen instantly. I encourage you to accept that you're unlikely to make any meaningful online connections immediately. Building relationships and an online persona takes time, but it also brings the possibility of exponential opportunity from the network effects of the web. Establish ten amazing relationships with your customers and the next hundred may come more quickly… and from places that you might not have even anticipated.

Consider it a "conversation"

This notion of conversation is popular in social media marketing circles, and with good reason. In the past, you could just barf out a noisy message with limited ramifications. New communication tools come with the ability for the recipients to respond to these same messages. This means you'll have to accept that yours isn't the final-word and that some may criticize and perhaps even change it.

The upside? This is your opportunity to get down on the floor with everyone else, and hear what they have to say, direct and unfiltered. Get out there, talk to people and respond to comments. You could even become involved in relevant forums and become one of the regulars there. Contribute and share, perhaps without initially making any mention of what you sell. Give away the "good stuff" and encourage them to interact with you as one of them.

By getting active in these communities and speaking frankly with others, you stand a chance of turning naysayers into champions. Instead of trying to sweep criticism aside, you have an opportunity to get closer, ask questions, and find out exactly what's going on. From there you can make things better for your customers and correct misunderstandings.

I don't know about you, but I loathe finding myself at a party where one person monopolizes the conversation with stories about their dietary problems. I'm comfortable discussing almost any subject matter, but I believe a few basic rules apply. Being interesting doesn't necessarily call for mystery and intrigue, but it usually involves varying subject matter and asking a few questions. This isn't so different on the web: engage with your audience, encourage discussion, and find out what others are interested in. Sometimes this is as easy as commenting on others' posts or sending an email to someone you admire. It seems to me that interesting people are equally interested in others.

Aside from a few exceptions, broadcasting via social media is largely pointless. Instead, I urge you to concentrate on connecting with smaller groups and individuals. This approach simply fits with social media more appropriately than bulk-mailing a single message to thousands of people. Part of this will require being as interested in the people you're speaking with, as you want them to be of you. (This is a concept quite foreign in traditional advertising.) There's little room for one-sided communication or relationships in this setting.

CHAPTER 20

Making It Work for Your Company

We've talked about the changing landscape and how you fit into all of this. Let's look more directly at how you can use social media, and the web in general, in your company's brand building and marketing. I'd like to address a few things you can do well with these means, specifically concentrating on those opportunities that were lacking or absent in more traditional media. We'll begin with a few thoughts on how to make your efforts in this area work best.

Figure out what you want to accomplish

One thing that bewilders me regarding the advent of new technology is how we seem to lose our minds for a short while upon its introduction. Take how conventional business logic was thrown out the window during the heyday of the web. All of a sudden people started talking like there would no longer be a need for traditional storefronts. In retrospect, this seems silly, but at the time, some really believed that the days of bricks and mortar companies had passed.

Social media may currently be the phrase on every marketer's lips, but I have a prediction: we'll soon see it less as a novelty and more as a means to an end. I believe it is as important as ever to determine clear goals prior to selecting the method of deployment. As sobriety overtakes our early hubris, we'll act sensibly and measure how close we come to meeting our goals.

In my mind, the worst kind of marketing starts from a buzzword being thrown about in an overly cavalier fashion. This is often the result of someone in a leadership role hearing about a new "unmissable" phenomenon that's quite likely spoken of as "game-changing." Shortly thereafter, said company has the acquisition, or creation, of such a thing in the works. You can almost hear it right now, can't you? "Julie, I don't know anything about mobile, but my old pal Tom says it's going to be huge! Look into this and find out how quickly we can do it too. I don't want to miss out on this!"

I'm not criticizing those who get excited about new technology (heck—I'm one of those people), but I get a little uncomfortable with phrases like "the next big thing." Such proclamations often leave me wondering if an ulterior motive is at work, and that such things are said to fulfill some kind of self-interest. I love new advancements, and I'm always interested in exploring how we might integrate these ideas. Still, I am made nervous by any strategy that is predicated solely on employing a new technology.

The web makes certain things easier for businesses, but it doesn't replace the need for sensible thinking. Similarly, blogs are great for connecting with people and sharing insights; forums are effective in collecting user responses and minimizing telephone support; and, wikis can be useful in creating shared data resources. Still none of these can save your company from a poor product, bad service, or spending more money than you make.

Technology remains a means and not an end. Some companies will benefit from social media while others will find different tools to meet their marketing and business needs. Determine what you want to do, and then you can explore whether social media is suitable for the task at hand.

Find a problem and then consider the solution

I like buying things so much that I sometimes jump before I know what to do with them. My feeling is that a lot of us do something very similar when it comes to marketing our companies. We get excited about video intros for websites and rapidly put them in place. We hear about some new ads shown on televisions in elevators and we place ours there. Then this social media thing shows up, and we go a little bonkers, getting one of everything. "MySpace page? Why not?"

A friend of mine (who runs a firm similar to ours) recently asked what I thought he should do with their Flickr (a photo-sharing site) account. I didn't really know how to respond. Although I could think of many things that one might do with such a tool, it seemed like a strange approach. I likened it to the notion to buying a screwdriver and then running around looking for something to fix. We don't do this sort of thing, because such actions would be foolish. When it comes to marketing, though, we often behave in rather nutty ways.

By thinking more sensibly, we're better able to find a sense of balance and perspective in our marketing and online efforts. It doesn't matter that there are lathes, calipers, monkey-wrenches, and acetylene torches if you don't have anything that needs to be built or fixed. Just the same, you can forget about all of the tools online until you have a project that calls for them. Photo pools, micro-blogging services, virtual worlds, and lots of other things exist. That doesn't mean you have to burden yourself with any of them. Just start by figuring out what problem you have; then determine whether one of those tools might be right for you.

Leveraging shared knowledge

We might as well have started our company smashLAB in a vacuum. On our own, with little idea of how to begin, we hung up our shingle (figuratively—there really wasn't much space to actually do such a thing) and got to work. We worked early, we worked late, we worked hard, and we worked for very little compensation, but we learned an awful lot. That was only a short while ago (2000), but what seemed so much harder to do then, was tap the information we needed. Search, for example, allowed us to find some information—the problem was that we didn't really know what to search for. We could have saved a lot of time if we would have had better places to ask questions.

Not so long ago, I needed to find background music for a video we were producing. It was a simple podcast and we threw the piece together in a couple of days. Our budget was limited, so I couldn't justify spending much money to license music. I thought there had to be other options out there. I spent the afternoon searching fruitlessly for some kind of music, but found it hard to know where to look. Thinking little of it, I made a quick note on Twitter about how frustrating the search had become. Within two hours I had received eight suggestions for places to look, and an offer from a band (The One Eyed Jacks) to use some of their music. We inserted the track and credited them for their contribution. As a result, they gained a little visibility and we got access to some great music. All it took was to ask. Social media makes it easier to do just that.

Connecting and asking people questions

In a world in which almost any information is readily available, the challenge becomes one of knowing where to look. From my experience, this can be incredibly frustrating. We know the answer is out there, but where do we start? As evidenced in my attempt to find background music, problems that seem challenging are often easily addressed by connecting with those who hold relevant expertise.

Part of the usefulness of social networks is found in how they help leverage greater access to a broad set of individuals with unique skill sets. This is beneficial for both the party in need of such expertise, as well as the one who can sell, barter, or exchange their knowledge or skills in this area. It's also interesting to see how people can use their connections to help facilitate ones between otherwise unconnected individuals.

Last weekend a friend and I were chatting. She had left her job four months earlier and had taken the summer off. Along the way she decided to move from marketing for a public organization to a similar role in high tech. For all of her experience, she doesn't have many connections in the high-tech sector. Not surprisingly she isn't getting the interviews she should. As we spoke, I kept thinking that she'd make a great hire for someone and offered to lend a hand. The next day I took an hour out to introduce her—via my social networks—to some people in the industry, and a few well-connected mavens. By the end of the afternoon she had confirmed a half-dozen meetings and had others in the works. I had little to gain from any of this, but enjoyed lending a hand. Plus, it's always nice to be the one who connects good people.

Social networks can help you reach appropriate people and ask questions about something you're working on. I've noted my frustration with focus groups, but that doesn't mean I don't believe in research. Let's pretend you're having a new website designed and you need to find out if a key function is easy for users to figure out. Why not just crowdsource the question with those who actually use the site? Post a quick note on a forum asking people to try it out and share their thoughts. It's so easy to do this and you'll likely find that people are eager to tell you what they think.

Spreading the word

Asking for feedback is one thing, but social networks are truly awesome for getting the word out on something notable. Let's say you designed something as playful as the Wario Land YouTube page: in it, video of game-play results in pieces of the screen shaking loose and falling off it.[93] It's a brilliant idea that's nicely executed, and surprises the viewer. (Perhaps less so for you, as I've let the cat out of the bag; nevertheless, you'll still probably think it's neat. Take a look: http://de.youtube.com/experiencewii)

If you were one of the people behind this, a nice way to share it would be through social networks. Post the link, send a message to friends, and leave it at that. If it's good, people will talk about it, link to it, share it, and sometimes even embed it on their own pages. It's not that this couldn't have been done with traditional websites—social networks and blogs just make it happen a little faster. Additionally, there's a social currency of sorts for those who find these things and share them first.

What I'm really talking about here is using social media to seed a viral campaign. When viral works, it's awesome; but I generally see viral like the pot-of-gold at the end of the rainbow. It's a seductive notion, but I wouldn't bank on it. If you by chance do happen to create something that "goes viral," thank your lucky stars. It's a rare day, and it many be the only time you are ever a part of something like this. (I hate to seem pessimistic, but frankly, these things are hard to predict and engineer.)

What we're up to

Using social media to send updates about what you're working on can be a nice alternative to those coma inducing corporate newsletters and email blasts. Let's be honest, those things are generally about as interesting as Aunt Edna's annual Christmas card and letter, "We did this, and then this, and then this." (Ugh.) I do think some are interested to hear what you're up to and what's happening at your company though. Limiting your updates to the one-line status areas typically available on social networking sites is sometimes just enough. At smashLAB, I often make note of a new website we've launched, a blog post we've written, and other little occurrences.

The trick with all of this is to not bombard people with self-promotion. Don't treat social media as a cheap way to broadcast your marketing messages. One of these days someone will work out a ratio of how many of these messages you can send before you start to irritate people. My guess is that it's around one in twenty. I suggest you make note of things that are meaningful and of interest to your friends. Sending out numerous posts on how your moving business helped with another relocation—someone really did this to me—is probably not the best idea.

Alternately, when we sent out a free white paper on social media (you can read it here: http://www.smashlab.com/files/primer_in_social_media.pdf), we had a great response. It resulted in speaking events, was published in part in Advertising Age, and was distributed widely on the web. Why? Because it wasn't about directly selling anything. It simply helped people make sense of something new. Think twice about any promotional message you send. If you had to pick up the phone to share this message, would you still do it? If the answer is "no," I ask you to stop, step back, and take an existing client out for lunch instead. Bugging people isn't smart marketing in any way, shape or form—I recommend doing something meaningful instead.

Social media can be used to spread the word on almost anything. In my mind you're only limited by your own preconceived notions of what the medium is suited to. If I were looking to make a new hire, I'd certainly use social media to spread the word. Your friends would likely suggest someone who fits the bill, or at least pass your posting along to others. The nice part with this approach is that you're first connecting with people you know. When I bring a new person into our company, I'm typically on edge as I don't want to get screwed by hiring someone who's dishonest. I just feel more comfortable hiring someone who's been recommended by a person I trust.

Forget viral

I've tempted you a little with the notion of using the web to spread the word. In doing so, I feel it my responsibility to temper this suggestion with a brief caution. The word "viral" has become a common term in marketing. It is intended to represent a message so compelling that it will travel on its own, in turn "infecting" many others. As I've noted before, it can be wonderful when this sort of thing occurs, but it's not that easy to make happen. Additionally, people often confuse viral for just "getting lots of cheap publicity." I don't believe this to be a healthy strategy for marketing your company.

Viral success is like a lottery ticket... without an actual payoff. The odds of winning the lottery are low, but if you are so lucky you're left with gobs of cash to squander. With viral campaigns the loot is more elusive. Most things that go viral just don't do that much for your brand. Being part of such a phenomenon is certainly fun and exciting, but that doesn't guarantee that you'll see an actual sale as a result of it. I've seen some really neat viral things on the web, but few have led me to look more closely at the company. Instead, I tend to pass these things along and then look for something else amusing to watch.

I'm of the mind that "viral" is the perfect word for this phenomenon: it's something many of us become infected with for a moment that is quickly kicked out by our collective immune system. If you're a really big brand like Nike or Dove, you can likely justify these sorts of efforts as general brand building, and it may not be wrong to do so. Most of us have to acknowledge that we aren't playing at their level. The rest of us need a smarter way to look at this, and perhaps even a better word with less dramatic overtones.

We need to coin a term that doesn't lead us to fixate on clever gags and gimmicks. Ours needs to relate to saying things that resonate with people over the long-term. We should make it refer to a perpetual dialogue that people want to engage in, not just for a moment, but to return to time and again. We need stories that others want to share—ones that hold relevance beyond the first little rush of amusement. I don't know what this word is; my suggestion is something along the lines of "tell-able," "sharable," or perhaps "reminisce-able." None of these are particularly good, but they might lend themselves better to stories that resonate with us and lend themselves to being retold over the longer term.

As noted, I don't think I've hit the right word here. Then of course, I'm probably not the guy to create it anyway. This is the beauty of the web today: as people come to this notion and explore it more, something will arise organically that makes sense—and likely sounds better than the ideas I've suggested.

Love your "fans"

I like to use social media to build stronger connections with "fans." I hesitate to use this word but if you stay in business long enough, you're likely to get a couple. Something about your company will resonate with people (perhaps not everyone, but probably a few) and these are the ones you'll want to get close to. They are going to be your best advocates and spokespeople.

Some might consider the term "fan" to be a pejorative one. I do not. With every project that we've launched, we have connected with a few people who have in turn raved about it. If I talk about our stuff, people will inevitably think it's a pitch (quite accurately). When others talk about these things, people tend to listen. Our fans get excited when we release new stuff; additionally, they tell us if they think that we've "missed the boat" on something. I appreciate how valuable each of these people is to our organization and I want to keep these people happy.

Perhaps the best example of how powerful these sorts of people are can be found in Apple fanatics. They are, in my mind, the most powerful aspect of Apple's marketing arsenal. In the completely hypothetical situation in which Apple were forced to cast off either their marketing department or their fans, I'd be inclined to axe their marketing. If you've spoken with an Apple fan, you'll probably appreciate why I feel this way. Truth be told, some of these folks seem half-nuts! Say one negative thing about Apple, and odds are that they'll take the next hour to explain to you why you're wrong, and how you should instead love Apple for this very same thing. This is outrageous loyalty, and it's far more valuable and convincing than even the most entertaining ad campaign.

Do whatever you can to connect with those who are passionate about what you do. Afford them special privileges and speak with them personally. Give them access to see new projects and stock as it arrives/develops, and ask for their feedback. Find any way you can to engage them in what you're doing; their enthusiasm is rocket-fuel.

Have a little fun

I believe fun to be pivotal in everything we do. Besides, how else do we keep ourselves interested for long enough to achieve breakthrough? It seems to me that most good things take time. Once this new thing is developed, it often takes even longer to make a connection with others, no matter how good it may be. This is why we hear about bands laughing at their apparent "overnight success"—often explaining that they whittled away in relative obscurity for a decade before reaching such a point. My bet is that if they hadn't liked what they were doing, they probably wouldn't have stayed the course.

Today we find ourselves facing an unprecedented opportunities to connect with others. Some have already found ways to make doing so as boring as oatmeal. Acronyms and vague references are thrown about by thousands of hacks self-professing their "guru" or "expert" status in social media—few of whom would you actually want to share a beer with. In years to come, "best practices" (how I hate that term) will likely be well-established for social media. Using these tools will become even more commonplace and systematic. Until then, I say it needs less "Kathie Lee Gifford" and a little more "Sid Vicious." This is interesting stuff—let's not beat all the fun out of it!

"Having fun" is rather difficult to prescribe. There's no single formula for making things "fun." I simply propose that you avoid thinking of marketing as a checklist of things to be completed. Instead, try to find opportunities to engage the people who like your stuff in a way that feels right to you. Some employ every single tool in a predictable fashion and have little to show for it. Alternately, others have done different, more personal things that have attracted massive attention and followings. Gary Vaynerchuk comes to mind for this. By taking a particularly irreverent and unpretentious approach to wine appreciation, he's become well known by many and has been coined "the wine world's new superstar."[94]

I'm not proposing that you do something unnecessarily outlandish. I simply believe that you have a unique voice that some would like to hear. I don't know what that voice is, and you might not have a handle on it quite yet. But in front of you is a massive control panel with all kinds of knobs begging to be turned. Say something that matters to you, and start to play a little. You never know where your experiments may lead you.

Watch the data

I've put off my cholesterol test for the past two years. I don't want to go, because I don't want to know. When I last had it checked it wasn't particularly bad, but I somewhat dread finding out that it has gotten worse and that I'll have to change my diet even more than I already have. Not knowing allows me to avoid taking action that might be less than pleasurable. Of course, there's a down-side to this approach: I might be risking a coronary just because I don't want to face facts.

I've seen almost identical behavior amongst businesses. They are happy to keep their heads in the sand regardless of how easy it would be to gain insight into the effectiveness of their marketing. It's hard, but not impossible, to create a smart and beautifully designed campaign—it's doubly-challenging to market in a way that results in action. Many happily put effort into building something beautiful but then fail to check the numbers and determine what works and what needs to be re-examined.

There's little excuse for this. It's easy (and cheap) to access data about incoming traffic, conversion rates, visitor click-paths, competitor comparison, and so on. Admittedly, a lot of this is what I call "wobbly data"; it can be misleading and does demand interpretation.

Monitoring it regularly will help you gain a better feel for what's occurring, and how you might act, in order to achieve what you desire.

Just because it worked for them

Guy Kawasaki (the author and venture capitalist) has gotten far on Twitter, but you probably won't. Amber Lee Ettinger's "Obama Girl" videos had a lot of views on YouTube, but I don't expect the same for you. Heather Armstrong's blog *Dooce* is huge, but yours? I think not so much.

The words "Who's this guy to tell me that no one will care about what I do?" might be passing through your mind at this moment. I admit, I may come off as a jerk here, but I'm likely right. The success that a few have found through these new communication tools is admirable, but that doesn't mean you'll do as well as they have. Don't bother. Really—don't even compare yourself to these people. What worked for them can likely be traced back to a specific set of circumstances that would be nearly impossible to duplicate. This is the strange—and wonderful—part about connecting with people using the tools at our disposal: you can cut your own path.

There's no single way to do this, but I think there's something to be said for isolating stories and themes that mean something to you. As you tap into these and start to define a voice for yourself, you give people something to identify with. From there, you open up the possibility of creating a unique dialogue that others would be hard-pressed to copy. You might do it with a blog, podcast, weekly video, or animated series. Or you might bypass some of the technology altogether and instead write a column for the local paper, put on workshops, teach classes, start a conference, or put on your own festival with other like-minded businesses.

I don't know what you'll do, but there's no reason to not make it uniquely yours. Who knows? In a couple of years time, people not so different from you might look at your success, trying to find a way to imitate it. At that point, you can tell them that they should "cut their own path," just like some noisy bald man once suggested.

CHAPTER 21

Ten (Digital) Marketing Stories

THIS IS A BONUS CHAPTER OF SORTS. My wife Amea and my good friend Hans have been reading over this and giving me feedback over the past couple of months. The unfortunate part with enlisting people whose opinions are good is that they often make you do more work, and indeed, they've done just that here. They've said over and over again that as interesting as this web and social media thing is, they wonder if I'm being too general in some of my observations.

What they say

They've also noted that they're not quite sure where the line between the person and the company falls. The fact is, that's an accurate observation. The web is fuzzy and there are countless ways to use it. Social media also blurs the lines between the individual and the organization. As a result, many of my suggestions intend to straddle this. In crafting this section, I've continually asked myself if a certain piece of advice would be applicable to a local plumbing contractor, destination ski lodge, or perhaps an interior design studio. Most of the time, I believe the answer would be "yes."

Still, I think it's worth taking a moment to look more closely at how this digital stuff could be applied in hard, tangible ways. To give this some kind of a framework, I'll look at ten different kinds of businesses, and what they could do right now with the web and social media. Most of these should be somewhat transferable to other types of businesses. *Please note that all of these are entirely hypothetical situations and not based on any actual party or situation.*

Case 1: The five-person travel outfitter offering tours of the Yukon

Based in Whitehorse (a small city in Northern Canada famous for its natural beauty), Jill and Rick have been running a small travel outfitter for the past 4 years. They use it to take people to untouched parts of the territory that are majestic and hard to describe. They work with three full-time staff guides, all of whom love the area and spend all of their spare time in the backcountry. Their operation is interesting because as far off the beaten path as they go, their expeditions are accessible to anyone and an awful lot of fun.

Over the past few years, they've had a great response from those who've taken the tours. Given the nature of these trips, though, most choose to do something else unique the year following. Some of them intend to come back again, but probably won't do so for another few years. In the meanwhile, they're having a hard time reaching new people and the poor global economy has slowed bookings drastically.

The group gets together for a huddle of sorts as they realize that the upcoming year's bookings just won't support the operation. As much as they love the work, they acknowledge that they need to sell more trips if they want to make a go of this. They meet over a weekend, go through some good wine, and try to figure out what to do next. Repeatedly they come back to the same observations.

People like the trips, but they aren't sharing these stories. Plus, the Yukon is quite distant for many. Those who do hear about the operation have a hard time imagining the experience and some even find it a little intimidating. They figure out that if they want to get people to book, they'll need to show them that their trips are accessible and fun. Meanwhile, they have to find a way to enable all of those excited past visitors to share their stories.

As the hours drift by (and they start to realize that their wine supply is almost gone) the gang comes up with a batch of ideas. The one idea that takes hold is to outfit their guests with small, inexpensive video cameras so they can record what they see and experience.

For doing so, each guest gets to keep their camera, which only costs the operator around $150 per unit. In exchange, the outfitter gets access to the video for promotional purposes.

They edit the final videos down to make two-minute travel diaries. They then upload these clips to the web, and send the link to the guests who took the video. Each one has a "share" button directly beneath, allowing them to add them to any social network they're a part of. So they get to share their travels with friends.

On top of this, the company starts carrying camera equipment with them wherever they go. In doing so, they start to collect a repository of breathtaking videos and photographs. They make all of these available to travel writers, media sources, and travel agencies; they also invite others to use these materials free of charge, so long as the outfitter is noted in the caption. Consequently, they receive what amounts to free advertising that showcases the beautiful sights and great times to be had on their tours.

Case 2: An interior design studio with a quirky sensibility

Siblings Bonnie and Boris run a small interior design studio in Portland. They're an attention grabbing pair, and self-declared "enemies of boredom." They loathed the dull and dreary houses they grew up in and decided that they wanted to fight such tediousness in their work. They like funky, playful, and sometimes weird spaces. To make these happen, they rummage around vintage shops and garage sales looking for one of a kind objects to help shape the homes they work on. They see every space as a new adventure and craft these around their clients' interests and lives.

Although they're really good at what they do, both of them absolutely abhor sales. Doing it makes them feel creepy, like they're somehow "selling out," and they just can't get over that feeling. The real problem is that once they're finished a project, their work is often unseen, as they mostly work on private residences. So they're always living hand-to-mouth, waiting for the next job to come in. They tried some ads in community papers, but found them rather unsuccessful. Most of the requests were for sterile and contemporary looks, or for that flowery country style they grew up in—and hated. Both of these types of requests make the two "feel like barfing."

It didn't take them long to figure out that advertising broadly was a waste of time for them. The masses simply won't "get" the kind of aesthetic they promote. That doesn't really matter because they don't need to appeal to everyone. Since some people delight in their approach, the challenge is for more of the *right* people to see their work.

The solution for Bonnie and Boris is to find ways to connect with more progressive people who want to have a little fun with their homes. They start with a simple photo blog showcasing the work they do. These images won't connect with everyone, which is good. This filters out those who wouldn't work well with them anyway. Then they decide to start a weekly online Q&A in which they answer others' space design questions.

Doing so accomplishes a few things. First, it showcases their projects to people who'd otherwise never see them; furthermore, it allows them to connect with like minds. Some won't be ready to hire them today, but will likely remember them when they are ready to. Most importantly, this gives people something to tune in to weekly and talk about with friends. In a spot like this, the weirder the design, the better, as people will be curious to check in again and see what the duo are up to.

Case 3: A software company focused on billing solutions

Paolo develops simple software that makes billing easier for home-based companies. People like his software's ease of use. Therefore he's been selling more every month. Since then he's added two other developers to his team and the software is getting good reviews.

Although they're getting some traction, Paolo realizes that they still don't make much money—especially given they work such long hours. These days he feels like he can hardly get on top of things while he juggles development, sales, QA testing, and customer support. He can't find the time to market his software sufficiently, and at their size, he also can't afford a full-time marketing person. Meanwhile, their customers are asking for additions and plug-ins that they just don't have the time to produce. Sometimes they feel like the whole thing is a hump that's impossible to get past.

Nevertheless, Paolo's actually pretty well connected. He knows a batch of other developers through his teaching at the local college. He's also involved in the PHP community and his friends there have expressed interest in developing modules for his software. He can't afford to bring them onboard as full-time staff members, but realizes that he doesn't need to.

Paolo decides to harness the power of his community. He opens up his software as a platform for others to develop on. This allows independent developers to build out new tools and make money for themselves. This adds to the depth of his software and modules available for customers. All of these people working with him results in them becoming advocates for the software. Better yet, these connections help him test new versions of the software and share notes on how it could be improved. At no cost to Paolo, he's expanded his product development team, enabled a committed testing team, and harnessed the power of word of mouth.

Case 4: A struggling not-for-profit addressing homelessness

A group of 20 recent university grads wanted to address issues surrounding homelessness. Being resourceful and smart, they banded together to start their own not-for-profit. They employ three full-time staff and the others volunteer on evenings and weekends. Many attest to them making a real difference, in part by getting out on the street and working directly with the people at risk

Lately though, the volunteers are increasingly forced to do bureaucratic paperwork; so many of them are getting burnt out. They signed on to work with the people and make a difference, not to fill in forms. With the economy being bad though, government funding has dried up. If they want to spread this work out a little, they'll have to actively solicit new funds.

Most of the members of the team use social networks on a daily basis; they're also longtime residents of the city. This makes them a pretty well connected bunch. They're convinced that if more people knew what they were up to, they'd be able to generate the funds they require. This would allow them to hire more support staff, allowing the volunteers to concentrate on the work they love.

Their needs are to spread the word and afford a way for people to donate to them easily. They start by creating a website that contains information about what they're doing; thereafter, they create a Facebook fan page and use it to spread the word amongst those they know. Meanwhile, they connect with some local ad people and create a pro bono campaign to connect with others. These ads are showcased on YouTube, and can be embedded anywhere. A number of their friends decide to post them on their blogs and user profiles. The cherry on top is a simply micropayment service that allows people to donate small sums to the group without hassle.

Case 5: An illustrator searching for a book deal

Cassie finished an art school illustration program five years ago. Since then, she's been working as a part-time assistant at the library. For fun, she's been writing and illustrating her own kids' books. All of the stories take place in a magical land with weird and wacky creatures. She's been testing them with the kids at the library and finds everyone loves them

She has contacted a number of publishers about the project, but few see her books as viable. The one that did offered a paltry contract and wanted substantial changes to the story and her style. None of this really worked for her. She's convinced that the books work exactly as they are and she really wants to maintain her unique voice. From her experience at the library, she's convinced that there's a market for her books.

Upon talking to some friends about the dilemma, she learns about POD (print on demand) services like Lulu, CreateSpace, and Lightning Source. These allow anyone to publish immediately, without a traditional publisher. With limited setup costs, she can get something out to market the way she wants. Additionally, her creative abilities are a huge asset that will help her build community around the book and perhaps even inform upcoming releases.

Cassie takes the bull by the horns, self-publishing her book and making it available online. On the last page of her book, she invites readers to visit a little website she created. Here, readers find a number of things that allow them to extend the fun. They can read bonus sections, suggest ideas for future stories, and even upload their own artwork based on the book to be featured in the site gallery.

Along with this, she also makes a batch of t-shirts, hats, and other neat items based on the book. These are manufactured by another company like Zazzle that takes care of all the logistics of printing, warehousing, sales, and shipping. The beauty of this is that she never even has to touch the products. She simply showcases the merchandise on her site, and takes a cut from the sales.

The way she really connects with others is by actively interacting with users and building her network of fans. She does so by allowing readers to sign up for updates, which she calls "magic dispatches." Some of these messages come in the form of personal emails from the characters, written directly to the kids. Additionally, she emails notes on new merchandise and releases as she makes them available. Oh, right—whenever she gets a "fan" letter, she asks these readers to write a positive review on Amazon.

Case 6: An independent accountant working to grow her company

Jayden just became certified as an accountant. She graduated at the top of the class and is really excited about this new career. Although she received a number of job offers from larger operations, she has decided that she'd like to go it alone. After some basic business planning and all of the other associated tasks, she starts her own firm and gets down to work.

The problem for Jayden is that she's just moved to a new town and doesn't really know anyone. She also has limited experience running a business and is sometimes intimidated by all of the tasks that face her. In her first couple of months, she's managed to setup the office and get the basics working. Now that she's done with all of that though, she isn't sure what to do next.

She decides that it would be great to connect with other entrepreneurs, perhaps through some kind of a networking group or club. After a little searching though, she comes up empty. It seems as though there are no such groups in town. This surprises her, as she has noticed a number of new businesses and shops opening their doors over the past few months. This gives her an idea. First of all, she realizes many of these businesses could likely use help with their accounting. She also figures there's plenty of knowledge that can be pooled amongst all of these folks.

Jayden uses Meetup to create a local entrepreneurs group. This takes her only a few moments, and once she's done she starts to invite other interesting young business owners to join and share their expertise. This gives her a lovely "reason" to introduce herself to prospective clients and talk a little about her offering. Plus, with all of these people coming from such varied backgrounds, they can share tips on how they're addressing common entrepreneurial challenges.

As she builds this network, she also starts a series of free bookkeeping workshops "sponsored" by her firm. She spreads the word through some ads focused on reaching entrepreneurs that run on local websites and in the newspaper. At these events, she invites people to email any of their questions to her. She then answers these questions publicly on a blog. In doing so she shows how interested she is in helping others. It also helps establish credibility in the community and also build link strength for her company's website.

Case 7: A home-based sustainable maternity clothing startup

Gabriella and Jose just welcomed their first child to the world. As they awaited their daughter's birth, they found themselves increasingly worried about the state of the planet due to climate change. They tried to start living in a "greener" fashion, but as they searched for more sustainable options, they found that few were available. They committed to doing their best to make the world a better place.

They toyed with a number of business ideas, but the one that stuck related to creating more sustainable maternity clothes. After six months of research, they had learned a great deal about sustainability; plus, they'd sourced some more environmentally-friendly methods and materials for their line of clothing.

All of this was going well, but they soon realized that their decisions around ethics and sustainability significantly increased the cost of their garments. They found that manufacturing locally, ethically, and with more sustainable materials made it tough to compete with those making less sustainable garments offshore. They're getting rather concerned about all of this, realizing that there's little possibility of their clothing appealing to retailers at its current price point.

Although Gabriella and Jose are both concerned about this wrinkle, they're positive that sustainability is an important issue that will resonate with others. They figure what they really need to do is get people to realize that their purchases make a real difference. Ultimately, they acknowledge that theirs largely is an issue of education and they need to share this information with others.

Gabriella and Jose have limited money on hand to advertise, but they do have some time—well, at least that small amount in between burping the baby and changing diapers. They decide to put aside a few hours a day to reach out and tell their story. First, they print a series of small cards that accompany each garment, extolling the importance of sustainable clothing. The cards also provide a link to their website containing additional information on sustainable clothing. When people read this page they're offered 25 percent off on their next purchase and an additional 10 percent off if they convince a friend to try the company.

Jose starts to write to those who blog about maternity and parenting, asking them if they'd like to try out the product. He's clear to them that there are no strings attached, but that if they like the product, they'd welcome any support. Jose's particularly careful about how he does this: every email he sends is addressed individually, and he ensures the recipient is interested in this sort of information. He doesn't want them to think that this is a bulk message or spam.

Gabriella also starts to document her experiences as a recent mom. These stories often relate to being more sustainable and what a pain in the ass it can be. Her posts are funny and candid, and in sharing them she builds up a bit of a following. New people find her blog and learn about their company. More than that though, she asks buyers to email them with any problems. From this feedback they're able to fix little issues and continually refine their products.

Case 8: A blues club based in a major center

Dan loves the blues. Scratch that—he's crazy about the blues. After twenty years of working in a factory, he's finally made his dream a reality. Recently he managed to get an operating loan, and his application for a liquor license was approved. Last May he opened his bar, and he's been working night and day since. He never minds though—this is the most fun he's ever had.

Even though he's been able to get some good acts to play there, his bar is a little out of the way. The only people who tend to visit are those who've made advance plans to do so. The problem here is that with it so quiet, the spirit of the place just isn't what it is on nights when it's rocking.

After talking with a few friends, Dan realizes that his bar isn't just a venue—it's a place of worship for those who love this kind of music. He reasons that perhaps the answer is to just remind those who share this interest that his place isn't that far away. He also starts asking how he can convert one-time visitors into regulars. He decides that the trick to all of this is to talk less about the bar, and instead, concentrate on his love of the blues.

Dan creates a simple blog in which he shares just these stories. His posts come in the form of personal experiences and photos from the shows that they've put on at the bar. He shares links to the websites of those who are planning to play at his bar. He does all of this simply—he doesn't even pay a designer to make it look nice. It's plain and sort of raw, but it comes from the heart. Slowly, he gets a bit of a following amongst local blues fans.

To learn more about what's happening on this blog, he installs Google Analytics. He realizes that although his traffic was quite high at first, it has since gone flat. So he starts to place some small ads Facebook that are keyword and geography targeted to reach those who love the blues in his town. He also runs ads on local entertainment sites. Most of these ads link right back to his blog where people can get up-to-date news on upcoming acts. He watches the analytics data daily in order to see which ads work the best. He then tests variations in order to get the best value.

When people come to the bar, he gives away free t-shirts and bumper stickers. Each one reads "I'm crazy for the blues." Admittedly, it's not a great slogan, but somehow it catches on. The hook is that he puts his web address beneath this slogan. Doing so results in other blues fanatics (almost inadvertently) spreading the word for him.

The pièce de résistance is in the way Dan uses his blog as a way to connect with blues legends. He writes to a bunch of them asking for interviews on his blog. Most ignore him, but a few agree to a brief back and forth. With each that he manages to connect with, he asks them to stop by if they're ever in town. Sure, some won't ever do so. But by extending the opportunity there's a possibility. Better yet, he's had a chance to chat with some of his idols. He sure didn't get to do that back at the factory!

Case 9: Independent filmmakers promoting their first release

Baraz and Parvana left Iran when they felt that the political climate in their country had became too unstable. They resettled in the United States five years ago, but never forgot about how things were in their home country.

Parvana is a born storyteller, and in recent years Baraz has became skilled in video production. Realizing that few knew about the situation in Iran, they saw an opportunity to use their skills to create awareness surrounding the injustices occurring there. They returned to Iran and started to make a documentary. There was a lot of risk for them in telling this story, but they finally got a finished film in place.

After completing the film, they thought the worst was over. It turns out that this was only one part of the job. Although they see their story as being important, the process of getting it to market seems daunting. Even if they get into film festivals, they worry that two few people will hear their message. Plus, they need to make some money from the film to keep promoting it.

Parvana and Baraz decide the most important thing to them is to spread the film's message. As they discuss their options, they see that people in Iran and around the world are using Twitter to talk about the situation. They realize by tapping the power of these individuals, they can work together to achieve a common goal.

The pair decides to initially forgo a standard method for releasing a film, instead showing the entire movie for free online. Directly beside the video is a note about the costs associated in making the film. They ask those who found it important to donate a small sum to help them promote it, and recover what they've already invested.

Meanwhile, they get on Twitter and connect with everyone talking about Iran. They ask each of these people to view the film and to consider spreading the word. Additionally, they connect with a number of Persian websites and write individual notes to the site owners.

On their website, they not only showcase the movie, but also discuss ways to take action. They do so by creating a forum for discussion that allows engagement on visitors' behalf. They provide downloadable graphics and advertisements promoting the film for anyone who wants to lend a hand.

Case 10: An auto mechanic who works only on select imports

Rob loves European cars. He's tinkered with them for years, and finally got his dream job at a BMW shop called PPJB Imports. After only six months though, the owner decided to retire. This led Rob to borrow money from his family to buy the business.

After a month on his own he learned that the financials weren't as good as they had once seemed. Worse yet, he learned the past owner didn't have a very good reputation. He feels bad about this and wishes he'd done more research before agreeing to the deal. It's sort of a shame though. He's affording good service and new customers seem pretty happy. Unfortunately, some just won't get past its spotty history. No matter how hard he works to change it, he's inherited a bad reputation and it's hard to shake that.

As noted, Rob has been doing a great job for customers, regardless of the shop's history. The new customers are saying good things and this leads Rob to realize he needs to quash the old legacy that's getting in the way so much. He has to plant his own flag and send a clear message that his shop will be different.

Realizing that he can't change every association with PPJB, he renames the shop. With the old name out of the way, he's free to build a new legacy. He changes the storefront to reflect this, and advertises in local media to publicize the new name and his message of new ownership. He recognizes this is just a first step, and he needs to concentrate on the good word that he's starting to establish.

He talks personally to all of his happy customers about the challenge he's facing and what he's trying to do. He asks them if they might help by visiting review sites like Yelp and talking about their experience with his shop. He hires a design company to create a little website for him, and asks them to showcase some of these reviews—both good and bad.

Bigger yet though, he asks for suggestions on how to make his business better. Part of this is accomplished by using cheap tools that others have developed. For example, Get Satisfaction helps him collect customer feedback and address it quickly and publicly. He also uses some services to track what's being said about his shop online, Anytime he finds something negative, he picks up the phone and calls the frustrated party. He insists on nipping any bad reviews in the bud. If someone isn't happy, he'll do whatever it takes to change that. Sometimes he gives these folks $100 off their next repair; for others, he offers to redo the job and even throw in a free oil change to make up for the trouble.

In doing all of this, he takes control of his shop's online reputation while getting real—and up-to-date—dialogue on his quality of service. Another nice perk is that when you search for BMW repair in his city, his shop comes up first every time!

The tip of the iceberg

Clearly, these suggestions represent just a few of the things you can do to connect with others, using these new tools. You really owe it to yourself to examine your personal situation carefully, experiment with different options, and determine appropriate ways to make it work for you.

PART FIVE
ACTING AND ADAPTING

Finally we'll look at how you can put all of this to work for your company. In this final passage, we'll start to craft a plan for your brand and marketing that you'll actually use. You'll also learn how to make change work for you, as well as how to find good partners and work with them. For fun we'll go over a few ways to screw the whole thing up! I don't think you have to worry much about that though.

CHAPTER 22

The Inverted Pyramid

I'D LIKE TO PROVIDE A FRAMEWORK of sorts for developing an over-arching plan for your brand and marketing efforts. While there isn't room in this chapter to address every single consideration, this will help you start.

"Big" does come with privileges

If you were in a marketing role at a big company you'd probably be part of a vastly different scene. Certain things would be clearly de-termined, allowing you to get focused on more well-defined proj-ects. On top of that, you probably wouldn't be left with so many big picture questions. The boss wouldn't walk into your office and ask, "What matters most to us?" or "Are we going to be happy doing this sort of work?" or "Do we really want to grow?"

Instead, they'd figure all of those things out, leaving you with mission statements, identity standards documentation, and maybe even some data regarding your customers and their habits. All of these are great things to have and tend to make a marketer's job that much easier. Once you have all of these great things determined, you can concentrate on more highly defined tasks with clearer goals and objectives. You might even have an organizational marketing plan in place, allowing you to concentrate on very specific efforts with the support of other more senior people to help you through.

Around here, it's different

It isn't really like this for most small companies. From what we've seen, small companies face an altogether different side of marketing. Most of them have very few of these things clearly defined. Perhaps they have an old business plan that hasn't been consulted in years. Maybe they had some conversations a while ago regarding the company's mission and values, but everyone felt weird about them. What came of that was vague and hard to buy in to.

Most small companies are just trying to fight through the day with rarely an extra moment to spare. We're typically bombarded by a seemingly endless stream of things to do and choices to make. Amidst all of this hustle and bustle, marketing tends to get kind of "piecemeal." When The Yellow Pages calls, an ad is prepared and placed. When you're asked to give a talk, you stay up past midnight for days trying to make a nice looking PowerPoint presentation. When a patron tells you that your website sucks, you're left trying to figure out why they'd say such a mean thing and asking what isn't working.

I believe this way of working is exponentially time wasting. While one of these considerations opens a can of worms, combined with the rest, it gets even worse. Every one of these things has an impact on the other tools and channels you employ. Few realize this, as they're mostly scrambling from one thing to the next. When they do finally have a chance to sit back and look at these elements together, they realize their marketing is scattershot and awkward.

When you're rushing to put out fires, it's hard to think about how your actions impact the big picture. Your website says one thing, but it's not echoed in your telephone manner, or the promise made in your ads. Getting each of these things to function alone is hard enough; without a clear direction, making them work together becomes almost impossible. These inconsistencies come with an added price: to the outsider it seems like your company is out of tune. Worse yet, it leads them to doubt if you can deliver on what you propose.

The "sauce"

Allow me a brief tangent. This whole mess reminds me of something

I once concocted in a high school cooking class. I didn't have much experience in the kitchen, but I suppose I likened myself to a culinary daredevil of sorts. I made the bold decision to... experiment. In my pursuit of finding new gastronomic delights I felt it best to be unencumbered of any rules or restrictions. To support this, I began with no clear direction or end goal in mind.

I began by frying some onions and adding assorted ingredients. Soon it seemed like I was making some kind of soup. I continued with this for a while, until it started to seem a little dull. To counter this I decided that it would be "neat" to make into something a little heartier—perhaps a stew. I then used dollops of flour to thicken the mixture. Next I added tomatoes, carrots, peppers—come to think of it, I might have even tossed some pickles in the mix. I started to hesitate at this point, and realized that no, it really should be more "soup-like." I added some water to thin it once again.

This fiasco carried on for some time and by the end of the afternoon, I was left with what might be characterized as a grayish mush. For dinner that night we ate something I'd rather forget. My parents christened it "the sauce." I still think that was a more generous name than it really deserved. My invention didn't taste like much of anything—largely because I didn't ever figure out what I wanted to make. To this day, you can ask my parents about the sauce and they'll laugh.

Some companies make "the sauce" when it comes to their marketing. They start with a little of this and add a little of that. They veer from one thought to the next, largely led by how they feel at the given moment. Perhaps they stumble upon something interesting here or "sort of neat" there. Unfortunately, without a clear direction in mind, a company's marketing can quickly turn into bland and uninteresting mush.

Zooming out

I recognize many readers of this book probably don't even have a marketing plan. I'd wager that the ones who do find theirs isn't working as they desire. Regardless of one's dislike of such things, it's important to come up with a plan that is well suited for your organization. I believe that the size of your operation may necessitate a kind of plan that's tailored around your unique challenges and needs.

My problem with some marketing plans is found in how they are often outward facing: concentrated solely on customers, competitors, market forces, and the like. If you're a company like General Mills and you're working to bring a new consumer product to market, such a lens makes a great deal of sense. If, on the other hand, you're a small video production company, your considerations are different. You might be wise to step a little further back yet, and look inward first.

While I can't speak to your specific situation, I can share what we've witnessed at our agency. In our experience, small companies generally make disconnected moves that result in that aforementioned mush. They bounce from one thing to the next, each time becoming more confused. By the time they reach us, they don't really know what to do, nor in what order.

We've found that it's been helpful to "zoom out" and ask them some more general (or perhaps bigger) questions. We're often able to help them isolate the root of the problems they face. In working through this process, it seems that other opportunities and a logical course of action are clarified. I suppose it's almost absurd to suggest any other result, isn't it? Many only address their marketing when a specific task demands their attention, instead of putting aside adequate time to outline expectations and develop a plan. Can you think of another setting in which such action make any sense? Just think of how silly it would be to start building a house by assembling the cabinets!

Most would instead start by asking what their life is like, what they want out of a house, and how much they can afford. Once those things were determined, they might hire a contractor to help them find (or draw) plans for something suitable. I've never built a house, but I'd expect from that point forth they'd take a series of steps, each informed by the one prior. We like to think that crafting a company's brand and marketing isn't altogether that different.

The inverted pyramid

Given the size of the companies we work with, we've found some ways to help our clients get a handle on things and determine a course of action. The nice part is that this all boils down to a fairly simple way for small companies to develop a big picture plan. Our approach has evolved over the years and I'll touch upon the high points here. You can fill in the rest, either on your own, or with the team you bring in to assist with such efforts.

I visualize our approach as an inverted pyramid. Imagine an upside down triangle comprised of four stacked layers. Each of these tiers represents a broad set of considerations and choices, and each follows the next in a defined order. From this characteristic, decisions made on one level inform the following ones. As this occurs, the direction, strategy, messaging and method of delivery are clarified.

This works well because it asks us to consider the long-term; meanwhile, it forces us to take subsequent steps that lead us further down this road. In turn, we're left with an approach that fits the organization's long-term needs but can still be implemented immediately.

I suspect that your marketing—not to mention your business— has forced you to face more questions than you had ever anticipated. I want to lighten the load, leaving you with fewer questions to deal with. Working through this process can do just that. The questions you'll be left with are made more manageable given that they operate within a less ambiguous context. This means the questions you do ask will be the right ones. Let's take a brief look at those four layers.

The first layer: Direction

Many believe they are facing a marketing problem when they are actually dealing with a direction problem. Worse yet, some have no direction. If you're inundated with challenges in your marketing, I ask you to take some time to stop concentrating on it so closely—instead let's pull back to examine and articulate what it is you want out of your life and your business. Knowing this will make everything that follows substantially easier.

To some, this might feel like an unnecessary step backwards. Even if feels cumbersome, it's highly important and worthy of added consideration. Should you have already determined all of these points, you can look at this as a good refresher that shouldn't take much time. A great many companies flail from one service to the next because they didn't ever take a "time out" and give suitable deliberation to their direction. This moment—this *very* moment—is the absolute best time to ensure you are on track. By asking, some may even determine that they don't have a track. If that's the case for you, count your lucky stars! When better than now, to learn of this and address it?

Clarifying your direction first requires an honest appraisal of who you are and what you really *want*. I emphasize this last point because it is so highly personal. Lots of people are trying to build a business that is like their neighbors'; yet, if they actually achieved it, they might find that it wasn't at all what they had expected. So... what do you want from the organization you're building? Are you growth focused or are you in it for the cash? Is your business focused on allowing you to maintain a certain lifestyle? Are you perhaps in it more for the art (or craft) of what you do? Are there some aspects of what you do that are simply more rewarding than other parts?

Asking and finding appropriate answers to these questions is pivotal to the small company. Sure, it steps back into business plan territory, but it's so important to your brand that it deserves reflection. Some have a great brand strategy and marketing plan, but are unmotivated to continue. If you hate what you have to do every day, what's the point?

I've met with a number of people who have given up on a particular kind of work (which may have been quite lucrative) to do something that better suits their desires. Some find that they are best off doing something other than what they had once planned. Personally, it makes little difference to me what you choose to do, or for what reasons. The purpose of this exercise is to align whatever desires you have with a method for building your business. You need to define what your company means to you, on your own terms. This way, if all of your marketing works, you land in the right spot.

From here I think it's important to look at the Hedgehog Concept as illustrated by Jim Collin's Venn diagram in his book *Good to Great*.[95] In it he takes three circles, each defining a simple measure of your situation. He breaks these down to the following questions:

"What you are deeply passionate about?"; "What you can be the best in the world at?"; and "What drives your economic engine?" I like to simplify these to: passion, capacity, and money. Either way, there's likely an answer of sorts for you where those three circles overlap.

You should think about or have already determined all of these considerations. On the other hand, I suggest that some of us have drifted a little over the years and perhaps even lost our way. Let's take pause, and run your current direction (and offering) against these measures. How do your expectations and plans stack up? Honestly— are you in good form or do you need to redefine your direction?

The second layer: Strategy

Defining where you want to go is a huge step. Many of us struggle throughout our careers, changing path many times as boredom sets in or our interests shift. This same challenge is compounded when one starts a company. We wrestle with all the same considerations, in fact, it's sometimes harder as more people tend to be involved. This makes the path even more difficult to navigate. Now that you have a clear direction, it will help you reduce the number of variables that you have to contend with. Better yet, you can start to come up with a way to achieve these ambitions.

There are countless ways to craft a plan for your organization, and I accept that I'm skimming over many relevant considerations. The thing is, I'm biased. While I'm obsessive about planning things out, I don't want you to get burdened by details prematurely. Instead, I'd like you to get the broad strokes in place. Once those work, you can always pin down all of the specifics.

I guess I should just say it here: I hate mission statements. They're long, vague, and difficult to act upon. Part of the problem is that we think a mission statement has to sound like a mission statement. They often do that but little else. This leaves one with a block of text that seems "right," but is rarely ever considered again or even used. On the other hand, I like sentences—particularly the ones that don't require fancy words. For these next points, I ask you to vehemently avoid the vapid bullshit that's endemic of those wanting to seem smart, important, or business-like. Get down to clear answers. If you

do so right, you should be able to share your responses with someone completely uninterested, and still have them understand what
you're doing.

I think there are a few key questions you need to answer clearly
for your organization's strategy. The first is purpose: What do we
want this company to accomplish? This is like a mission statement,
but much more plain and actionable. In a sentence, can you tell me
what you're about? You get bonus points if you can do so with only a
few words. By the way, most people would address this earlier. I put
it later as think it's important to first determine what you want as a
person, and then see how your company's mission fits with that.

The second, and closely related one, comes down to offering:
what does our company do? I admit this seems like something that
should be implicit; yet, if you ask some business owners this same
question they'll hum and haw before stumbling through a vague and
overly long description.

The third question relates to value: What do our customers get
from buying from us? I probably don't have to say it, but this goes
past the hard goods and services you provide, and relates to the
greater value you afford to them. Finally, we're left with positioning:
How are we unique from everyone else in the market? This last question can alone uncover some of the answers for how you can most
effectively market your organization.

These may seem like very simple questions. If you find them so,
I ask if you are truly giving them the time and deliberation they deserve. Alternately, having these answers could mean that you know
exactly who you are and how you are situated amongst competitors.

Casting aside the apparent straightforwardness of these questions, you'll likely find that each requires you to think further and
do a little legwork. For example, you'll need to define your organization's vision and goals. You'll also have to carefully identify and reflect
upon your audience, asking: who buys our stuff? Is there someone
more suitable—or profitable—to consider selling to instead? What
are these people like, and what do they need?

You'll also need to boil down exactly what you offer and why
this is relevant amongst all of your competitors. This will force you
to assess the landscape. You can do so by examining your competi-

tors, their messaging, and asking what gaps exist in the marketplace. Along the way you might find certain patterns. Perhaps there's an opportunity in between what you offer that what others haven't really concentrated on.

Knowing where you're going, understanding the landscape, and clearly articulating your value. That's what you have now cemented. You're now set to hone your organization's voice and craft the tools with which you connect.

The third layer: Messaging

A challenge that many run into with their marketing relates to how they envision its function. We see this quite regularly at our agency when new clients come to us wanting what we call the, "magic marketing key." This fantasy basically equates to: "Here's some money. Build me a new _____. How soon will our sales increase?" While I'd love for marketing to be this clear-cut, it rarely is as direct as this notion implies.

In marketing, you don't just insert your dollar and have a treat pop out at the bottom of the machine. I argue that to be effective in your efforts, you need to think of marketing as a more holistic practice. By this I mean that all of the dots need to connect, forming one clear presence for the consumer. This is largely tangible through an organization's messaging and it has an awful lot to do with alignment. If you want to do one thing, but you say something else, you're going to confuse people. While some think marketing has to be clever, I say it instead needs to just be really clear.

Tying all of your messaging elements together (and by this I mean all touchpoints for your organization) removes doubt in the customer's mind. I use the term messaging very loosely here and intend it to reference any way in which others interface with your company. So your corporate identity, its styles, treatments, sensibilities, and the resulting emotions, all fit into this. You could think of this as your company's "look," and it manifests itself in your signage, displays, website, brochures, name tags, and business cards.

More than this, it relates to how your organization communicates in the broadest terms. This means the way you approach people when they enter your premises, how you respond to customer calls, the text you use in advertisements, the promises you make in your marketing materials, and so on. Such a list can get pretty long and intimidate some people, as it brings a lot of decisions to make. By having all those earlier steps sorted out, this becomes much easier. Establishing your messaging allows you to know what all of these things should look, sound, and feel like.

In doing so, you'll find that even the smallest decisions are affected by these earlier decisions. If you're part of an organization concentrated on environmental sustainability, you probably won't print oversized brochures on thick, metallic stock that can't be recycled. Similarly, if you're company is big on being friendly and accessible, you probably won't use ten-dollar words in your ad copy. If you want your organization to seem exclusive, you might not choose to advertise for staff on craigslist.

If you do all of this well—and you really should take the time to do this well—you'll save headaches in the long run, as well as money and time. Doing it this way will keep you from starting from scratch every time you need to implement a new marketing tool. By not having to experiment with each individual task so closely, you won't waste so much money building and rebuilding.

The fourth layer: Delivery

Finally, we arrive at the delivery stage, and you're ready for it because you went through the steps in a logical order. This is radically different from how most small companies reach this point; some just skip all of the above steps and start right here. That's why this stage gets so confusing for most of those folks. They find themselves tasked with picking the right tool, before they know what their plan or purpose is. As we've addressed, you're in an entirely different position. You know what you want to do. You have a plan for how to do it. Additionally, you've clarified the way you're going to say it. With all of that resolved, you just need to figure out *where* to do so.

This really comes down to a few basic considerations. The first is to determine what you want to achieve through your marketing; or, as some would say, you need to determine your goals and objectives.

Remember that there is a difference between the two. Sure, you'll want to feel out what you generally want to accomplish, but you'll also need to get more specific. What objectives can you quantifiably define and set as hard targets? In doing this, you'll be able to set out on a course and have established a hard set of measures for what you want to achieve.

From here, we can look more closely at your audience. Earlier you covered who they are, but this is a good time to get more detailed in our questioning. Where are they? What matters to them? What's the most suitable—and highest value—way to engage them? Meanwhile, I think you'll need to carefully consider the resources you have at hand. Do you have the necessary funds for a particular tool/venue? Let's be blunt: there's terribly little point in looking at ad rates for major magazines if you only have $10,000 in your annual marketing budget. Money is just one matter—you also need to consider how much of your valuable time can realistically be invested in your marketing efforts.

For example, lots of people get excited about creating their own content. I suggest that such thinking can prove dangerous. Creating a great video series, online resource, or blog takes time. Managing your company's interaction on social networks is something that can take a real bite out of your day. Even if the tool seems inexpensive or free to use, think carefully about the time you have available. Can you really allocate enough to pull these things off effectively?

There are countless ways to spread your message but I have a hard time believing that any one thing is inherently better than the rest. I ask that you instead seek out the ones that work best for you. In part you can do this by fixating on which vehicle might be most effective in conveying your message to an interested audience. You may choose to test some selective advertising that leads people to your website. Perhaps you'll concentrate on directly contacting qualified leads. You might start a frequent customer program. Giving away a new product to loyal customers could work well. Alternately, it might make sense to start an online advice forum centered on your area of expertise. Or, you could do several of these things. It all comes down to your company and what gets the word out best for you.

And then you refine

By doing all of the above, the inverted pyramid is formed. In a way You could look at this as map of sorts. Occasionally you might deviate from it or try another route. That's OK—it doesn't matter that you'll sometimes change course. The point is the destination remains consistent. Meanwhile, you have a method of getting "there," even if there's a little drifting along the way.

You'll want to come back to the plan you've established here repeatedly as you move ahead. Some things won't resonate, requiring you to augment your approach. Others may be hugely successful revealing new avenues worth exploring. All of these things involve some unknowns. You need to be responsive to information as it unfolds itself to you. The nice part is that by knowing your direction you can make tweaks as necessary. For example: an advertisement doesn't result in traffic? Try a different venue. People can't find something in the shop? Move it. No one reads your blog posts? Test some different ones and see which resonate. Better yet: ask some people why they don't find them engaging.

Yawn

It's easy to confuse marketing for fun. Many people get wrapped up in working with interesting creative folks, thinking that they'll be able to, "push the envelope." They look at every marketing exercise as an opportunity to "play" and say things like "this is going to be fun" or "let's do something out of the box!" Conversely, I say by following the plans you've made earlier, such comments should occur less frequently. Actually, doing all of this might make some of the process surrounding your marketing and associated design work seem almost boring. Try to remind yourself this isn't about make art or having fun. You simply need to do what's in line with your organization.

Recently, a client came to us. They were struggling terribly with their marketing and were quite frustrated. When we spoke (early in the process) they had all kinds of ideas for things to try, but they didn't have a way to gauge which made the most sense. They were rather lost, but certainly not ready to give in. At one point they asked,

"Should we do something funny to get some attention?" My response was simply, "Are you a funny company?" Well, they weren't, and with that query I was able to make a point. By getting the right plan in place for an organization and aligning all of the pieces, such a question wouldn't have been asked in the first place.

At around the same time, we were working with a more long-standing client of ours. They needed us to create the design for their trade show booth. We crafted no creative briefs or lengthy concept documents; there wasn't even much back-and-forth or discussion. We spoke briefly and gathered the specifications; then we built something that fit with their brand. The associated questions were limited because there were only so many ways to design this piece. They signed off on the artwork and it ran without a single revision. Knowing where you're going makes the path easier.

CHAPTER 23

Finding and Enabling Great Partners

Although I keep saying you're the best person to market your company, it would be unwise for you to go it all alone. Actually, I'm being too generous here; not bringing in others to lend their knowledge and expertise might doom you to failure. I can't tell you how many times I've met with a beleaguered entrepreneur who is still regretting having cut costs by trusting certain choices to an amateur.

In this section, I'll provide some thoughts on how to access people who are great at what they do. You'll be able to rely on their capabilities, which leaves you with more time to concentrate on what you are great at.

People who speak human

Whether they want to work with us or for us, I generally chose people over their "pitches." I look for people who are interested in helping me understand; meanwhile, I generally steer clear of those who can't present things simply. I tend to end meetings when I hear things like: "The ROI on our SEO, as a result of the PHP integration, will synergize with our Brand Asset Management system before Q3!" That phrase, by the way, is complete nonsense... I have, however, heard people spout things almost as asinine.

If your supplier uses an unending parade of fancy terms and acronyms, I'd ask if they're perhaps trying to bamboozle you. It sounds mean, but it's a fair question. The other day I was asked if our firm employed a particular brand management system purportedly used by one of the big agencies (they had a really convoluted name for it). It's funny; all the name really meant was that their clients could call and ask questions when they arose. I responded that we do the same thing, but call it, "answering our clients' questions."

There are times when highly-specialized terms are necessary. Every once in a while I use industry-specific language out of habit. That being said, if you're looking to hire a brand or marketing company, and their every second word sounds like code, I'd pass on them. I don't believe in making things unnecessarily complex and if something in marketing can't be explained simply, I start to wonder if it's a con. Any good provider should be able to explain plainly how they can be of service. In my experience, those who try to intimidate with vague, jargon-laden language aren't worth considering.

Those who have all the answers

Every time I open another brand, design, or marketing book, I'm confronted by how little I actually know. This perplexes me; after so many years of doing this work, shouldn't I know more? Of course, with the number of facets involved in this practice, there's always more to learn. This leads me to the thought that "knowing" may be less important than being willing to ask questions.

I have a bit of a soft spot for certain kinds of people/suppliers. The ones I like tend to be comfortable admitting that they don't know everything. Sure, they know their practice, but they don't think this makes them an expert in your business. Good partners will understand that this kind of work requires the active involvement of (at least) two parties. They'll bring certain domain knowledge you don't have access to; meanwhile, they'll rely on you to educate them on the nature and nuances of your business.

The practitioners I most admire come to the table with few preconceived notions, and instead ask questions and listen carefully to their client's responses. It seems to me that it's all too easy to hastily prescribe a solution. I think it's important for those you bring in to start with a clean slate—minds scrubbed of any baggage that might get in the way of a unique and workable solution. Theirs should be a pursuit of identifying the root problem, seeking out truths, and crafting suitable solutions.

Meanwhile, egos should be left at the door. I know a lot of people in this field and most are curious, interesting, and articulate people. Those who aren't willing to explain the logic behind suggestions and proposed plans are part of a very small minority—I'd look upon such a lack of willingness to communicate as a *big* warning sign.

With that said, I think you need to find someone who'll push you. Actually, I believe the worst practitioners are those who agree with every idea proposed by a client. Doing so represents either an inexperienced party lacking the confidence to challenge your observations, or, someone who has lost interest and just wants to get a job done—but not necessarily the right one. We earn our keep when we question some of our clients' preconceived notions—particularly if it seems that these ideas are getting in their way.

Lead us

Working on a branding, marketing, or design effort is rarely a walk in the park. While buying a new company car is a rather simple process, crafting a story or determining the value proposition for an organization is rarely as straightforward or commonplace. These projects tend to bring with them a certain amount of stress. This can in part be assuaged by choosing good partners and clearly delineating the parties responsible for each aspect of the work.

This is easier by not allowing unbridled enthusiasm to confuse roles and responsibilities. While few in your operation are likely interested in lending their voice to your selection of legal representation, tasks containing creative aspects tend to bring interested parties and critics out of the woodwork. While most professional practices are acknowledged as outside of one's particular expertise, most everyone will take an interest in (and proclaim an aptitude for) marketing, design, and communications related issues. Of the many projects I've taken part in, the most toxic problems relate to involving too many individuals who then become confused about their roles.

As the one calling the shots, you have to lead by concentrating on the big picture. This necessitates establishing a clear set of goals for the project at hand. It also might entail relinquishing your personal vision. I don't mean to imply that you shouldn't exchange ideas and insights; it's your company and you ultimately have the most "say" in the matter. At the same time, thinking that your marketing partners will do their best even if they don't have your trust is unrealistic.

This, of course, is the big problem in client/supplier relationships when it comes to such projects. You are the one who has to live with the devised solution, but in many ways you're the least capable of seeing this sort of thing objectively. You're in the eye of the storm and this might limit your ability to see things clearly.

A little breathing room

Your role is largely that of ensuring the goals you established at the outset are achieved by the team you've employed. If you want to create a microsite that engages teenagers with your energy drink brand for example, you should expect them to deliver a sound strategy aimed at doing just that. You're also entitled to hold the team's feet to the fire and demand that they defend their proposed strategy and implementation coherently. If their logic doesn't hold, they'll have to go back to the drawing board and make it work. But you need to concentrate on whether the end result actually works, not whether your husband, "doesn't like the blue in the background."

It may seem odd that I bring up an example like this. In my experience, though, things like this are more likely to compromise a project than bigger, more strategic concerns. I've been present at many meetings in which ten guys in gray suits get into a long-winded (and ill informed) debate about color or typefaces, instead of the underlying strategy and messaging. I suppose this is a good time to say it: the more people at the table, the harder it will be. Likewise, the smaller and more focused the team, the better. This is a rule that I have yet to see challenged effectively. As Charles F. Kettering so beautifully put it, "If you want to kill any idea in the world, get a committee working on it."

I've watched great ideas die from fear introduced by too many people wanting to drive. In some respects, yours is an exercise in restraint; set your bearings, stay the course, and turn if you're going to hit a rock. Let's just not put everyone's hands on the wheel.

Plans that work

When we started our company, we met with a young fellow who had recently completed his business degree and was eager to share his insights. His eyes opened wide as he sat down with us, and a little froth formed at the corner of his mouth as he said, "Let's talk about your business plan." Every time we met, he'd do the same, and it became almost a chant of sorts, "Business plan! Ya, ya, ya, ya! Business plan! Ya, ya, ya, ya! Business plan! Ya, ya, ya, ya!"

After a while it all started to sound pretty convincing. Meanwhile, we reasoned that we didn't know much about business, so we spent days crafting an elaborate document that ultimately sat untouched in a desk drawer for several years. What's strange is that we've spent a lot of time planning since then, but never in quite that fashion.

Planning is a core component of every project we take on, be it for a client or an internal project. In my experience, this is done best when plans are kept simple, short, and free of rhetoric. As you look at your marketing efforts, I suggest you do the same. Outline details as succinctly as possible. If one word will do the work of five, use it. This isn't a book report, and you don't get extra points for fulfilling a word count. Good plans should also be flexible and easy to augment; we've even taken to crafting them in emails or shared files, so that they can be quickly revised by key stakeholders. We also tend to limit these documents to a single page, to hold everyone's attention when we review them.

Read a few marketing books and you'll end up with all kinds of things to think about and employ. This is problematic as it can embroil you in marketing discussion, instead of focusing on the job at hand. Take your short, simple plan and go through it verbally with another team member. Ask them to call "bullshit" on points that are overly aspirational or vague. You need clear, tangible goals and tasks that can be acted upon.

Starting a fire

The part you probably don't want to hear is that little of this comes for free. Some combat this by cutting corners, piecemealing efforts, or employing unproven partners whose sole benefit is price. I assure you, someone can always offer a lower price; most times you get what you pay for.

This piecemeal approach to marketing can obstruct a company's efforts. Many are eager to create a one-off with hopes that it will prove a catalyst for change. This is hardly ever the case, and often results in frustration as sporadic efforts tend to bear little fruit. With this in mind, I ask you to instead look at such efforts as ongoing.

The analogy I liken this to is one of lighting a fire. Most small organizations put countless hours and resources into collecting dry kindling, finding matches, and getting it started, only to walk away once a small flame takes hold. A week, month, or year later they return to find that their fire has burnt out, and needs to be restarted. So they begin again, hoping for something different, only to repeat the process ad infinitum.

Fires need perpetual attention to grow. Once you have it going, the hardest part is over; from there you need to stoke it from time to time and add some dry wood when necessary. It's not hard, but it does require consistent attention. By keeping at it like this, you can build a roaring fire. If you're lucky, it might even turn into a wildfire, bigger than you ever anticipated. The trick is to *keep going*.

It's going to cost something

Marketing involves time, attention, and money. Look over your projections for the year and determine what you can reasonably allocate to your marketing. As with any budget, establishing this number helps you and your team determine what you can afford to do and in what sequence. Perhaps this isn't the year for a complete identity overhaul, but those funds might be more than ample to pinpoint a particular market and connect with them.

Some are fearful that a marketing or design team will simply match their quote to whichever number is provided. In my mind, this only happens with the shadiest of firms. Determining that number will help the team determine if they can work with you, and if so, what projects might be undertaken with the allocated funds. Keep in mind you don't need to spend your whole budget with one firm, but knowing what you have allocated is certainly useful. All too often we're confronted by clients with a fixed budget which they are unprepared to reveal. This seems a little like showing up at a car dealership and saying "I need a car, but I'm not going to tell you how much I have to spend." To get you into the right one, they'll need to know what you require, and how much you can afford.

I'll also caution you that almost all companies underestimate the cost of design and marketing services. Don't get me wrong, most in this field enjoy helping people out, but there are hard costs associated with this kind of work. Meanwhile, anyone who's good will want to be compensated fairly for their efforts.

Marketing is a "long haul" kind of thing. Look for good people who you can trust, knowing that you can always pull the plug if things don't go as they should. There are a lot of smart, talented, and capable people out there. Finding a good team that you can trust will make your job easier.

Get it done

Why all this talk about making it happen? Mostly because you're one of the little guys. You don't have focus groups, assistants, budgets to fall back on, or possibly even time to spare. The moments you do have available are right in between getting all of the other work done and perhaps watering the office plants.

Others may have the luxury of taking an extra day to get marketing in place but you don't. As one of the small guys you have to take every opportunity you can get. One of the strongest advantages you have comes down to pure sweat. When everyone else goes home, you can still be working. More to the point: for everything you complete ahead of schedule, you earn time to address one more thing. Take every one of those opportunities you can.

CHAPTER 24

Embracing Change

Many of us resist new methods and technologies, instead relying on things we've grown accustomed to. Once we take the plunge, it's easy to get excited and confuse this new thing as the only option. Think of how resistant we were to embrace webmail services like Hotmail when they first became available. We were so ensconced in the world of desktop email clients we couldn't imagine moving to an online version, regardless of the benefits gained. The same thing happens all the time; we get comfortable with something and turn off the possibility of other options.

Missing out on such advancements can make us vulnerable to those who more aggressively test and deploy new tools. This challenge is compounded by the rate of change in a connected world. Tools that are seen as critical in marketing today may not have even existed two years ago. Once such a technology reaches a tipping point, we find ourselves in a landslide of momentum around it. The new tools available to us, particularly on the web, are awfully easy to get excited about. Some will last while others might mutate or fall away. I'd like to provide suggestions on how to keep one's head above water in this environment.

Get liquid

Before all of this new technology, marketers spent a lot of time coming up with a good plan and then executing on it, given how costly it was to put such campaigns together and deploy them. That cost, although still substantial, doesn't need to be quite so prohibitive any longer. We can now establish a strategy and act on it quickly and with less fear. Should the plan not quite work, we can always change course. It might seem messy, but adapting like this is pretty fast these days. You're left with a great advantage since you don't need to employ an army to spread your messages.

Trends and technologies will continue to change, with new ones emerging all the time. This doesn't mean you should embrace every new tool, but I'd remain open to the possibility of exploring them. You may launch a blog only to find that it doesn't resonate with your audience. At such a time, there's no reason for you to not see if your message might work better in a video blog, podcast, newsletter, or some other medium. Perhaps the approach you're taking just isn't the best fit. If this is the case, adapt.

I recently had lunch with a colleague who shared such an example with me. His team had connected with a local grocery chain regarding a website redesign project. In examining their situation, he observed that there were areas more deserving of consideration. Although the website was in need of an update, they advised their client to forgo this step in favor of building content in order to increase interest. The firm was subsequently hired and started to toy with the content. With time, they learned that the most popular aspect of the site was in the recipes offered to interested shoppers. They amplified this content and traffic increased manyfold in spite of a rather hackneyed website.

Given the number of new technologies, approaches, and expectations we're faced with these days, we just have to adapt more readily. Part of this relates to divorcing ourselves from sentimentality regarding the way we used to do things. Just because it once worked doesn't necessarily mean it will today. Why would anyone voluntarily limit themselves to methods that weren't the most effective? The only benefit in doing so is comfort. Don't let fear get in the way of your marketing goals.

You may have to get uncomfortable to gain familiarity with new methods. Once you do, you'll more objectively determine which tools best suit your purposes. It's equally important is to be wary of change for its own sake. The existence of a new method doesn't necessarily render a working one obsolete.

Rethink the importance of ample funds

Advertising works well—particularly for big brands with lots of money. If you aren't a big brand, you have to find a way to achieve the same end with what you do have. Sometimes the same effect—or a better one—can be had by exploring methods that others would have discounted due to their low cost. A lack of cash can actually prove an advantage; it can even open you up to new methods of differentiating.

If they're making sexy, polished ads, perhaps you need to go the other way. Where they have high-paid models, you bring in local teenagers whose knowledge of posing is limited to the fictional Zoolander's "Blue Steel."[96] They utilize high-resolution photographs that cost $20,000 a piece, so you get an old Polaroid and have fun. They hire a famous actor to narrate the commercial, so you bring in a funny kid with a weird voice who makes people laugh. Some of the best albums in rock and roll history were made by unproven musicians whose bad equipment was outshined by pure "guts." The same applies here. Money isn't the answer you think it is, so don't let it stop you. Instead, ask how you can do better with what you've got.

It doesn't end with advertising. They bring their best clients on all expense paid golf trips; you invite yours to a wild house party. You could even "up the ante" by bringing in a fire-eater or local band that hasn't quite cracked, but still "rocks." Their offices have fancy boardrooms and luxurious chairs; you buy some lawn chairs and beach umbrellas, replacing ostentatiousness with a bit of spirit and fun. They send wasteful gift baskets with overpriced crackers at Christmas; you call your clients in January offering a temporary price cut to minimize the credit card "hangover" they're perhaps suffering from.

If you're reading this book, you're probably part of a small company. Most small companies don't have mountains of cash to help them look like everyone else. There's no point in trying to keep up with them on that level. I won't tell you how to spend your dollars, but I do think there's waste in blindly doing things the "proper" way. You don't need a wheelbarrow full of currency so long as you're willing to use your brain.

Break rules

I don't advise doing things differently just for the sake of having done so. Still, there are a lot of bad rules out there that many follow to a fault. These are rules we rarely question, just because everyone else seems to take them at face value. I think we have to ask exactly why we're following such rules and ponder whether they benefit us or get in the way.

Maybe you don't need an extensive website with all the bells and whistles. Perhaps all your restaurant needs is a single web page without even an image—just a menu and contact information. As a hotel, you might bypass a website altogether and simply redirect to a page of reviews from Yelp, Expedia or Trip Advisor. One agency, called Boone Oakley decided to forgo a traditional website and instead use a series of playful YouTube videos in its place.[97] All of these are viable—and possibly noteworthy—approaches that one could arrive at simply by asking, "What do we actually need to accomplish here?"

As I've noted before, truly different stuff can be scary to most people. It's also where the greatest opportunity tends to lie. Few believed in the Herman Miller Aeron chair when it was conceived and some thought it a "monstrosity."[98] It has since become an icon and one of the company's most successful products. No one would have made that chair by trying to incrementally improve on what already existed. They needed to look at what such a thing could be, and then rethink the entire notion of seating.

Iterate

In the software development world there are many different methods of programming. One of the most common ones is the waterfall method, in which a project is exhaustively planned, crafted, refined, and finally released once deemed fit for public use. Another method, which is on the opposite end of the spectrum, is the agile approach. Using this method, a product is released early with only a small set of features, and then augmented as users interact with it, helping to isolate bugs and note desired additions.

When software was distributed physically, the former method was the most common, given the associated time and cost required to distribute updates. As we've increasingly moved to the web, many have gravitated to the latter method. The logic behind doing so is largely rooted in the development team being able to quickly adapt to real client needs instead of ones only anticipated in a vacuum.

The agile approach is quite fashionable at present, and there are a number of people championing this way of working. I was first exposed to this notion a couple of years ago and we've made efforts to integrate it into our operations—particularly in developing marketing strategies. The nice part about working in this fashion is that it is concentrated on getting something in play quickly, instead of polishing a potentially ineffective approach endlessly. Come up with a plan, get the minimum required elements in place, see how they work, then revise. That's "agile" in a nutshell and it isn't by any means limited to software. Ask yourself how you might benefit from such an approach and test whether it's a fit for your marketing. It doesn't always work, but it's certainly worth experimenting with.

Disposable ideas

The problem with ideas is that we fall in love with them all too easily. Once we do, we put a lot of time into getting them off the ground. Some of us go to the far ends of the earth just to bring them to life. Although some look at this in a romantic way, I think it's pure silliness. Contrary to popular belief, ideas are never in short supply. Tying ourselves to one that doesn't work simply limits us from uncovering one that does.

Some people think that the creative process requires great toil and sweat. They come up with hundreds of ideas and select the best one. Then they sort through thousands of photographs to pick the one that feels perfect. They carefully draft the text and sift through it for any areas that could possibly be misread. They work closely with the production team to ensure precise execution, quibbling over the most mundane and inconsequential points. These become long, labored battles that result in outbursts, arguments, and stress. What happens if the idea doesn't work? Well, that's when the animosity really builds, people burn out, and the good scotch gets downed.

It's not that I think hard work isn't a factor in coming up with a good idea, I just wonder if we need to operate quite like this. I've come to accept that some of the things we do just suck. So we do our best to limit our emotional investment in an idea. Instead, we try to come to solutions quickly, test them out, and work with them if they seem viable. When they're not, I think it's acceptable to put that one out of our minds and simply move on to another.

Few plan their wedding in detail before the first date. Tell the truth, I know a couple of people who did so and they were pretty let down when things didn't work as they'd imagined. Most of us keep things casual until we meet someone great. When we know that it's a fit, we might start planning things, looking at place settings or what have you. I wonder if we should look at our ideas the same way. Let's not "put out" for them until they've proven that they're worth it.

Hack

A large part of Hotmail's success comes down to one brilliant little move. Was it a huge giveaway or perhaps an award winning television campaign? Did they pay for product placement in a popular movie? Nope! They "hacked" their way to success by placing just nine words in a spot they had full access to. By appending the note "Sign up for your free email account at Hotmail" to each message sent through their system, they created enormous awareness for their product and effectively built a household name.[99]

Sadly, this probably won't work for you. So many people have talked about this particular success that everyone thinks they can do the same. With such approaches being more commonplace, they to register as noise, with few grabbing our attention. You yet again may have to find your own way to connect. I suggest is you think less about what you're supposed to do, and instead concentrate on how you can make things work in your favor. (Whether they were intended to work this way or not.)

Hacking basically relates to using existing tools in an unintended fashion. Doing it will allow you to cover ground others most likely haven't. You won't find the way to do this in marketing books or from consultants—once these things have been done once, they tend to be less effective. That being said, there's almost always a faster, simpler, and more elegant way to achieve what you wish. You simply have to remain open to some less familiar ways of getting the job done.

CHAPTER 25

Screwing Up
and the Long Run

We've spent many pages together, talking about theories and strategies that might rely too heavily on analogy and metaphor. (I know—I have a predilection for that sort of thing. Sorry.) For the sake of argument, let's pretend that you do everything exactly as I suggested. Will it work?

I don't know.

Some marketing dude I am; aren't I? You bought the book, read carefully, and actually did this stuff; yet, the best I can do is, "I don't know." Pathetic—I agree. The fact is, it would be hard for anyone to promise any more. There are recipes and formulas for almost everything out there. In reality, the path isn't all that clearly marked no matter how much we might like it to be. It's a personal journey, one that you'll have to figure out for yourself as you move along. I'll suggest a few things to consider as you do so. Let's first look at how you can screw the whole thing up.

Lose interest

Few expect to turn into bad spouses. Similarly, not that many of us think that we'll ever grow negligent in servicing our customers. As we sit there, planning our companies, we dream of the kind we might be, "We'll offer great service! No, no… better than that! We'll make our customers feel like kings and queens—they'll only ever say the greatest things about how hard we've worked to make them happy!" Then, real life sets in. We get busy, errands pile up, and we get pulled in several directions. Or, we get so many orders that we just can't give all of our customers the attention we might like.

We can talk about marketing until we're blue in the face, but most of us treat it as something that helps bring people in, instead of a way to keep the clients we already have. Losing interest in the people who already buy from us is costly. Still, people struggle with the notion of "a bird in the hand is worth two in the bush."[100] I ask you to market your company as much to the people who already buy from you as those newcomers you hope to eventually seduce.

Companies get excited about new business, and lose interest in what they think of as boring "customer service." They are fools; the way you treat your existing customers is as important as any marketing you do. Always remind your customers that they're important.

"Hold out for a management position"

Standing back from your company's marketing, or pawning it off on a staff member, can be tempting. Once the initial shine of "doing something creative" wears off, we realize that it's work just like anything else. Thing is, it's really important work. The voice you speak to customers with; the way you present your company; the promises you make: none of these should be put solely in the hands of another. You'll want to pull in others with specific expertise, but don't confuse this kind of work for something that can be shuffled off entirely.

All too often creative teams are brought together to explore strategies for how to best market the company. Concepts are presented, ideas tested, and assets produced with the notion that all the relevant decision makers have been involved in the process. Then, at the last meeting (just before moving ahead with the campaign), the team learns of an influential person who just decides to "pop in." Midway through we hear, "Wait a second! This isn't us! We can't say this sort of thing!" This is accompanied by a deafening roar of time and money spontaneously bursting into flame and vanishing forever. The frustrated and emotionally exhausted team is forced to begin again.

This sort of derailment is common, and it's awfully effective if you want to wear out your people and squander precious resources. If instead you'd like to concentrate on getting the job done, there's one way to bypass this nonsense altogether: get involved from the first moment and take an active role in messaging and marketing your company. If you're going to make the final call on what "goes to press" anyway, you had best be well aware of the process and the directions presented, entertained, discarded, and developed. When it comes to marketing, you just have to get your hands in the dirt.

Getting cheap with your customers

While waiting to order a burrito at a franchised taco stand in the food court, I spied a sign that was intended only for their staff members. Management created it to remind those negligent workers to not become overly generous. It nagged them to portion their servings carefully, as not doing so would cost the company valuable dollars. While I appreciate the need to manage costs, messages like this should remain hidden from customers. The last thing we need to know is that you're scrimping on us.

Most of the time, such things aren't really that big of a deal anyway. What's the actual cost of throwing a few extra fries on the plate or giving a piece of pie to a regular? What's the cost/loyalty ratio for taking a few moments to sweep the steps well after mowing your customers' lawn? As a moving company, are you making more money by rushing and breaking furniture, or are you just sacrificing customers for a quick buck?

Part of keeping customers, and getting them to talk about you, relates to making them feel like the most important people in the world. You don't get cheap with friends; likewise, doing so with customers will only hurt your company.

Tell me how much I should love you

You know, I'm a pretty good looking guy. I make lots of money and I drive a shiny red sports car. Last week I met with Richard Branson on his private island and we smoked up together. Next week I'm getting together with Dick Cheney to play bridge and make jokes about all the "crazy shit" he did without Bush ever knowing. I once swam with dolphins, but got bored. So I taught a few of them how to do karaoke. Yup... I can't complain; life's good.*

How long do you think I could go on before you'd stop reading? Or, as the Gaping Void cartoon reads, "If you talked to people the way advertising talked to people, they'd punch you in the face."[101] Few companies actually take even a moment to think about this. Instead they spend all kinds of money taking out ads that talk only about themselves. "We brought on five new salespeople!", "We won a bunch of awards!", "We were rated best in class!" Some of these messages may need to be shared, but there are tasteful ways to do so; meanwhile, this kind should only be the exception. You aren't the star of the show—your customer is.

BTW: As you likely guessed, none of that first paragraph is actually true. (Except for the dolphin part—marine mammals really know how to rock the house.)

Bug the hell out of me

We all fall into patterns. Some are good for us, like running every day or checking in with customers once a month. Sometimes, we also find ourselves in less constructive patterns. Automation is in part to blame for this. Most of us send out email newsletters once a month regardless of whether we have anything to say. We need to build awareness, so we just keep on sending.

This isn't marketing; it's simply annoyance. I stress this point again: every message you send should be clearly considered and have a goal in mind. Moreover, it's important we broadcast only messages that the recipient will find value in. I may be happy to receive a not-so-frequent email from you containing running tips and notices for upcoming races in my neighborhood. On the other hand, getting a weekly email about bargains at your shop will probably piss me off rather quickly. At best it will be deleted on arrival; worse, I'll add you to a spam list.

This isn't limited to email. Sales calls that aren't spaced adequately, overly frequent mailers, and waiters who visit our table too often calling me "buddy" all fall into this category. There's a fine line between being helpful and interrupting your patrons. An introduction may be useful, and subsequent ones may serve as helpful reminders. But without editing, even the most welcome messages become noise.

Get sneaky

When Mark Bayard at Belkin decided that reviews of their Wireless F5U301 USB2.0 hub and dongle weren't quite what one might hope for, he took things into his own hands. Did he explore improvements, or assemble a group to determine why people weren't in love with this product? Nope. Who needs to improve the product when the problem is really with the reviews? Instead, he enlisted the help of a service called Mechanical Turk, paying them 65 cents for every positive review they wrote for the product.[102]

Sadly (for the Belkin folks) someone let the cat out of the bag. Word quickly spread that they were trying to game the system like this. Belkin earned press for the story, but probably not the kind they wanted. Let this be a lesson for all of us. The temptation to rig the system in our favor is always there, but it comes with a steep price. I say the cost is far too great, and it's all too easy to get caught. This makes the answer simple: play fair! You leave a trail wherever you go, whether it's a traceable IP address or simply a line of people you've wronged. Posting reviews under fake names, tricking people into buying, making things sound like something they're not... we all should know better.

Let's move on to a few brief thoughts on how to look at your efforts as you get underway.

Does it feel right?

Regardless of what you do to market your company, you're going to have moments when you're unsure whether you've taken the right course. At times like these, it may help to bring in people you trust and voice your concerns. Meanwhile, you might also have to call on your internal sensibilities for direction. I should note that it's not uncommon to feel uneasy when you're first presented with a new idea. This isn't what I'm referring to here. A lot of good ideas force us into new waters. I'm talking about whether it seems like "you."

We often feel like different people from one day to the next as our moods shift and we see things in a different light. Nevertheless, some things don't fit. When we learn of this, we have good reason to look critically at what we're doing. For example, do you make excuses for some aspect of your messaging? (e.g., "I don't get it, but they tell me the kids are crazy about it.") If so, I'd take a moment to really think about what you're doing.

Sure, some things that make sense to the rest of the team just won't resonate with you personally, and that's OK. My suggestion, is to just keep your "fake-meter" active as you develop messages and determine execution strategies. If it sounds like bullshit, well…

Are they talking?

Being polite doesn't necessarily result in additional awareness. Sure, you have to treat customers with care and respect. You certainly won't get far by acting unethically. But sometimes the worry of being seen as "impolite" scares us off of doing things that might work.

I ask you to look carefully at the marketing efforts you undertake—specifically those aimed at generating awareness—and ask if they are the kind of thing that people will feel the need to discuss. If not, I think it's a good time to ask why and determine if it's acceptable to keep moving on this path. If your message is not remarkable in any way, there's little point to wasting time and money or trying to get people to remember you.

It's often better to ruffle some feathers than go unnoticed. Sure, you might upset a few people, but there are always some casualties in marketing. Getting a few people to take notice and act is worth losing a few who might not have cared anyway.

Patterns versus wild swerving

In the *Embracing Change* section of this book, I talked at length about being ready to change when the need to do so presents itself.

At this moment, I'd like to temper those suggestions with a degree of caution—hopefully without negating those points I've already made. While there are good times to consider a change of course, doing so does come with associated costs.

As a teenager with a newly minted driver's license, I once found myself caught in some loose gravel as a result of edging too close to the shoulder of the road. It sucked me in and threatened to toss the car in the ditch. I rashly turned the wheel to correct this, forcing the car to lurch abruptly to the other side of the road. I did this once more before learning to correct more subtly. Those aggressive corrections were only creating other, equally dangerous movements.

Marketers often lose confidence in a direction, only to swerve wildly to correct course. While the impetus for doing so is understandable, it's no less hazardous. Instead of jerking around wildly, changes need to be made tactically and with careful consideration of the potential ramifications.

A memorable brand can't be achieved if your marketing changes course every few months. Your purpose and associated messages need repetition and constant confirmation. Someone once suggested an analogy to me of marketing being like hammering a nail into a board. No one expects it to be done in one swing, but by repeating the same action a few times you'll get the job done.

Change for the sake of change can be awfully seductive. To avoid giving in to temptation, I ask you to carefully contemplate what you expect from altering your plan. If your efforts are working, stay the course. As Markus Frind, founder of the successful free dating site Plenty Of Fish noted in his 2009 interview with *INC Magazine*, "The site works ... why should I change what works?"[103] There are plenty of things he could do to improve his site, but the fear of messing up a formula that works keeps him from acting prematurely.

It's not easy for anyone

Remember that movie *The Blair Witch Project*? It was an independent film with a budget of $22,000 that went on to generate over $248 million in revenue.[104] This massive success was in part achieved by employing a nontraditional marketing campaign that created massive buzz. That film was released to theaters in July 1999, which has left Hollywood with over ten years to learn from those tactics and repeat them. If they would have managed to do so they'd be able to create films that return revenues of 11,000 times the original investment. What happened?

The studios went back to work and created *Book of Shadows: Blair Witch 2*, which was largely a dud. The new film generated less than $50 million, with a $15 million budget.[105] Now, I'd be happy with $35 million in profit, but I can see how they might have looked at this as a failure. Meanwhile, it stands to reason that without the momentum of its predecessor, it wouldn't have even had this measure of success.

The bigger question, is why the marketing methods from the original film didn't serve as the new blueprint for every film marketing project to follow? How did this first attempt succeed in a way that the brightest marketers in Hollywood couldn't reverse engineer and replicate? The answer is likely manyfold; perhaps it was tied to the fact that the story of its underground success and low budget was part of the movie's plot and therefore difficult to effectively replicate. My feeling is that it's just hard to make magic happen twice.

We know this from life experience. Sometimes we throw a party that turns out to be one of the most memorable nights of our lives. The summer breeze is light, and the moon in the night sky is crystal clear. Everyone just connects, and the conversations are electric. The barbecue is mouthwatering, and the smell in the air is sweet. This only happens every once in a while, so we have to hold on to such moments. The same exact steps taken a week later, with all the same ingredients, might result in a completely different experience—void of any magic.

As much as we might like, we just can't bottle this stuff. That's simply the way it is. Some things have patterns you can learn from, but winning the lottery in no way predisposes you to repeating this act. Instead we need to bank on a few general principles that ready us for luck when it strikes. We clarify what we're about, remain open to possibility, and experiment with some variations. Meanwhile, we work hard and repeat our message and values until we make enough connections. Instead of putting unreasonable demands on ourselves to create "blockbuster" campaigns, we accept that most of the things we do just are just another swing of the hammer.

Keep on truckin'

My bet is that the first thing you do to market your company will not be a resounding success. The nice part is that it doesn't matter that much. You have plenty of time to get it right. Some will argue this, saying that there's little time to waste. This isn't altogether untrue, but I fear that such thinking can result in haphazard efforts that don't pay off as one might hope.

I like to think of marketing as a cumulative set of efforts. Planned well, it stitches into your daily activities without requiring Herculean gestures. This way there's room to think, plan, test, augment, and repeat, perpetually moving in one direction appropriate for your company. As marketers, we're all doing something akin to running a marathon. We're rewarded for reaching our destination, not for making random bursts along the way.

Sometimes this takes years, and you'll find yourself frustrated, just trying to figure out what will work and when. This can drive you crazy. Sadly, there just aren't a lot of good shortcuts out there, and I'd advise against trusting those who suggest there are. Just keep at it and remain open to new possibilities that get you closer to your overall goal. In my mind it's not about being right today; it's about getting it right in the long run.

It's easy to beat yourself up

I find it both curious and somewhat disheartening to think of how readily people criticize those who fail in business, or those who don't immediately succeed. The fact is, it's easy to sit on the sidelines and toss about opinions. I suppose for such people, there's little to lose. Perhaps there's even some comfort to be found in judging, when one fears that they don't have the guts to try for themselves.

You, though? You're in business and you're putting it out there. I respect the hell out of people like you for actually putting some skin in the game. At times you might find yourself frustrated that your business isn't doing quite as well as you had once hoped. Perhaps you're looking at competitors, thinking they have it all worked out and this is putting you into a bit of a funk. Don't sweat it. In my experience, almost no one has it "figured out." You know, some put on a really convincing show, but are still stressing out behind the scenes.

I don't know anyone who thinks business is a cake walk. The tricky part is that even if someone does have this experience, theirs is probably a pretty unique situation. It seems to me that the rules are different for every player. Think of your business and marketing as its own unique race and try to not obsess over what all the other guys are doing. That can really only lead to "grass is greener" thinking.

Perhaps you feel like you've made the wrong marketing decisions up to this point. You haven't. Everything you've done is part of your journey and will inform your actions as you determine the next step. Some lessons may be hard-won, but those tend to be the most illuminating ones. There's no time for lamenting what's done; just pick up and move on!

Perhaps you're uncomfortable about trying a new marketing approach because you've experienced some failures in the past. Cast those worries aside. Inaction and waffling won't get you anywhere. Get to work and keep trying. Even if you fail, you'll have learned something. Standing still teaches you very little, if anything.

My son Ari is seven months old and he *really* wants to move. He lies on his belly and rocks back and forth. He wiggles and squirms, trying to coordinate his movements. He gets mad and visibly demonstrates his frustration in not being able to make it happen. All of these struggles lead to something. Last week he finally linked it together and started making his way across the room. Nothing will stop him now!

When you get to a point at which it feels like you're just not making any headway, I ask you to reconsider where you're at. Maybe your marketing is just a second from "happening" and you're on the verge of connecting with people who love what you do. It could be the things that you're doing *are* working, but they just haven't quite connected *yet*. No one can say when it will come together for you. Keep struggling—it's your fight to win!

ENDS AND ODDS

COMMUNICATING

I've always been interested in connecting with people in one way or another, but I think the movie *Turk 182!* was what hooked me. Timothy Hutton played a guy named Jimmy Lynch. Angry about the city denying his injured brother (a firefighter) benefits, he sets off on a mission to embarrass the mayor by placing the message "Turk 182!" in spots throughout the city.[106] Little of this movie remains memorable to me, aside from the notion that a message could provoke controversy and even action.

Shortly thereafter I joined with a friend of mine to craft similar (although largely pointless) messages that we later peppered around our elementary school. Admittedly, it was all rather silly. I believe our tag was "Nerf 482" or something similarly derivative. We scrawled this message on bathroom walls and in cryptic notes—well, as cryptic as they come when you're twelve years old. Ultimately, we were caught, and the jig was up. For the following day or two we did "hard time," washing walls around the school.

The whole thing was a clumsy exercise, but I still look back upon it as an important event in my life. While our principal believed us to be bratty vandals, he actually missed the point. (Not that we likely would have articulated it all that well.) We weren't interested in ruining anything; we just wanted to engage people in a mystery. In our minds, success was getting a few people to wonder what that message meant, and why it kept appearing.

I design things and spend a lot of time writing. I help to develop marketing strategies and have also worked on some interesting self-directed projects. But I often struggle with how to describe what I do for a living. Recently it struck me that the common thread in my work relates to communicating. Whether to share ideas about marketing, ask people to try out one of our networks, or help a group clarify their value proposition and story. It all relates to crafting and spreading messages.

What excites me today is the multitude of ways we can do this. In the past, a limited few had access to publishing media, but the playing field has been fundamentally leveled. This is an unprecedented democratization, and it affords companies like yours the opportunity to outmaneuver those who have traditionally ruled—largely because of their mass. For customers this can mean access to significantly better and more committed businesses that otherwise might have gone unnoticed.

To do this, we need to clearly establish who we are. Then it's up to us to spread this message effectively using these new channels along with some of the old ones. The new opportunities represent seismic changes, but we can't expect them to do the work for us. We need to be smarter, more lucid, and better storytellers than our overgrown brethren. In doing so, we can connect with people who may very well help us thrive.

Most will continue to look upon marketing as a prescriptive practice. They'll lurch about grasping for quick remedies. Such chaotic and disconnected efforts will cycle into an endless parade of false promises, one-offs, and unfulfilled expectations. It's only by working methodically and seducing customers with unforgettable stories and experiences that we can break free of the violent and exhausting cycles that many of our companies are prone to.

Little of this comes easily but that doesn't make it any less important. Similarly, little of it is out of reach for anyone compelled to build a great company. An open mind and keen interest in building meaningful connections gets you in the door. From there on, the sky's the limit.

Worst case: You probably won't have to wash graffiti off the walls.

NOTES

CHAPTER 1: BIG ISN'T THE ONLY OPTION

1. Schultz, Howard, and Yang, Dori Jones. *Pour Your Heart Into It: How Starbucks Built a Company One Cup at a Time.* (New York: Hyperion, 1997).
2. Kiviat, Barbara. "Starbucks Goes From Venti to Grande." *TIME,* 2 July 2008. Available from http://www.time.com/time/business/article/0,8599,1819839,00.html.
3. Muskal, Michael. "Starbucks to cut 6,700 jobs." *The Los Angeles Times,* 29 January 2009. Available from http://articles.latimes.com/2009/jan/29/business/fi-layoffs-starbucks29.
4. Starbucks Gossip. *Starbucks chairman warns of "the commoditization of the Starbucks experience."* (23 February 2007; cited 11 September 2009) Available online http://starbucksgossip.typepad.com/_/2007/02/starbucks_chair_2.html.
5. Kiesler, Sara. "Capitol Hill to get a second stealth Starbucks." *seattlepi.com,* 27 August 2009. Available from http://www2.seattlepi.com/articles/409629.html.
6. Starbucks. *Company Factsheet – February 2008.* Available online http://http://www.starbucks.com/aboutus/Company_Factsheet.pdf (Accessed October 14, 2009).
7. Hoovers. *Starbucks Corporation Factsheet.* Available online http://www.hoovers.com/starbucks/--ID__15745--/free-co-factsheet.xhtml (Accessed October 14, 2009).
8. Mann, Charles. "Beyond Detroit." *Wired,* June 2009, 101-107.
9. U.S. Small Business Administration. *Frequently Asked Questions,* 2009. (PDF version of document downloaded September 2009).
10. Etsy. *What is Etsy?* Available online http://www.etsy.com/about.php (Accessed September 11, 2009).
11. Browne, David. "Blogs to Riches: Perez Hilton Migrates Into Cosmetics, Fashion and Music." *Wired,* 18 August 2008. Available from http://www.wired.com/techbiz/people/magazine/16-09/mf_perez.
12. Quantcast. *perezhilton.com.* (Accessed October 6, 2009) Available online from http://www.quantcast.com/perezhilton.com.
13. Quantcast. *starmagazine.com.* (Accessed October 6, 2009) Available online from http://www.quantcast.com/starmagazine.com.
14. Maestri, Nicole and Sage, Alexandria. "Amazon.com buying shoe seller Zappos for $928 mln." *Forbes.com,* 17 July 2009. Available from http://www.forbes.com/feeds/afx/2009/07/22/afx6689231.html.
15. Zmuda, Natalie. "Marketer of the Year 2008: Zappos, Customer Service

First—and a Daily Obsession." *Advertising Age,* 17 October 2008. Available from http://adage.com/moy2008/article?article_id=131759.

16. "Social Media." *Wikipedia, The Free Encyclopedia,* http://en.wikipedia.org/ wiki/Social_media (Accessed September 11, 2009).

CHAPTER 2: THANK GOODNESS YOU'RE SMALL

17. Chafkin, Max. "The Startup Guru" *Inc.,* 1 June 2009. Available online: http://www.inc.com/magazine/20090601/the-startup-guru-y-combina- tors-paul-graham.html

18. Facts About Microsoft. *microsoft.com.* (Accessed October 6, 2009) Avail- able online from http://www.microsoft.com/presspass/inside_ms.mspx.

19. "Forbidden City Starbucks closes." *BBC News,* 14 July 2007. Available from http://news.bbc.co.uk/go/pr/fr/-/2/hi/asia-pacific/6898629.stm.

20. Ihlwan, Moon, and Kiley, David. "Hyundai Gains with Marketing Blitz." *BusinessWeek,* 17 September 2009. Available from http://www.business- week.com/globalbiz/content/sep2009/gb20090917_167667.htm.

21. J.D Power and Associates. *2009 Initial Quality Study.* (Accessed September 28, 2009) Available online http://www.jdpower.com/autos/ratings/quality- ratings-by-brand/sortcolumn-1/ascending/page-#page-anchor.

22. Ingrassia, Paul. "Why Hyundai Is an American Hit." *The Wall Street Jour- nal,* 13 September 2009. Available from http://online.wsj.com/article/SB10 001424052970203917304574410692912072328.html?mod=googlenews_wsj.

23. Howard, Theresa. "Ads challenge people to 'rethink' Hyundai." *USA Today,* 8 October 2006. Available from http://www.usatoday.com/ money/advertising/adtrack/2006-10-08-track-hyundai_x.htm.

CHAPTER 3: STARTUP THINKING

24. Hamm, Steve, and Symonds, William C. "Mistakes Made On The Road To Innovation." *BusinessWeek,* 27 November 2006. Available from http:// www.businessweek.com/magazine/content/06_48/b4011421.htm.

25. Andrejczak, Matt. "Kodak to cut jobs as it swings to $137 million loss." *MarketWatch,* 29 January 2009. Available from http://www.marketwatch. com/story/kodak-shares-sink-22-on-big-loss-job-cuts?dist=msr_1.

CHAPTER 4: MARKETING IS A BIG LOAD OF BOLOGNA

26. Harry Nilsson. "Everybody's Talkin'." *Midnight Cowboy.* EMI America, 1989. CD.

27. Perrone, Matthew. "FDA takes issue with Cheerios health claims." *USA Today,* 12 May 2009. Available from http://www.usatoday.com/news/

health/2009-05-12-cheerios-fda_N.htm.

28. Mortished, Carl. "McDonald's salad is more fattening than a burger." *TimesOnline,* 9 March 2004. http://www.timesonline.co.uk/tol/news/uk/ article1041265.ece.

29. *Heart Attack Grill - Extreme Pigouts!* [Video] (April 2009). Retrieved October 11, 2009, from http://www.youtube.com/watch?v=KTKysI59HAw.

CHAPTER 5: THE PROBLEM WITH ADVERTISING

30. Horovitz, Bruce. "Domino's nightmare holds lessons for marketers." *USA Today,* 16 April 2009. Available from http://www.usatoday.com/money/ industries/food/2009-04-15-kitchen-pr-dominos-pizza_N.htm.

CHAPTER 7: WHAT A BRAND IS

31. Hof, Robert D. "Jeff Bezos on Word of mouth Power." *BusinessWeek,* 2 August 2004. Available online: http://www.businessweek.com/magazine/ content/04_31/b3894101.htm.

32. *Microsoft Jerry Seinfeld and Bill Gates Commercial* [Video] (2008). Retrieved September 10, 2009, from http://www.youtube.com/ watch?v=ImyK29QLs_A.

33. Central Intelligence Agency. *The World Factbook – People.* (Updated 10 September 2009; cited 11 October 2009) Available online https://www.cia. gov/library/publications/the-world-factbook/geos/xx.html.

34. Ries, Al, and Trout, Jack. *Positioning, The battle for your mind.* (New York: McGraw-Hill Inc., 2000).

35. *Make The Logo Bigger!* [Video] (2007). Retrieved September 10, 2009, from http://www.youtube.com/watch?v=-cGSn5Um0zI.

36. Agency Fusion. *Make My Logo Bigger.* (November 2007; cited 9 September 2009) Available online http://www.makemylogobiggercream.com.

37. Burke, Monty. "On the Run." *Forbes.com,* 11 February 2008. Available online: http://www.forbes.com/global/2008/0211/044.html.

38. Wilson, Thomas. *Swastika the Earliest Known Symbol and its Migrations.* (Whitefish: Kessinger Publishing, 2000).

CHAPTER 8: BRAND COMMANDMENTS

39. Shaw, Gillian. "Robeez shoes sells for $30.5 million." *The Vancouver Sun,* 7 September 2006. Available online: http://www.canada.com/vancouver-sun/news/business/story.html?id=8052a119-bc3b-43c5-813e-b203d04f0205.

CHAPTER 9: FOCUS AND DIFFERENTIATION

40. *City Slickers.* Produced by Billy Crystal and Irby Smith, directed by Ron Underwood. 112 min. Castle Rock Entertainment, 1991. Videocassette.

41. Collins, Jim. *Good to Great: Why Some Companies Make the Leap... and Others Don't.* (New York: HarperBusiness, 2001), p. 164-187.

42. "McDonald's products." *Wikipedia, The Free Encyclopedia,* http://en.wikipedia.org/wiki/McDonald%27s_products (Accessed October 11, 2009).

43. McDonalds. "Pizza!" *Cossette Communication Group,* 1992. Available online: http://theadwiki.com/wiki/McDonald%27s_Pizza:_Pizza!

44. Shapiro, Eben. "McDonald's Hopes Pizza Will Be the Next McHit." *The New York Times,* 20 September 2006. Available from http://www.nytimes.com/1989/09/20/business/mcdonald-s-hopes-pizza-will-be-the-next-mchit.html.

45. Old-Computers.com. *Systems Released In ~ 1985 ~.* (Cited 11 October 2009) Available online http://www.old-computers.com/MUSEUM/year.asp?st=1&y=1985.

46. "Apricot UK hits the end of the road" *computing.co.uk,* 18 March 1999. Available online: http://www.computing.co.uk/computing/news/2066110/apricot-uk-hits-road.

47. Apricot Computers. *Homepage.* (Cited 11 October 2009) Available online http://www.apricotcomputers.com.

48. "Volkswagen." *Wikipedia, The Free Encyclopedia,* http://en.wikipedia.org/wiki/Volkswagen (Accessed September 11, 2009).

49. Kiley, David. *Getting the bugs out: the rise, fall, and comeback of Volkswagen in America.* (New York: John Wiley & Sons, Inc, 2002).

50. Clausager, Anders Ditlev. "Ivan Hirst: Englishman who made Volkswagen part of the German economic miracle." *guardian.co.uk,* 18 March 2006. Available from http://www.guardian.co.uk/news/2000/mar/18/guardianobituaries.

51. "About the Company: Legacy" *Volkswagen Group America,* http://www.volkswagengroupamerica.com/company/legacy.htm (Accessed October 22, 2009).

52. Volkswagen. "Think Small." *Doyle Dane Bernbach,* 1959.

53. AdAge. *Top 100 Advertising Campaigns.* (Accessed September 11, 2009) Available online http://adage.com/century/campaigns.html

54. Frank, Thomas. *The Conquest of Cool: Business Culture, Counterculture, and the Rise of Hip Consumerism.* (Chicago: University Of Chicago Press, 1998), p. 57.

CHAPTER 10: STORYTELLING

55. *J.J. Abrams' mystery box* [Video] (2008). Retrieved September 11, 2009, from http://www.ted.com/talks/j_j_abrams_mystery_box.html.

56. *Go Further.* Produced by Sharon Brooks, Bill Imperial, Ron Mann, Sebastian Rotstein, and Daniel J. Victor, directed by Ron Mann. 100 min. Mongrel Media, 2003. DVD.

57. *Surfwise.* Produced by Graydon Carter, Mark Cuban, Amir Feingold, Jason Kliot, Tony Lord, Tommy Means, Dana Merwin, Jonathan Paskowitz, Jonathan Pine, Stef Smith, Joana Vicente, Todd Wagner, and Matt Weaver, directed by Doug Pray. 93 min. Magnolia Pictures, 2007. DVD.

58. *Helvetica.* Produced by Andrew Dreskin, Gary Hustwit, and Jakob Trollbeck, directed by Gary Hustwit. 80 min. Swiss Dots, 2007. DVD.

59. Moleskineerie. *Moleskine Musings.* (08 April 2005; cited 11 September 2009) Available online http://www.moleskinerie.com/2005/04/Moleskine_musin.html.

60. Fortt, Jon. "Are Google's nerds destroying design?" *CNN Money.com*, 20 March 2009. Available online: http://brainstormtech.blogs.fortune.cnn.com/2009/03/20/are-googles-nerds-destroying-design.

61. Nudie Jeans. *This is Nudie.* (2008; cited 11 September 2009) Available online http://www.nudiejeans.com/thisisnudie.

62. Lev-Ram, Michal. "Want the biggest iPod in the world?" *CNN Money.com*, 1 May 2009. Available online: http://money.cnn.com/2009/04/30/small-business/bling_your_ipod.fsb/index.htm.

63. Cocoa West Chocolatier. *Chocolates.* (Cited 11 October 2009) Available online http://www.cocoawest.com.

64. Hunch. *What blog should I read? Signal vs. Noise (by 37signals).* (Cited 11 October 2009) Available online http://www.hunch.com/blogs/signal-vs-noise-by-37signals/904904/.

65. Signal vs. Noise. *Homepage.* (Cited 11 October 2009) Available online http://37signals.com/svn/.

66. Howe, Robert F. "Wild Thing." *Smithsonian Magazine*, August 2003. Available online: http://www.smithsonianmag.com/history-archaeology/Wild_Thing.html?c=y&page=1.

67. Finkelstein, Sydney, Charles Harvey and Thomas Lawton. *Breakout Strategy: Meeting the Challenge of Double-Digit Growth.* (Columbus: McGraw-Hill, 2006), p. 156-157.

68. Interbrand. *Best Global Brands List 2009.* (Accessed October 11, 2009). Available online: http://www.interbrand.com/best_global_brands.aspx.

CHAPTER 11: AUTHENTICITY AND THE ZELLERS PARADOX

69. Miller, Stephen. "Rose Mattus, 90, Co-Founder of Häagen-Dazs." *The New York Sun,* 1 December 2006. Available from http://www.nysun.com/ obituaries/rose-mattus-90-co-founder-of-hagen-dazs/44436/.

70. Foulkes, Nick. "Old Brands, New Tricks." *Newsweek*, 2 June 2008. Available online: http://www.newsweek.com/id/138367.

71. Parry, John Horace. *The Spanish Seaborne Empire.* (Los Angeles: University of California Press, 1990), p. 265.

72. "Surprise! American Icons That Aren't American." *AOL Money&Finance.* Available online: http://money.aol.com/special/american-icons-that-are-foreign-owned (Accessed September 11, 2009).

73. "Apple Pie." *Wikipedia, The Free Encyclopedia,* http://en.wikipedia.org/ wiki/Apple_pie (Accessed September 11, 2009).

74. DJ Z-Trip and DJ P, "Uneasy Listening, Vol. 1." 2001, ZTRIP. http://djztrip. unknownvariable.com/audio/Uneasy_Listening_Vol1_Pt1.mp3

75. LaMotta, Lisa. "Starbucks: Ooh, That Smell." *Forbes.com*, 31 January 2008. Available online: http://www.forbes.com/2008/01/31/starbucks-sandwiches-mcdonalds-markets-equity-cx_lal_0131markets24.html.

76. Breen, Bill. "Who Do You Love?" *Fast Company*, 19 December 2007. Available online: http://www.fastcompany.com/magazine/115/features-who-do-you-love.html.

77. McMahon, Shannon. "Skating to the top." *San Diego Union-Tribune*, 25 September 2005. Available online: http://www.signonsandiego.com/ uniontrib/20050925/news_mz1b25skate.html.

CHAPTER 12: DO THEY LOVE YOU?

78. Christian, James L. *Philosophy: An Introduction to the Art of Wondering.* (Belmont: Wadsworth Publishing, 2008), p. 153.

CHAPTER 13: DO THEY KNOW YOU?

79. Flam, Jack D. *Matisse and Picasso: The Story of Their Rivalry and Friendship.* (Boulder: Westview Press, 2003), p. 65.

CHAPTER 14: HOW TO FLIRT WITH YOUR CUSTOMERS

80. Postrel, Virginia. *The Substance of Style: How the Rise of Aesthetic Value Is Remaking Commerce.* (New York: HarperCollins, 2003), p. 14, 56.

81. Method: Home Care and Personal Products. *Company information.* (Cited 11 October 2009) Available online http://www.methodhome.com/

overlay/company-info.aspx.

82. Sacks, Danielle. "The World's Most Innovative Companies." *Fast Company*, 14 August 2008. Available online: http://www.fastcompany.com/magazine/123/the-worlds-most-innovative-companies.html.

83. LinkedIn. *Companies: Hyatt Hotels Corporation.* (Cited 11 October 2009) Available online http://www.linkedin.com/companies/hyatt-hotels-corporation.

CHAPTER 15: BE NICE TO PEOPLE

84. "Holiday travellers peeved about airline's handling of flight delays." *CBC-News.ca*, 24 December 2008. Available from http://www.cbc.ca/canada/story/2008/12/27/airline-complaints.html.

85. Giles, Lee. "WestJet or Air Canada?" *Red Deer Advocate*, 10 April 2009. Available from http://www.albertalocalnews.com/reddeeradvocate/opinion/advocate_view/WestJet_or_Air_Canada_42760697.html.

86. Adams, Sharon. "Handling disaster fallout? Be accountable." *Business Edge*, 17 August 2006. Available from http://www.businessedge.ca/article.cfm/newsID/13264.cfm.

87. Crerar, David A. "The Bane and Antidote Must Be Taken Together: a Recent British Columbia Court of Appeal Decision Reassures Publishers and Journalists." *MastheadOnline*, 29 September 2005. Available from http://www.mastheadonline.com/library/law/law20.shtml.

CHAPTER 16: SELLING WITHOUT SELLING

88. *Glengarry Glen Ross.* Produced by Joseph M. Caracciolo Jr., Nava Levin, Karen L. Oliver, Morris Ruskin, Jerry Tokofsky, and Stanley R. Zupnik, directed by James Foley. 100 min. New Line Cinema, 1992. Videocassette.

89. Hughes, Pat. *Open Ice.* (New York: Laurel-Leaf, 2007), p. 97.

90. Brooks, Fred. *The Mythical Man-Month: Essays on Software Engineering.* (Upper Saddle River: Addison-Wesley, 1995).

CHAPTER 17: NEW TOOLS

91. Morrissey, Brian. "Small Brands Teach Big Lessons: Bacon Salt serves as an example of social media's power to help young companies grow quickly." *AdWeek*, 27 October 2008. Available online: http://www.adweek.com/aw/content_display/news/digital/e3ia353f77f11f28ab9dc52553ff7d92e84?pn=1.

92. Collins, Glenn. "COMPANY NEWS; Ten Years Later, Coca-Cola Laughs at 'New Coke.'" *The New York Times*, 11 April 1995. Available online: http://

www.nytimes.com/1995/04/11/business/company-news-ten-years-later-coca-cola-laughs-at-new-coke.html.

CHAPTER 20: MAKING IT WORK FOR YOUR COMPANY

93. Nintendo. *Wario Land: Shake It—Amazing footage!* (September 2008; cited 11 September 2009) Available online http://www.youtube.com/wariolandshakeit2008.

94. Foley, Stephen. "Gary Vaynerchuk: The wine world's new superstar." *The Independent*, 4 August 2008. Available online: http://www.independent.co.uk/life-style/food-and-drink/features/gary-vaynerchuk-the-wine-worlds-new-superstar-884063.html.

CHAPTER 22: THE INVERTED PYRAMID

95. Collins, Jim. *Good to Great: Why Some Companies Make the Leap... and Others Don't.* (New York: HarperBusiness, 2001), p. 90-119.

CHAPTER 24: EMBRACING CHANGE

96. *Zoolander.* Produced by Stuart Cornfeld, Celia D. Costas, Joel Gallen, Monica Levinson, Scott Rudin, Adam Schroeder, Ben Stiller, and Lauren Zalaznick, directed by Ben Stiller. 89 min. Paramount Pictures, 2001. DVD.

97. Boone Oakley. *BooneOakley.com - Home Page.* (28 May 2009; cited 11 September 2009) Available online http://www.youtube.com/watch?v=Elo7WeIydh8.

98. Gladwell, Malcolm. *Blink: The Power of Thinking Without Thinking.* (New York: Little, Brown and Company, 2005), p. 168-172.

99. Jurvetson, Steve. "What is viral marketing?" *cnet*, 22 June 2000. Available online: http://news.cnet.com/2010-1071-281328.html.

CHAPTER 25: SCREWING UP AND THE LONG RUN

100. Fuller, Linda K. and Shilling, Lilless M. *Dictionary of Quotations in Communications.* (Westport: Greenwood, 1997), p. 51.

101. Gaping Void. *if you talked to people.* (9 May 2006; cited 11 Sept. 2009) Available online http://www.gapingvoid.com/ifyoutalkedtopeople.jpg.

102. Parsa, Arlen. "Belkin's Development Rep is Hiring People to Write Fake Positive Amazon Reviews." *The Daily Background*, 16 January 2009. Available online: http://www.thedailybackground.com/2009/01/16/exclusive-belkins-development-rep-is-hiring-people-to-write-fake-positive-ama-

zon-reviews.

103. Chafkin, Max. "And the Money Comes Rolling In." *Inc.*, 1 January 2009. Available online: http://www.inc.com/magazine/20090101/and-the-money-comes-rolling-in.html.

104. Quenqua, Douglas. "Vampires coming on HBO, after months of warnings." *The New York Times*, 15 July 2008. Available online: http://www.nytimes.com/2008/07/15/business/worldbusiness/15iht-15adco.14494903.html.

105. IMDB - The Internet Movie Database. *Box office / business for Book of Shadows: Blair Witch 2.* (Accessed October 11, 2009). Available online: http://www.imdb.com/title/tt0229260/business.

COMMUNICATING

106. *Turk 182!* Produced by Robert W. Cort, René Dupont, Ted Field, Gary Goch, and Peter Samuelson, directed by Bob Clark. 102 min. Twentieth Century-Fox Film Corporation, 1985. Videocassette.

Acknowledgements

This book was crafted over approximately fourteen months, but it's the result of many years of discussions, debates and sometimes even arguments. I'm grateful to all of those kind people who have shared their time and insights.

Our clients have invited us into their lives and allowed us to work with them and experiment. In this arena, learning is a perpetual exercise, and I believe we've gained a great deal from these partnerships. Meanwhile, we've been fortunate to have a number of colleagues who've happily shared in an open exchange of ideas and perspectives. There's only so much you can do on your own. Having some peers to exchange war stories and insights with can make all the difference in between feeling we're moving forward or treading water in isolation.

Along the way, a few mentors have shared their struggles and successes, and we've gained depth from them. The design and marketing community is particularly vital and verbal, and they've expanded our perspectives and sometimes fortified our arguments by exchanging their opinions, both in person and in lengthy comment threads on *ideasonideas.com*. Some of these folks have become friends of ours even if we've never met in person. They've sent emails of encouragement, support, and sometimes highly personal stories, which have made us feel like we're connected.

A few folks meet with us regularly for coffee or lunch to swap and debate ideas. This is something that we greatly appreciate—doing so makes it more fun to come into the office, knowing that an engaging lunch meeting might fuel us for days to come. Meanwhile, we're particularly thankful to our families who indulge our long hours, and for their willingness to listen to the challenges and opportunities we talk about, sometimes without the ability to edit ourselves.

As you may have noticed, I've used the pronoun "we" in the text above. That's because this book isn't a singular effort, but rather one that was shared with my brilliant and levelheaded business partner Eric Shelkie. We started our business with a great deal of enthusiasm and ambition, but were hardly aware of how much we had (and still have) to learn. I'm particularly thankful to share this journey with such a nice guy.

On a personal note, I want to thank my parents, Lauri and Helina, for our daily talks, and for being a voice of reason and support at some rather harrowing moments. Meanwhile, I owe a debt of gratitude to my good friend Hans Saefkow, who has vetted this piece and voiced his thoughtful suggestions and rebuttals. Thank you for all the great discussions, my friend! Similarly, I'm very happy that Tom Biederbeck was been kind enough to lend his keen eye to this, helping isolate problems and smooth out a number of rough edges. My brother Mark, who is perhaps the most rational individual I know, has also generously investigated this book and pointed out some of the little slips that would have otherwise fallen through the cracks.

The three people I owe the most to are my wife Amea and our two little boys, Ari and Oscar. They've permitted my absence on many evenings, weekends, and even a summer vacation in order to allow me time to finish this. I suspect that one day I'll regret having squandered those days for a book, given what a wonderful gang they are; without that sacrifice, though, I doubt this would have seen the light of day.

Finally, I thank you: the individual whose passion to make something good gives all of us something to look forward to. I appreciate you taking the time to read this book and sincerely hope it helps galvanize your efforts in some way. I know how difficult it can be for small companies at times. Thanks for keeping up the good fight!

Eᴙɪᴄ Kᴀʀᴊᴀʟᴜᴏᴛᴏ ɪs ᴀ ғᴏᴜɴᴅɪɴɢ ᴘᴀʀᴛɴᴇʀ of the digital agency smashLAB. He has directed projects for groups including CN, Tourism Vancouver, and Canadian Heritage. He is a strong advocate of strategy and pragmatism in design.

In 2007 he spearheaded Design Can Change, an effort to unite designers and address climate change. The team at smashLAB has also launched the online community MakeFive and a crowdsourced design and marketing site called undrln. *TIME*, the Lotus Awards, and ICOGRADA have recognized his work; meanwhile, the agency has been featured in *The Globe and Mail*, *The Vancouver Sun*, and *Studio 4*.

Eric writes about design, brands, and experience at *ideasonideas. com* and has spoken at events for the AIGA, SEGD, and GDC. Eric studied at the Emily Carr Institute and lives in Vancouver with his lovely wife and two delightful little boys. (He still talks to his mom and dad almost every day.)

www.speakhuman.com

3752025